The Antonine Constitution

Impact of Empire

ROMAN EMPIRE, C. 200 B.C.–A.D. 476

Edited by

Olivier Hekster (*Radboud University, Nijmegen, The Netherlands*)

Editorial Board

Stéphane Benoist
Angelos Chaniotis
Lien Foubert
Anne Kolb
Luuk de Ligt
Elio Lo Cascio
Bernhard Palme
Michael Peachin
Francisco Pina Polo
Rubina Raja
Christian Witschel
Greg Woolf

VOLUME 29

The titles published in this series are listed at *brill.com/imem*

The Antonine Constitution

An Edict for the Caracallan Empire

By

Alex Imrie

BRILL

LEIDEN | BOSTON

Cover Illustration: Giessen, University Library, P. Giss. 40 / P. Giss. inv. 15.

The Library of Congress Cataloging-in-Publication Data is available online at http://catalog.loc.gov

Typeface for the Latin, Greek, and Cyrillic scripts: "Brill". See and download: brill.com/brill-typeface.

ISSN 1572-0500
ISBN 978-90-04-36822-4 (hardback)
ISBN 978-90-04-36823-1 (e-book)

Copyright 2018 by Koninklijke Brill NV, Leiden, The Netherlands.
Koninklijke Brill NV incorporates the imprints Brill, Brill Hes & De Graaf, Brill Nijhoff, Brill Rodopi, Brill Sense and Hotei Publishing.
All rights reserved. No part of this publication may be reproduced, translated, stored in a retrieval system, or transmitted in any form or by any means, electronic, mechanical, photocopying, recording or otherwise, without prior written permission from the publisher.
Authorization to photocopy items for internal or personal use is granted by Koninklijke Brill NV provided that the appropriate fees are paid directly to The Copyright Clearance Center, 222 Rosewood Drive, Suite 910, Danvers, MA 01923, USA. Fees are subject to change.

This book is printed on acid-free paper and produced in a sustainable manner.

To Sandra
Optima Magistra

Contents

Preface IX
List of Abbreviations XI
List of Figures, Table and Illustration XV

Introduction 1
    The Antonine Constitution in Scholarship 2
    An Edict for the Caracallan Empire 6

1 Contexts 11
    The Historical Context: 193–212 CE 12
    The Antonine Constitution in Ancient Literature 30
    The Role of the Jurists 33
    The Antonine Constitution and the Giessen Papyrus 39

2 The Fiscal Rationale 50
    Early Imperial Economic Activity 52
    Decline and Crisis in the High Empire 53
    The Severan Recovery 59
    The Economy under Caracalla 61
    The Economic Function of the Antonine Constitution 65
    The Vicesima Hereditatum 72
    The Purpose of Caracallan Fiscal Innovation 75

3 The Military Rationale 81
    Obstacles to Legionary Recruitment 83
    The Severan Reforms 91
    The Military Application of the Antonine Constitution 93

4 Alexander Imitatio 99
    Alexandrian Influences in the Antonine Constitution 100
    Alexander Iconography in the Caracallan Empire 104
    The Political Significance of Alexander Iconography 107

5 Securing the Caracallan Empire   113
      The Drive for Aequitas   114
      Re-writing the Severan Past   117
      A Religious Offering   122
      The Indulgentissimus Princeps   127
      A Social Contract   130

   Epilogue   134

   Appendix   139
      Text, Translation and Commentary of the Giessen Papyrus   139
   Bibliography   154
   Index of Names   171
   Index of Places   173
   General Index   174

Preface

The Antonine Constitution is nowadays regarded as one of the most globally important constitutional documents in history. In 2017, it was formally inscribed into the UNESCO *Memory of the World Register*, placing it alongside other charters such as Magna Carta, the Golden Bull of Emperor Charles IV, and the Declaration of Human and Civil Rights introduced by the French National assembly in 1789. It is, with good reason, seen as the genesis for many later concepts of citizenship in Europe and beyond. But the Antonine Constitution remains apart from its eventual successors. It was not predicated on any singular European centre or national statute: it established a uniquely transnational network of citizens, whose own local and customary rights were simultaneously preserved.

The universal significance of the Antonine Constitution, however, rests somewhat uncomfortably against the image of the Roman emperor responsible for its promulgation. Caracalla is best known for his allegedly murderous rage, ordering the assassination of his own brother to secure his grasp on the imperial throne, and accused of laying waste to the city of Alexandria with little provocation. The apparently progressive and avant-garde *Constitutio Antoniniana* seems a bizarre and almost incredible act on the part of an autocratic ruler whose self-identity was characterised predominantly by militaristic iconography and a message that his regime was divinely sanctioned. In this book, I aim to address this paradox, and to shed some light on the emperor's rationale for introducing such a revolutionary constitutional change.

This monograph would not have been possible without the input and assistance of many people. The doctoral thesis that forms the core of this publication was generously sponsored by the Kerr-Fry fund in Edinburgh. Their willingness to support my postgraduate research, from Masters onwards, was gratefully received. Indeed, it undoubtedly removed many of the worst financial anxieties that are an unfortunate component of the modern PhD experience for the majority.

The School of History, Classics and Archaeology at the University of Edinburgh has presented me with a stimulating and supportive environment since my earliest days as an undergraduate in 2003. As a first-generation university attendee, I had little familiarity with the world of academia, but the knowledge, enthusiasm and opportunity presented to me by various members of faculty were significant enough to help me overcome most of my fears, and set out towards a career in the discipline. Foremost among these is Sandra Bingham, whose passionate belief in my project and abilities as a scholar have been a constant source of confidence and motivation. With her support, I felt able to write on the subjects that I wanted to, rather than conforming to others' assessments of the field. She has been instrumental in making me the classicist that I am today. Lucy Grig has also been an important influence in my development. Her readiness to challenge and play devil's advocate with my ideas has always pushed me to test my attachment to any hypothesis that I have pursued. I hope that this book, the summation of our years spent working together, makes them as happy as it does me.

Many others have read my work and have offered helpful thoughts, comments and suggestions. I am grateful to Olivier Hekster for his continual assistance in refining my doctoral thesis into this monograph. Our first meeting was during my final PhD defence, in which he acted as an examiner. I confess to being more than a little awestruck and intimidated by his fierce intellect, initially, but I could not have asked for a better champion for my work thereafter. He has been a continually positive correspondent, and a driving force in my path towards a first book. Similarly, Andrew Erskine has been a welcome adviser in this process, whose own wealth of experience has been an invaluable source of information. I have been fortunate to work alongside a number of talented classicists, both during my PhD and beyond. Amy Bratton, Nicole Cleary, Raphaëla Dubreuil, Juan Lewis, Fiona Mowat, Peter Morton, Katie Thostenson and Cas Valachova all deserve recognition for reading parts of my work as it developed, and for their continued friendship and camaraderie. Special mention goes to David Greenwood, for his dry wit and his sense of perspective; and Belinda Washington, for her unerring ability to motivate me and make me laugh, even at my lowest ebb.

Without the love and support of those above and following, I doubt that I could have completed this book. I am grateful to my parents, Rose and Alexander, for nurturing my love of learning, and for working relentlessly in order that I might pursue my goals and attend university; to Darren Maley, for two decades' worth of stimulating conversations, and for his unfailing friendship; and to my wife Rachael, for being the part of me that I was missing until I met her. It is nearly impossible to articulate everything that I owe to Rachael. Her selfless devotion to sharing my aspirations made it possible for me to make the very most of my time as a doctoral student. More generally, though, my life would be inestimably poorer for her absence. She is and ever will be my muse and inspiration.

List of Abbreviations

Ancient Authors and Works

Ael. Ar.	Aelius Aristides
Or.	*Orations*
Amm. Marc.	Ammianus Marcellinus
Arr.	Arrian
Anab.	*Anabasis*
Aur. Vict.	Aurelius Victor
Caes.	*Caesars*
Cic.	Cicero
Har. Resp.	*De Haruspicum Responso*
CTh.	*Theodosian Code*
Dig.	*Digest of Justinian*
Dio	Cassius Dio
Diod. Sic.	Diodorus Siculus
Eutrop.	Eutropius
Gaius *Inst.*	Gaius, *Institutes*
HA	*Historia Augusta*
Avid.	*Life of Avidius Cassius*
Car.	*Life of Caracalla*
Comm.	*Life of Commodus*
Geta.	*Life of Geta*
Hadr.	*Life of Hadrian*
Marc.	*Life of Marcus Aurelius*
Niger.	*Life of Pescennius Niger*
Pius.	*Life of Antoninus Pius*
Quad. Tyr.	*Lives of the Four Tyrants*
Sev.	*Life of Septimius Severus*
Ver.	*Life of Lucius Verus*
Hdn.	Herodian
Jerome	Hieronymous (Jerome)
Livy	Livy
Lucian	Lucian
Alex.	*Alexander*
M. Aur.	Marcus Aurelius
Med.	*Meditations*

Oros.	*Orosius*
Plin.	Pliny the Elder/Pliny the Younger
Ep.	*Letters of the Younger Pliny*
HN	*Natural History*
Pan.	*Panegyricus*
Plut.	Plutarch
Alex.	*Life of Alexander*
Moralia.	*Moralia*
Polyb.	Polybius
Sen.	Seneca the Younger
De Ben.	*De beneficiis*
Suet.	Suetonius
Aug.	*Life of Augustus*
Cal.	*Life of Gaius (Caligula)*
Dom.	*Life of Domitian*
Nero.	*Life of Nero*
Vesp.	*Life of Vespasian*
Tac.	Tacitius
Ann.	*The Annals*
Hist.	*The Histories*
Tert.	Tertullian
Apol.	*Apologeticus*
Resurr.	*De resurrectione carnis*
Vall. Pater.	Valleius Paterculus
Veg.	Vegetius

Modern Titles

AE	*L'Année Epigraphique*
Aegyptus	*Aegyptus: rivista italiana di eggitologia e di papirologia*
AJA	*American Journal of Archaeology*
AJN	*American Journal of Numismatics*
AJP	*American Journal of Philology*
AJPhA	*American Journal of Physical Anthropology*
ANRW	*Aufstieg und Niedergang der Römischen Welt*
Arctos	*Arctos: acta philologica Fennica*
Athenaeum	*Athenaeum: studi di letteratura e storia dell'antichità*
BABesch	*Babesch: bulletin antieke beschaving*
BASP	*Bulletin of the American Society of Papyrologists*

LIST OF ABBREVIATIONS

BMCRE	*Coins of the Roman Empire in the British Museum*
Britannia	*Britannia: a journal of Romano-British and kindred studies*
CdE	*Chronique d'Égypte*
Chiron	*Chiron: Mitteilungen der Kommission für Alte Geschichte und Epigraphik des Deutschen Archäologischen Instituts*
CIL	*Corpus Inscriptionum Latinarum*
CJ	*The Classical Journal*
CQ	*Classical Quarterly*
CRAI	*Comptes rendus / Académie des inscriptions et belles-lettres*
EA	*Epigraphica Anatolica: Zeitschrift für Epigraphik und historiche Geographie Anatoliens*
Eos	*Eos: organ Polskiego Towarzystwa Filologicznego*
G&R	*Greece and Rome*
Gerión	*Gerión*
GIC	*Greek Imperial Coinage*
Hermes	*Hermes: Zeitschrift für klassische Philologie*
Historia	*Historia: Zeitschrift für Alte Geschichte*
Histos	*Histos: the new electronic journal of ancient historiography*
IAM	*Inscriptions antiques du Maroc*
IGRR	*Inscriptiones Graecae ad res Romanas pertinentes*
ILAfr	*Inscriptions latines d'Afrique (Tripolitaine, Tunisie, Maroc)*
ILS	*Inscriptiones Latinae Selectae*
JAH	*Journal of Ancient History*
JEA	*Journal of Egyptian Archaeology*
JHS	*Journal of Hellenic Studies*
JJP	*Journal of Juristic Papyrology*
JRA	*Journal of Roman Archaeolgy*
JRS	*Journal of Roman Studies*
Klio	*Klio: Beiträge zur Alten Geschichte*
Ktèma	*Ktèma: civilisations de l'Orient, de la Grèce et de Rome antiques*
Latomus	*Latomus: revue d'études latines*
MBAH	*Münstersche Beiträge zur antiken Handelsgeschichte*
Mnemosyne	*Mnemosyne: bibliotheca classica Batava*
Oliver	*Greek Constitutions of Early Roman Emperors from Inscriptions and Papyri*
Opus	*Opus: rivista internazionale per la storia economica e sociale dell'antichità*
PBSR	*Papers of the British School at Rome*
Philologus	*Philologus: Zeitschrift für antike Literatur und ihre Rezeption*
Phoenix	*Phoenix: journal of the Classical Association of Canada*

PNAS	*Proceedings of the National Academy of Sciences of the United States*
RBN	*Revue belge de Numismatique et de Sillographie*
RIC	*The Roman Imperial Coinage*
RIN	*Rivista italiana di numismatica e scienze affini*
RSA	*Rivista storia dell'Antichità*
SDHI	*Studia et documenta historiae et iuris*
TPAPA	*Transactions and Proceedings of the American Philological Association*
Topoi	*Topoi: Orient-Occident*
ZPE	*Zeitschrift für Papyrologie und Epigraphik*
ZRG	*Zeitschrift der Savigny-Stiftung für Rechtsgeschichte. Romanistische Abteilung*

Citations of papyri included in this study conform to the standard abbreviations contained in the *Checklist of Editions of Greek, Latin, Demotic, and Coptic Papyri, Ostraca and Tablets,* which is continuously updated at: http://library.duke.edu/rubenstein/scriptorium/papyrus/texts/clist.html.

List of Figures, Table and Illustration

Figures

1 Graph illustrating the decline in median fineness of *denarii* 63
2 Graph illustrating fluctuation in weight of *aurei* and *denarii* 64

Table

1 Table illustrating the changing legal status of auxiliaries 89

Illustration

1 Giessen, University Library, P. Giss. 40 / P. Giss. inv. 15 152

Introduction

In July 212, the emperor M. Aurelius Severus Antoninus Pius, better known simply as Caracalla, fundamentally and irrevocably changed the constitutional nature of the Roman Empire.[1] In one proclamation, he extended the previously exclusive rights of *civitas* to nearly every single free person living within his realm. Since the discovery of a papyrus thought to contain a copy of the edict at the opening of the twentieth century, Caracalla's Antonine Constitution (*Constitutio Antoniniana*) has proven to be one of the most perplexing and controversial artefacts to survive from the Roman imperial period. It has piqued the interest of historians and archaeologists, linguists and papyrologists, and has provoked a profusion of publications in every decade since its discovery.[2] If anything, academic interest in the edict has intensified in recent years, thanks in no small part to the 1800th anniversary of its promulgation falling in 2012.

Despite such consistent interest in the Antonine Constitution, however, there are still remarkably few areas in which consensus has been reached regarding the legislation. Nearly every aspect of the *constitutio* has proven divisive, including the question of its fundamental significance. In turn, this situation has elicited a variety of scholarly reactions, and created a long and convoluted historiography. In this book, I concern myself with the question of Caracalla's rationale for introducing the legislation in 212. In the past, studies have been conducted that assess the Antonine Constitution against individual motivating factors, but this study takes the hitherto unprecedented step of gathering these potential prompts together and setting them against one another. The ultimate purpose of this exercise is to offer a comprehensive assessment of the emperor's reasons for extending the franchise. By examining numerous motivating factors collectively, we thus avoid the methodological pitfall of affording an inflated or exaggerated sense of importance to any one, individual element. The net result of this approach is an image of the *Constitutio Antoniniana* that reflects the complex and precarious political milieu in which the young emperor found himself in 212. Indeed, it is only by placing Caracalla's edict into a properly embedded context that one can begin to make sense of it.

---

1 The dating of Caracalla's legislation remains disputed. This will be discussed in the next chapter.
2 By the time Christoph Sasse published his literature review of the edict in 1962, the figure had surpassed ninety major publications.

Before we can begin to assess how the Antonine Constitution functioned within Caracalla's contemporary milieu, it is first necessary to consider the nature of the current scholarship on the edict. To a large extent, the *constitutio* remains controversial and divisive owing to the dearth of ancient evidence relating to it. In fact, one of the few areas of modern consensus to be found regarding the edict is a shared sense of disbelief in how little direct evidence survives.[3] Apart from the famous Giessen papyrus, the only contemporary references to the *Constitutio Antoniniana* are to be found in a brief mention by Cassius Dio, and a similarly fleeting description by Ulpian, now preserved in the Justinianic *Digest*.[4] Given this meagre selection of sources, it is hardly surprising that some still regard the legislation to be 'shrouded in mystery', and possessing a suspiciously small historical echo.[5] While the lack of any sizeable corpus of evidence is obviously frustrating, it should not lead us to the conclusion that Caracalla's edict was somehow meaningless or insignificant: absence of evidence is, after all, hardly evidence of absence.[6] Indeed, it is precisely the aura of enigma surrounding the *constitutio* that still draws academics to it.

The Antonine Constitution in Scholarship

Research on Caracalla's edict can be roughly divided into studies focused in three key areas: the Giessen papyrus as a historical source; the implications and consequences of mass enfranchisement, and the emperor's rationale in promulgating the decree. Each of these elements contains its own controversies. As noted above, the question of why Caracalla chose to extend the franchise is the primary focus of this study, but it remains essential to be aware of the different ways in which this unique legislation has been approached previously.

Owing to its significance as the only surviving copy of the edict's text, it is unsurprising that the majority of scholarly attention has been devoted to *Papyrus Gissensis* 40.[7] Historically, scholars of this text have been faced with the vexed

---

3   De Blois (2014) 1014; Hekster (2008) 45; Buraselis (2007) 1–3.
4   *P. Giss.* 40. 1; Dio 78.9.5 (all references to Dio employ the Loeb numbering system); *Dig.* 1.5.17. All of these sources will be considered further in the wider contextualisation of the *constitutio* in Chapter 1.
5   Ando (2012) 52. Also see Buraselis (2007) 2–3.
6   Hekster (2008) 55.
7   Bryen (2016) 29; Modrzejewski (1990); Sasse (1962). For sake of clarity and convenience, I have included my own consideration of the Giessen text, with an accompanying apparatus, in the appendix accompanying this work.

issue of the artefact's highly fragmentary state. This unavoidable problem has prompted disagreement on how it should be reconstructed which, in turn, has caused the subsequent discussion of the edict's importance to become 'enmeshed in papyrological and epigraphic debates.'[8] Early attempts to restore the text are problematic inasmuch as they often contain extensive conjectural reconstructions that, while eloquent, are based on the survival of isolated characters.[9] Furthermore, these editions often fail to acknowledge the precarious nature of such a method.

This cavalier approach towards the Giessen papyrus was eventually challenged, particularly in the 1970s, but the result was a strikingly negative assessment of the evidence. Far from the creative compositions of the early twentieth century, some began to voice doubt regarding how far the papyrus should even be associated with the Antonine Constitution.[10] This nihilistic trend reached its zenith in Wolff's assessment, in which the artefact was distanced from the study of the *constitutio* completely, paraphrased here by Millar: 'we cannot use *P. Giss.* 40, which cannot be proven to refer to the *Constitutio*, or even to have come from Caracalla.'[11] Only in far more recent years has a moderate position been achieved. While scholars remain divided on numerous points of detail, most now agree that the Giessen papyrus contains a copy of at least part of the Antonine Constitution.[12]

Another aspect of the *Constitutio Antoniniana* that has enthralled modern scholarship concerns how the edict was implemented, and the legal and social consequences of mass enfranchisement in the era post-212.[13] This area of study has proven popular owing both to the greater availability of surviving evidence and the opportunity to identify developments in the conceptualisation of citizenship across the span of European history, even into modernity.[14]

---

8   Tuori (2007) 42.
9   For selected examples, see Laqueur (1927) 15–20, and Heichelheim (1941) 10–22. For more detail on the nature of the problems encountered in these works, see Lukaszewicz (1990a).
10 Sherwin-White (1973a) 380–81.
11 Millar (1979) 235; Wolff (1977) 193–209.
12 Bryen (2016) 29–43; Van Minnen (2016) 205–21; Kuhlmann (2012) 51–52 and (1994) 215–56; Torrent (2011) 11–20; Rocco (2010) 131–35; Hekster (2008) 45; Oliver (1989) 500–5.
13 Sherwin-White (1973a) 386 argued, for example, that the tangible effects of the *constitutio* were far more important than the detail of its terminology. For a more recent investigation of the consequences of the edict, see Sessa (2014); Kantor (2016) 45–62, and Moatti (2016) 63–98.
14 A prime example of this is to be found in the recent edited volume offered by Clifford Ando: *Citizenship and Empire in Europe, 200–1900: The Antonine Constitution after 1800 years* (Stuttgart, 2016).

The currently prevailing *communis opinio* on the impact of the Antonine Constitution is itself the product of an evolutionary process. Early attempts to gauge the consequences of the edict were influenced by the colonial notion of an orderly Roman *Rechtsstaat* being imposed across the empire in its entirety.[15] More recent assessments of the legislation have questioned the extent to which such a system was likely in antiquity or, indeed, if it was even enforceable.[16] It is therefore clear that while it is possible to hypothesise in broad strokes regarding the impact of the *constitutio* in the long term, the immediate consequences of the edict are more difficult to assess, the situation likely being far more complex and nuanced than was acknowledged, historically.

Whereas the restoration of the Giessen papyrus and the consequences of the Antonine Constitution form the focus of many conflicting studies, it is the question of Caracalla's motivation and intentions in promulgating the *constitutio* that remains the most controversial. A cursory examination of recent historiography reveals that the debate includes even the fundamental question of whether or not the emperor possessed a definite reason for introducing the edict at all. It has been argued, for example, that the legislation was the result of nothing more than an unpredictable whim on Caracalla's part, an impulsive act that was poorly conceived: 'the edict of Caracalla came out of the blue. No one had anticipated it, least of all his provincial subjects. It was an act neither of necessity nor, if we follow Dio, of statesmanship.'[17] This dismissive analysis has been countered by others who view the legislation as the logical culmination of a process in which citizenship was gradually extended from the imperial heartland to the peripheries.[18] Key to this argument is the idea that the *Constitutio Antoniniana* was an initiative that was completely germane to the early third century, fitting the zeitgeist of an age in which imperial power resided with the emperor himself, rather than in the city of Rome.[19] Far from being introduced spontaneously, these scholars view Caracalla's edict as an end point to a process that had been underway prior even to the foundation of the Principate.

---

15   Tuori (2007) 39.
16   Garnsey (2004) 143, for example, correctly questions how many people would have truly been affected by the *constitutio*, and how many were permitted to 'slip through the net'. Also see Van Minnen (2016) 220.
17   Garnsey (2004) 137.
18   Nicolet (1980) 17. Sherwin-White (1973a) remains the magisterial source on this, to a large extent, with his work clearly demarking phases of expansion from the Republic and through the Empire.
19   Honoré (2004) 114–15; Simelon (2010) 810.

Both of these approaches are flawed, to an extent. On the one hand, the notion that the *constitutio* was the result of little more than a passing whim is an unusually absolute position that not only ignores other contextual factors that might have prompted the emperor, but also allows the notion of Caracalla's volatile temperament (itself the result of a hostile source tradition) to dominate the question.[20] On the other hand, while it is evident that the franchise was gradually expanding within the provinces as the imperial period progressed, the conclusion that Caracalla was merely adding a final flourish to a *fait accompli* does not reflect the reality that citizens still represented a distinct minority of the empire's population at the opening of 212.[21] It is clear that the Antonine Constitution was neither a foregone conclusion, nor the mere result of youthful impetuosity. The reality is ultimately more complex and dependent on a multitude of contextual factors.

Further attempts to explain the introduction of the *constitutio* have been made by scholars analysing the edict through the lens of individual subjects. This trend can be seen most visibly in earlier studies assessing the veracity of Dio's fiscal explanation for the legislation.[22] These scholars are not alone in attempting to attribute a single causal factor to the Antonine Constitution, though, with others forging links between the edict and Caracalla's hero-worship of Alexander the Great, or his more general military ambitions.[23] Nevertheless, this methodology remains troublesome, with the inherent risk that one places an exaggerated sense of importance onto the individual element under discussion which, in turn, may lead to an unrepresentative view of the legislation that is detached entirely from its wider contemporary milieu.

This situation has improved in more recent years, as scholars have acknowledged that is it unlikely that Caracalla was moved to promulgate the *Constitutio Antoniniana* on the basis of a single issue. In fact, there was a variety

---

20 Even more recent studies have fallen foul of allowing the notion of Caracalla's temper and anger to impact upon the question. For examples, see Kemezis (2014) 30; García (2009) 100–2; Honoré (2002) 85; Sherwin-White (1973a) 287.

21 Garnsey (2004) 135. Recently, Lavan (2016) 3–46 has offered a quantification of the citizen body prior to 212. While this is evidently based on a number of necessarily arbitrary factors, his analysis has suggested that before Caracalla's edict, only around 22% of the population of the empire were fully enfranchised.

22 Dio 78.9.5 claimed that the edict was the result of Caracalla's desire to reap a vastly increased tax yield, a claim that will be considered in greater detail in Chapter 2. For early examples of scholars following this line, see Jones (1974) 194; Gilliam (1952) 405; Bell (1947) 17–23; Sherman (1928) 33–47.

23 These potential explanations for the legislation will be analysed in the third and fourth chapters of this book. Also see González-Fernández and Fernández Ardanaz (2010).

of pressures and inspirations that motivated the emperor to legislate and, moreover, none of these need be mutually exclusive.[24] The most comprehensive modern study in this regard is that of Buraselis, who sought to interpret the *constitutio* within the wider political philosophy of the Severan dynasty.[25] His work remains authoritative in many ways, providing a solid base from which to approach Caracalla's edict, finally removed from the inflammatory rhetoric of Cassius Dio.

While scholarship on the Antonine Constitution has become increasingly nuanced and sophisticated, then, there remain fundamental problems that restrict how far we can achieve a properly holistic impression of the edict and the circumstances surrounding its introduction. The myriad studies regarding the Giessen papyrus are invaluable to any modern analysis, but the nature of the reconstruction required means that the historical role and importance of the *constitutio* is often lost among the artefact's linguistic controversies.[26] Attempts to view the legacy of Caracalla's edict in later history can provide any number of interesting observations on the concept of citizenship in the post-Caracallan world, but the legislation itself only rarely forms the primary focus of these studies, meaning that little can be deduced regarding its importance to its own era. Finally, attempts to study the *Constitutio Antoniniana* through individual lenses can be as problematic as they are illuminating. They inevitably remove the edict from its own context, to some degree, and thereby force artificial comparisons between factors that cannot realistically be extricated from the wider historical milieu.

An Edict for the Caracallan Empire

To date, there has never been an attempt to consider the various possible motives for the Antonine Constitution together in one study. And yet it is only when the edict is analysed in a fully embedded context that the relationship between the different motivations and pressures bearing on Caracalla in 212 can be properly observed. This monograph attempts, then, to build upon the existing scholarship relating to the *Constitutio Antoniniana*, and to add a new layer of interpretation to the discussion. It represents the first study of its kind, the fundamental purpose of which is to bring together the major elements that served to prompt the emperor to introduce his famous edict. Throughout the

---

24   Hekster (2008) 50.
25   Buraselis (2007) 14–87.
26   Sherwin-White (1973a) 381.

course of this investigation, I will endeavour to offer a more grounded and cohesive image of the *constitutio*, demonstrating that it was an important political initiative, combining practical and propagandistic values at a crucial point in Caracalla's fledgling sole reign.

It is necessary at the outset to consider the extent to which it is correct to label the Antonine Constitution as a vehicle of Caracallan imperial propaganda. This function of the edict will be a feature repeatedly evaluated throughout this study, particularly in discussion relating to the emperor's exploitation of the Alexander mythos, and his attempts to legitimise his sole rule of the empire. The use of the term 'propaganda' in connection with ancient evidence, particularly that released by the imperial household, has proven contentious, though. Historically, the objection to 'propaganda' is based upon the absence of an equivalent term in Latin, and the view that the label has absorbed inappropriate undertones from the Fascist and National Socialist regimes of the 1930s and 1940s. Burnett, for example, addressed the issue in connection with imperial coinage. He argued that for the term to become acceptable, it must first be stripped of two elements, namely the idea of a deliberate falsehood and a systematic orchestration of public opinion.[27] Sensitivity regarding the use of 'propaganda' is not unique to Burnett, and has resulted in others offering alternative conceptual frameworks in describing how imperial media functioned. One popular such model discusses imperial iconography in terms reminiscent of modern brand marketing, for example.[28]

This problem is more apparent than real. It is self-evident that the precise nature and expression of propagandistic messages would differ between the ancient and modern eras, but this does not preclude Roman imperial initiatives and media from containing a propagandistic significance. Furthermore, the fact the ancients lacked a comparable term for the phenomenon hardly confirms that such a process was non-existent.[29] While it is true that a direct comparison between the Roman Empire and modern totalitarian powers is inappropriate, we must also be careful not to sanitise the imperial regime, or to deny its autocratic and dictatorial (even tyrannical) character, of which state propaganda is an obvious element. In fact, the value of the *Constitutio Antoniniana* in simultaneously promoting Caracalla's personal *pietas* and an official narrative surrounding the murder of his brother, Geta, can be seen to

---

27   Burnett (1987) 66.
28   Hekster (2003) 25.
29   Hannestad (1984) 9.

fit with even the more contentious definition of propaganda.[30] It represents a clear example of an emperor attempting to engineer a positive response to his regime among the populace, and impart a moralising quality to his version of Geta's assassination. In this study, then, the label 'propaganda' is taken to mean a deliberate initiative undertaken by the imperial regime, designed to orchestrate public opinion with a political objective.

The nature of this book means that it is necessary to approach the Antonine Constitution from a number of angles. As a consequence, chapters will be devoted to the different potential motivations affecting Caracalla, demonstrating the complexity in attributing individual factors to his decision to extend the franchise in 212. The first chapter will offer a contextualisation of Caracalla as emperor and of the *constitutio* itself. In historical terms, the period from the death of Commodus until the sole reign of Caracalla will be outlined, since I argue that the circumstances of the Severans' rise to power were an important background feature in Caracalla's decision to legislate in 212. The surviving evidence for the edict will then be considered, particularly the Giessen papyrus. Owing to the controversy surrounding this artefact, I have opted to compile my own edition of the text, one that compares and contrasts previous attempts to restore the fragmentary document. The result of this is an edition which remains heavily embedded within the pre-existing textual scholarship, but resists overreliance on any one previous reconstruction. In addition, the content of *P. Giss.* 40 will be analysed in an attempt to conclude how far we should identify Caracalla as the ultimate author and architect of the legislation, particularly given the prominence of jurists in the early third century.

Following this exercise in grounding the Antonine Constitution within the context of Caracalla's reign, the following chapters will be divided into two overarching sections. The first of these considers the potential factors prompting the emperor to legislate on a macro or state level. In Chapter 2, the economic application of the *constitutio* will be assessed. This is a thorny issue since, on the one hand, it is the only rationale offered for the edict by a contemporary source other than the Giessen papyrus. On the other hand, though, the economic claim derives from Cassius Dio, and therefore must be treated with careful scrutiny. By reading between the lines of the author's vitriol, and combining his account with surviving numismatic evidence, it becomes possible to identify a fiscal rationale for the legislation based on a liquidity crisis,

---

30   The rivalry between Caracalla and his younger brother will be covered in the next chapter, and the role of this animosity in prompting the Antonine Constitution will be discussed in Chapter 5.

rather than systemic economic failure. This position will be supported by a close reading of the Giessen papyrus, dismissing any supposed mention of the *dediticii* and replacing it with a reference to an assortment of fiscal privileges being denied by the emperor upon the grant of *civitas*.

To some degree, Chapter 3 forms an extension of the economic case for the *Constitutio Antoniniana*. One of the problems in accepting that Caracalla was engaged in a large scale programme to improve liquidity is that that there is little indication that the empire was in the grip of the financial stress that would be seen later in the military crisis of the third century. If a fiscal explanation for the edict is accepted, then the question of its ultimate purpose becomes all the more pertinent. The answer lies with Caracalla's programme of military reform and expenditure, particularly in the prelude to his fateful campaign against Parthia. Over and above the financial aspect of the *constitutio*, however, the immediate consequences of the legislation also lend credence to the theory that Caracalla desired to increase exponentially the pool of available manpower to fill the legionary levies. The combination of these factors will further serve to ground the Antonine Constitution in the contemporary context of Caracalla's reign and, furthermore, will offer a more rational analysis of the edict's fiscal dimension, without Dio's hostile account corrupting the picture.

The second section will consider the *Constitutio Antoniniana* on the micro level, that is to say by examining the factors that may have prompted Caracalla on a personal level, politically or otherwise, to introduce his edict in 212. Chapter 4 considers Caracalla's apparent obsession with Alexander the Great. It is necessary first to assess the nature of the emperor's Alexander *imitatio*, to discern how extraordinary or exaggerated it was. Caracalla was not the only emperor to invoke the legacy of the Macedonian, and so it is necessary to position him within the wider fashion of exploiting the political currency of the Alexander mythos. Rather than seeking to draw a direct link between Caracalla and the historical Alexander, the emphasis here is on the extent to which the emperor was shaped and inspired by the literary presentation of the conqueror found in writers such as Plutarch. It is this literary incarnation of Alexander the Great that appears to have formed a key facet of Caracalla's self-identity and, moreover, influenced his vocabulary when constructing the eventual extension of the Roman franchise.

Chapter 5 will combine a number of other potential motivations for the Antonine Constitution. I will examine the potential religious foundation for the edict, since this was the rationale that Caracalla himself actively promoted in the opening lines of the *constitutio*, such as we have it from the Giessen papyrus. Indeed, there is evidence to suggest that the legislation was merely one facet of a more general drive by the emperor to appear pious and favoured by the gods in his official state media.[31] In order to assess the religious dimension of Caracalla's edict in more depth, this programme must also be set against the general desire for consensus between the emperor and his subjects.

The primary objective of this final chapter is to position the *Constitutio Antoniniana* within the political context of the Severan era and, more specifically, the tense period of transition from a shared principate at the outset of 211 to Caracalla's sole reign commencing at the close of the same year. On a general level, the events surrounding the rise of the Severan dynasty had resulted in a process of social levelling between the equestrian and senatorial orders, particularly in terms of their relationship with the imperial household. The levelling tendency at the heart of the Antonine Constitution will be discussed against this backdrop. More pressing, however, is the question of how far Caracalla's rivalry with Geta was the dominant factor in his decision to institute the *constitutio* when he did. The relationship between the brothers and co-emperors had always been fractious, but the internecine violence observed in 211 had threatened to tear the imperial household apart. The surviving evidence for this period suggests that Caracalla was intensely mindful of his position in the opening half of 212, and took a variety of actions to consolidate and legitimise his principate, effectively rewriting the history of the Severan dynasty, and refocusing the regime around his persona alone. Within this dramatic context, the Antonine Constitution will be characterised as an act of political expediency, a powerful tool in dictating the narrative of Caracalla's regime, and in binding his subjects to him at the moment when his principate was potentially vulnerable.

The paucity of the ancient evidence means that, in many ways, the *Constitutio Antoniniana* remains a frustratingly enigmatic document. Nevertheless, despite its many controversies, it is possible to assess the legislation from a number of perspectives, and to consider them together when contemplating the emperor's intentions in promulgating it. To understand the purpose of the edict and to make sense of Caracalla's motivations, however, it is crucial that the Antonine Constitution is considered within a properly embedded context. Through this approach, the *constitutio* can be identified as a multifaceted initiative, addressing the emperor's military and fiscal concerns, but also functioning as a powerful example of Caracallan propaganda, stabilising the emperor's position at one of the most dramatic moments in Roman imperial history.

---

31 Buraselis (2007) 36–47. Also see Corbo (2008).

CHAPTER 1

Contexts

The introduction of the Antonine Constitution represents a turning point in imperial history, and was a defining moment in the life of Caracalla. By means of this legislation, he had ostensibly revolutionised the constitutional complexion of the Roman state, with the rights of citizenship eventually becoming the norm, rather than the preserve of an exclusive minority.[1] Its long term effects were social as well as legal. It is well established that the edict was a major step towards political homogenisation within the empire, and resulted in an increasing sense of *Romanitas* among formerly peregrine or barbarian communities that should not be underestimated in the increasingly turbulent context of the later Roman Empire.[2]

Despite this apparent importance, however, the act of situating the *Constitutio Antoniniana* within the period appropriately, and thereby assessing its wider significance, is made difficult owing to the paucity of the ancient material relating directly to the edict. The striking dearth of evidence relating to Caracalla's *constitutio* has suggested to some, for example, that it was simply not considered by its contemporaries to represent the ideological watershed that many modern readers are tempted to see.[3] Any assessment of the Antonine Constitution in terms of its rationale, then, must be founded not only upon a clear sense of the context into which it was being promulgated but, moreover, must also assess the nature of the few extant sources that record its introduction. This chapter will therefore offer a contextualisation of the *constitutio* in two parts. Firstly, the historical backdrop against which Caracalla legislated will be considered. The Severan dynasty was forged in violence and warfare, usurping an unpopular but legitimate emperor, and defending itself against a number of threats and opponents. Consequently, it is important to view Caracalla's edict against the wider history of the period stretching back to the accession of Pertinax in the early hours of 1st January 193. Secondly, the extant references to the Antonine Constitution that we possess will be examined, and their individual virtues and limitations outlined. Central to this examination is the Giessen papyrus which, as the most comprehensive record

---

1 Buraselis (2013) 1747–48; Garnsey (2004) 135.
2 Mathisen (2006) 1015–18; Hekster (2008) 45; Sherwin-White (1973a) 282–83.
3 Ando (2012) 77; Buraselis (2007) 2.

of the edict, raises a number of issues that must be highlighted before the analysis of Caracalla's motive can begin in earnest.

The Historical Context: 193–212 CE

The Reign of Pertinax

The year 192 ended in dramatic fashion. Only hours before its conclusion, the emperor Commodus fell victim to a court conspiracy, following years of ever-decreasing popularity. The conspirators were members of his inner circle; they had first tried to murder him by means of poison but, when this approach failed and the emperor's suspicions were aroused, they resorted to the more direct method of having him strangled to death.[4] While Dio claimed that Commodus had been 'guileless' rather than irredeemably wicked, the fact remains that many among the senatorial order must have been pleased at the news of his demise, owing to the troubled relationship between themselves and the increasingly erratic emperor.[5]

The first of January 193 thus began with a frenetic burst of political activity. Judging from accounts of the night presented by both Dio and Herodian, it would appear that the assassins of Commodus had made no substantive plan regarding who should succeed him.[6] Following private discussion, the conspirators agreed upon the aged Publius Helvius Pertinax. Dio claimed that they chose him on the basis of his rank and personal excellence, while Herodian similarly asserts that the conspirators considered him the most qualified statesman to step into the power vacuum caused by the fall of the Antonine dynasty.[7] Pertinax was an Italian senator and had enjoyed a long and varied career in the military and imperial government, not only under Commodus, but also under Marcus Aurelius and Antoninus Pius before him.[8] The nature of his career meant that, in theory, Pertinax was ideally placed to rule, an individual who might command the obedience and respect of both the army and the senate: as Ando sums up, 'Pertinax represented the establishment.'[9]

---

4 Dio 73.22; Hdn. 1.17.10–11; HA *Comm.* 17.1.
5 For an example of this tension, see Dio 73.21.1–2.
6 This is probably explained by the plotters feeling compelled to act, following Commodian threats against the consuls, in addition to his generally autocratic demeanour. See Dio 73.22.1–2.
7 Dio 74.1.1; Hdn. 2.1.3.
8 Southern (2015) 31.
9 Ando (2012) 19.

Pertinax' first act after being informed of Commodus' assassination was to visit the *Castra Praetoria*, seeking approval for his regime from the praetorian guard. This is an indicator of the political reality facing emperors of the late second century, since it would have been imprudent, almost futile, to attempt to rule from Rome without the acceptance of the guard, especially when succeeding a ruler such as Commodus, who had enjoyed considerable popularity with the praetorians.[10] This episode is also useful in observing something of the underlying tensions within Pertinax' government from the very outset. Herodian, for example, suggests that the urban populace were aware of the praetorians' attachment to Commodus, and so crowded the camp to ensure the troops' acceptance of the new regime.[11] The author of the *Historia Augusta* goes further, alleging that on 3rd January 193, the guard even tried to supplant the new emperor with their preferred senator, Triarius Maternus Lascivius; this account is questionable, though, and contains characteristically sensational elements.[12] According to Dio, a key figure in this drama was the praetorian prefect, Quintus Aemilius Laetus. Dio depicts him attempting to soothe initial tensions by speaking well of Pertinax in public, although the author is quick to observe that Laetus' loyalty was itself never fully guaranteed.[13] Despite Pertinax' offer of a sizeable donative, then, it would appear that there was unease among the praetorians regarding how their position might be affected by the new regime, especially given the new emperor's long-established reputation as a martinet.[14]

With the apparent support of the main pillars of state successfully garnered, the business of government could begin. Like the aged soldier-emperor Galba in 68, however, Pertinax inherited an empire facing considerable financial difficulties. The reign of Commodus had been disastrous in economic terms, be this the result of his lavish spending habit or through unforeseen expenditure in response to multiple crises.[15] Whatever the underlying causes, the result was that the new emperor faced severely depleted coffers, and an empire that

---

10   Potter (2014) 93. As Bingham (2013) 42, has shown, however, Commodus' rapid progression through several guard commanders suggests that even he was suspicious of the praetorians, especially later in his reign. Also see Hekster (2002) 69–70.
11   Hdn. 2.2.4–5.
12   HA *Pert*. 6.4–5. In this account, Maternus is terrified at the prospect of elevation, and flees naked to Pertinax before departing the capital.
13   Dio 74.6.
14   Dio 74.1.2–3.
15   The re-emergence of the Antonine Plague and the Great Fire of 191 stand out in particular. The economic stress observed in the Antonine period will be considered in Chapter 2.

was on the brink of financial exhaustion.[16] In response to the looming crisis, Pertinax pursued an austerity agenda designed to forestall economic collapse. Imperial assets were auctioned and spending was curtailed.[17] These initiatives proved to be a welcome change from Commodus' regime, at least in the eyes of the senatorial order. Dio spoke glowingly of Pertinax' careful consideration for the public good, noting: 'He at once reduced to order everything that had previously been irregular and confused'.[18]

While he was feted by the *ordo senatorius* during this period, the fact remains that after only 87 days in power, Pertinax fell to an assassin's blade. The weapon was brandished by a member of the praetorian guard, clearly illustrating that Pertinax had failed to convince everyone of the virtue in his regime. Whether or not the new emperor was attempting to refashion the post-Commodus imperial state too quickly is ultimately academic: Pertinax' policies and self-consciously moderate style of government represented an almost continual source of tension between the emperor and his bodyguard, one that was to have murderous consequences.

The reports of the final, deadly exchange between Pertinax and the praetorians found in our primary authors are clearly flawed. Both Dio and Herodian write from a position of hindsight, and with an openly hostile attitude towards the military. Thus, in these accounts, the guard is a selfish and rapacious organisation, baying for the blood of an emperor who dared to restrain their insatiable excesses.[19] According to Herodian, the guard were increasingly frustrated by Pertinax' attempts to rein them in, with a number of soldiers attacking the emperor *en masse* at an otherwise peaceful moment.[20] In Dio's version, the figure of the prefect Laetus once again features prominently. Despite exhorting Pertinax' virtues in the aftermath of Commodus' murder, he was soon implicated in a plot to overthrow the emperor, planning to supplant him with one of the consuls for 193, Sosius Falco.[21] Moreover, following Pertinax' decision to pardon Falco, Laetus is depicted stirring further anger and dissent among the

---

16 Dio 74.5.4.
17 Dio 74.5.4–5.
18 Dio 74.5.1. Herodian (2.3.9) similarly has Pertinax refer to a requirement for a more fiscally restrained mode of imperial government in his speech to the senate following his accession.
19 Bingham (2013) 43.
20 Hdn. 2.5.
21 Dio 74.8. This episode is mysterious. It is unclear why Laetus would have sought to replace Pertinax at that moment. Birley (1988) 94, has suggested that, if the prefect was indeed the architect of this affair, that he may have done so with the explicit intention of foiling it publically, thus improving his stock.

guardsmen.[22] Disaffected praetorians responded by entering the palace complex and stabbing the emperor, who had attempted to meet the insurrection head on, and calm the soldiers through discussion and rhetoric. In this version, Laetus is ultimately responsible for Pertinax' death, although the reasons for his duplicitous actions remain unclear.[23]

Didius Julianus and the March of Severus

The murder of Pertinax meant that the Roman Empire faced a second power vacuum in the space of four months. What followed is arguably one of the oddest moments of this dynamic period, labelled by an appalled Dio as 'a most disgraceful business and one unworthy of Rome': the episode commonly referred to as the 'auction' of the empire.[24] Apart from Herodian, who claims that there was an interregnum of around two days, our other sources for the period convey the speed with which news of Pertinax' murder spread across the capital.[25] In these versions, Didius Julianus, who had served as suffect consul alongside the slain emperor in 175, first went to the senate house before being directed to the praetorian camp with a view to staking his claim for the principate.[26] Opposing him was the Urban Prefect, and Pertinax' father-in-law, Flavius Sulpicianus. According to Dio, Sulpicianus had been dispatched to the *Castra Praetoria* by Pertinax to stem potential unrest there, though he was likely only to interact with the urban cohorts, in the first instance.[27]

The image of what followed in our main sources verges on farcical. The praetorians seized their chance to extort the largest donative from the would-be *principes*. Julianus, barred from entering the camp, was forced to make his case by shouting to troops on the walls or making placards.[28] Placing the theatrical language of the auction-room to one side, what remains is confusion regarding who should be named as Pertinax' successor.[29] Within this maelstrom of activity, the praetorians were clearly the deciding authority. It is noteworthy, then, that in addition to monetary promises, it was a fear of Sulpicianus exacting

---

22   Dio 74.9.1–2.
23   Dio 74.9.4–10.3.
24   Dio 74.11.3.
25   Hdn. 2.6.3; Dio 74.11.3–4; HA *Jul.* 2.4–5.
26   Potter (2014) 96. The detail of these events is furnished by the *Historia Augusta* (*Jul.* 2.4–5) which, for all of its problems, is noteworthy in providing at least some explanation of how Julianus came to arrive at the camp.
27   Dio 74.11.1; Bingham (2013) 44.
28   Dio 74.11.3–6; Hdn. 2.6.8; HA *Jul.* 2.6.
29   Bingham (2013) 44.

retribution for the murder of Pertinax that finally swayed the guard to proclaim his opponent emperor on March 28th 193.[30]

With the support of the guard, the senate had little option but to ratify the new *princeps*, but Julianus was soon to find the task of consolidating his position of power nearly impossible. Our main sources are mercilessly hostile towards him, criticising his weak leadership and his personal habits.[31] This picture is almost definitely the result of later Severan propaganda denigrating Julianus, with Herodian and the *Historia Augusta* offering completely opposed views of the emperor's predilection for luxury.[32] Nevertheless, it is clear that the urban populace stood opposed to his regime, protesting vigorously and even occupying the Circus Maximus for twenty-four hours.[33] During this demonstration, our sources allege that the urban mass exhorted the governor of Syria, Pescennius Niger, to liberate them. While Niger would eventually feature in the civil turmoil that was to follow, the immediate threat to Julianus' position was not to come from Syria, but from the governor of Upper Pannonia, Lucius Septimius Severus.

Septimius Severus was proclaimed emperor by his troops on April 9th. Given the time that it would have taken for news of Pertinax' assassination to reach the governor, any notion that Severus had not hitherto considered the prospect of seizing the throne for himself seems somewhat unconvincing. Herodian, following Severus' autobiography, claims that the general experienced a number of dreams and portents forecasting his rise to imperial power.[34] Even setting this supposedly divine providence to one side, Severus seems to have been well aware of Commodus' lack of an heir, and was probably consulting with potential supporters in the central provinces throughout early 193, even after swearing an oath of loyalty to Pertinax.[35] In this context, the events of March 28th gave Severus a perfect pretext upon which to base his offensive: he would position himself as the avenger of the slain emperor, marching on Rome to punish the assassins.[36]

---

30 Potter (2014) 96–97; Bingham (2013) 44.
31 Dio 74.14.1; Hdn. 2.7.1–2; HA *Jul.* 3.9–10.
32 Millar (1964) 136–38.
33 Dio 74.13.4–5; Hdn. 2.7.2–3. The incident is also recorded in the *Historia Augusta*: HA *Jul.* 4.7; *Nig.* 3.1. Ando (2012) 24, neatly depicts Julianus and the guard as 'co-dependent' but otherwise lacking in legitimacy.
34 Hdn. 2.9.4–7; Dio 75.3.
35 Southern (2015) 34–35; Potter (2014) 101. At the latest, it is also possible that Severus began forging arrangements with his contacts after news of Falco's abortive coup reached him. See Birley (1988) 97.
36 Hdn. 2.9.8–10; Dio 75.1.1, 75.4.1.

CONTEXTS 17

The Severan march on Rome was swift, with Julianus' lack of command authority in the capital becoming ever more apparent. Severus' forces were able to take Ravenna without bloodshed, according to Dio, and the troops that Julianus had sent to stall the advance had simply defected.[37] While the emperor struggled to fortify Rome itself, the extent of Severus' support network can be observed in his successful protection of his young children, whom he had been obliged to leave in the city during the period of his governorship.[38] Dio offers us a valuable insight into the increasing panic and desperation shown by Julianus, who executed the praetorian prefect Laetus, obviously fearing that the guard would turn on him, before finally offering to share power with his rival.[39] Severus, however, had already vowed to show clemency to the praetorians if they surrendered the assassins of Pertinax and did not otherwise oppose him, thus robbing the incumbent emperor of his final defences. By the time Severus' army arrived in Rome on 9th June, Julianus had been declared a public enemy by the senate and was subsequently stabbed to death in the palace; he had ruled the empire for sixty-six days.[40]

Severus spent a month in Rome, following his successful coup d'état, consolidating his power in the city. This process is most clearly seen in his almost immediate cashiering of the praetorian guard entire, filling the ranks with soldiers from his own legions.[41] He had successfully supplanted the incumbent (and legitimate) emperor, but his rule was far from uncontested. Severus was not the only military governor raised to the purple by the army in April 193. The news of Pertinax' murder spread quickly among the provinces, and it became clear that the governor of Upper Pannonia was not alone in laying groundwork for his own claim to the imperial throne. Severus found opponents at both extremes of the empire. In the east, the governor of Syria, Pescennius Niger (for whom the Roman populace had supposedly called) probably raised his standard shortly after Severus in mid-April, although later Severan propagandists were keen to stress that the former declared first.[42] At the same time in

---

37   Dio 74.16.5–17.1.
38   Hdn. 3.2.4; Potter (2014) 102.
39   Dio 74.17.1–2; Hdn. 2.12.3. For the murder of Laetus, see Dio 74.16.5. Julianus fares even worse in the *Historia Augusta*, with an accusation that he resorted to consulting magicians and engaged in bizarre rituals to shore up his faltering regime. See HA *Jul.* 7.9–10.
40   Dio 74.17.3–5; Hdn. 2.12.6–7. Southern (2015) 35–36; Ando (2012) 24.
41   Bingham (2013) 45, notes both the unprecedented nature of this change, and the speed with which it was implemented, further suggesting that Severus had been planning his advance in some detail.
42   Hdn. 2.8.1–6. Herodian later points to the use of Severus himself as a source in reconstructing the chronology of the pretenders' campaigns. Also see Ando (2012) 23; Potter (2014) 99.

the west, Clodius Albinus, the governor of Britain, was proclaimed emperor by his legions.[43] Following the death of Julianus, then, there were still three men claiming the title of Augustus simultaneously: civil war was inevitable.

The Wars of Succession—193-7 CE

Severus was to spend the majority of the following four years on campaign. Even during his *blitzkrieg* against Didius Julianus, it would have been apparent that he was in a potentially dangerous position, wedged between two other contenders for the throne. Writing with the benefit of hindsight, Dio characterised Severus as the most cunning of the three surviving competitors, reaching out to Clodius Albinus in an act designed to divide and conquer:

> Of the three leaders, Severus was the shrewdest. He understood in advance that after Julianus had been deposed the three would clash and fight against one another for the empire, and he therefore determined to win over the rival who was nearest to him. So he sent a letter by one of his trusted friends to Albinus, appointing him Caesar; as for Niger, who was proud of having been summoned by the populace, he had no hopes of him. Albinus, accordingly, in the belief that he was to share the rule with Severus, remained where he was.[44]

Herodian reported that Severus sent a messenger to Albinus, offering the position of Caesar in exchange for a pledge of non-aggression, during the former's preparations for war with Pescennius Niger.[45] It is more likely, though, that he was in contact with the governor of Britain even earlier, potentially as part of his attempts to secure the support of his colleagues following the death of Pertinax, and certainly before his advance on Rome.[46] A number of questions remain regarding the relationship between Severus and Albinus at this crucial juncture. Most importantly, given what was to follow, is the question of how far Albinus considered Severus' offer to be a genuine one. Dio notes that Albinus accepted the offer in good faith, while Herodian (again displaying something of later Severan propaganda) emphasises how far Severus was able to manipulate his rival's simple mind and sense of vanity, in order to outmanoeuvre him.[47] Whether or not Albinus truly believed the authenticity of the Severan offer,

---

43 Dio 74.14.3.
44 Dio 74.15.1-2. (tr. Cary).
45 Hdn. 2.15.3-4.
46 Hdn. 2.10.1-2.
47 Dio 74.15.2; Hdn. 2.15.3.

especially considering that the governor of Pannonia already had two young sons, it seems that he was willing to work with Severus, quickly adopting a new imperial name that declared his identification with the Septimian faction: Decimus Clodius Septimius Albinus Caesar.[48]

With a peace brokered in the west, Severus could direct his considerable military force eastwards. Our accounts of the war against Pescennius Niger suffer from the propagandistic traditions of later Severan historiography. Niger himself is characterised as a preening and self-important commander, hopelessly inadequate when met with any significant opposition.[49] The reality, however, is that Niger's cause was at a disadvantage from the beginning, and his forces fought with considerable resolve even after defeat was inevitable.

While Niger could call upon support from a vast expanse of territory in the east, ranging from Asia Minor down to Egypt, the military balance was heavily stacked in favour of Severus. Arrayed against the six legions under Niger's control were the sixteen legions of the Danube.[50] Speed was the vital element for both commanders. Niger had to strike swiftly, in the hope of destabilising the Septimian faction, while Severus could not afford to allow his opponent too much time to nurture a larger support base.[51] Contrary to the image of sloth associated with them in our main sources, the eastern faction was to draw first blood in this contest, with Niger's forces fortifying Byzantium and advancing as far westward as Perinthus, where they inflicted a high number of casualties on the Severan army under Fabius Cilo.[52]

Even if taken aback by this initial setback, the Septimian faction showed no sign of vulnerability and, by the end of the year, Severus' armies had organised and forced Niger's men back into Asia Minor, defeating the eastern legions at both Cyzicus and Nicaea.[53] As 194 began, it was apparent that Niger had little hope of redressing the balance, with a number of cities that had previously

---

48   RIC 2–12A *Clodius Albinus*. Also see Southern (2015) 36, who has noted that there is also some question surrounding whether Albinus even intended to press his imperial claim so quickly. The peaceful arrangement may have been seen, then, as a temporarily convenient one by Albinus as much as Severus.
49   Rubin (1980) 92–96.
50   Potter (2014) 103.
51   Southern (2015) 38; Potter (2014) 103.
52   Dio 75.6.3; Hdn. 2.14.7; HA *Sev.* 8.3; Southern (2015) 38–39; Potter (2014) 103; Ando (2012) 30; Birley (1988) 108. Byzantium was to resist Severus' eventual counter-offensive, and held out under siege until the end of 195.
53   Dio 75.6.4–7.8; Hdn. 3.2.1–6.

supported him defecting to Severus.[54] Niger's cause was shattered in May 194, following a comprehensive defeat on the field at Issus, a final irony in the career of one who is said to have viewed himself as a new Alexander.[55] Niger himself survived the battle, but was captured while fleeing eastwards and was subsequently murdered, his head sent to his former headquarters in Antioch before being transported for display in Rome.[56]

Following the defeat of Niger, Severus almost immediately launched an offensive against Parthia, either to punish those who had supported his enemy, to claim imperatorial titles without the stain of civil war or, alternatively, simply to provide a common enemy for the survivors of legions that had only just stopped warring against one another.[57] The campaign, labelled the First Parthian War, also allowed Severus to respond to the opportunistic revolt of Osrhoene and Adiabene.[58] A direct result of this offensive was the conquest of Mesopotamia and the sacking of Nisibis, actions that served to re-stabilise the eastern frontier, at least temporarily.[59] This 'short-term punitive war' was swiftly resolved by Severus, and he was back in Rome before the end of 196.[60] By the time of his arrival in the capital, the empire was once again in the grip of civil war, following the collapse of the fragile alliance between Severus and Clodius Albinus. This was a conflict of Severus' own making and, when viewed with hindsight, there can be little doubt that the emperor had planned to cast his Caesar aside when the time was right.[61]

---

54 Herodian states, for example, that the cities of Laodicea and Tyre were swift to recognise Severus in the aftermath of Niger's defeat at Nicaea. See Hdn. 3.3.3. The manner in which local rivalries between cities appear to have driven the civil conflict in the east during the war is one of its more intriguing facets. See Potter (2014) 104.

55 Dio 75.6.2a; Buraselis (2007) 28; Birley (1988) 135–36.

56 Dio 75.8.2–3; Hdn. 3.4.6–7. There is a suggestion that local potentates or vassals of the Parthian Empire had supported Niger, and that he was therefore fleeing to them: see Southern (2015) 39; Ando (2012) 31. It seems quite reasonable that Niger would seek assistance from Parthia, given his comparative lack of military strength compared to the Severan legions, but the extent to which it was actually delivered is difficult to know: see Potter (2014) 109.

57 Ando (2012) 31.

58 Dio 75.1–3; Sheldon (2010) 164–65.

59 Dio 75.2.3; HA *Sev.* 9.8–10. It is unclear if Severus also partitioned Syria into two provinces at this time or later, but there is an argument to be made for the logic of such a division immediately following the defeat of Niger; see Southern (2015) 41.

60 Birley (1988) 119.

61 Southern (2015) 40; Birley (1988) 117.

While still in the east, Severus took steps to consolidate his position of imperial power, and to ensure that his claim to legitimacy was both singular and unassailable. This was achieved primarily through retroactively adopting his family into that of the Antonines, thereafter referring to himself as the son of the Divine Marcus and rehabilitating the image of his 'brother', Commodus, eventually ordering his deification.[62] At around the same time as this act of adoption, he bestowed his wife, Julia Domna, with the honorific title *mater castrorum* (a clear allusion to Faustina) and promoted his eldest son, Caracalla, to the rank of Caesar, thus removing Albinus from the picture altogether.[63] This was an astonishing move: the 'adoption' was both entirely unprecedented and a reversal of his rhetoric regarding Commodus during his initial advance on Rome.[64] Moreover, this propagandistic shift was highly significant in other ways. It was to form the basis of one of the Severan household's strongest political themes in subsequent years (something that Caracalla would later be challenged to navigate, when promoting his own regime).[65] It also had the more immediate effect of making obvious Severus' intention to hold the imperial throne alone, removing Albinus from the equation entirely.

Although the precise chronology of what followed is not completely clear, the evidence shows that Albinus was far from passive as 197 began. He had always enjoyed popularity among the senate, owing to his prestigious lineage, and there is evidence to suggest that he had been in constant contact with many senators secretly, a number of them encouraging him to march on Rome in Severus' absence.[66] Once Severus' betrayal became apparent, Albinus claimed the title of Augustus for himself, advancing into Gaul.[67] Critically, the nearby German legions remained loyal to Severus, meaning that Albinus encountered a strategic disadvantage similar to that faced by Pescennius Niger. The pretender was to advance as far as Lyon, before being intercepted by a Septimian army, with Severus himself at its head.

---

62 Dio 76.7.4, 77.9.4; HA *Sev.* 11.4. For more on the process of self-adoption, see Hekster (2015) 209–17.

63 Southern (2015) 41; Ando (2012) 32–33; Kienast (2011) 162.

64 Dio 76.7.4–8.4; Hekster (2015) 208–17, has clearly shown that this new imperial image was carefully distributed to different groups through varying media in stages, rather than all at once.

65 Kemezis (2014) 55–74.

66 Dio 75.4.2; Hdn. 3.5.2; Bingham and Imrie (2015) 83. Severus was to execute a number of senators for supporting his rival, following his eventual victory.

67 Coinage struck for Albinus suggests a rapid promotion of his new titulature. For examples, see RIC 13–49 *Clodius Albinus*, struck at Lugdunum.

In his description of clash that followed, Dio claimed that both commanders fielded armies in excess of 150,000 men.[68] While this is almost certainly an exaggeration in the case of Albinus' force, the Battle of Lugdunum still represents the largest single mêlée of the civil wars.[69] Arrayed against the governor of Britain would have been a force assembled from multiple areas and legions; since the legions of the Rhine and Danube regions alone would, at full strength, have constituted a force of *c.* 200,000 men, the number assigned by Dio might not be too far removed from the reality of the Septimian host.[70]

For all of the disparity between the competing armies, however, the battle was a close affair.[71] While Albinus' army was forced to cede ground, it managed to feign a retreat, encouraging the Severan forces to charge headlong into concealed trenches that Albinus had ordered before the conflict.[72] This was enough to upset the balance of the battle temporarily, with a number of the Severan soldiers wavering and fleeing. In the ensuing confusion, Severus found himself in mortal danger, thrown from his horse and compelled to discard his imperial cloak, so as to obscure his identity. Dio claims that the emperor drew his sword and exhorted his retreating army forces to fight.[73] Herodian, by contrast, alleges that Severus and his praetorians simply fled after being repulsed by Albinus' battle-line.[74] Just as the fate of the empire hung in the balance, one of Severus' generals, Julius Laetus (not to be confused with the executed praetorian prefect), entered the fray with a large number of fresh cavalry, tipping the balance decisively in Severus' favour.[75] His army defeated, Albinus fled into the city of Lugdunum before eventually committing suicide.

With final victory achieved, Severus now held the imperial throne unchallenged. After sending the head of his last rival to be displayed in Rome, the

---

68   Dio 76.6.1.
69   Birley (1988) 124, has calculated that Albinus' force was more likely around 40,000 men, presuming that the pretender left some military force in Britain to retain control of the northern frontier.
70   Southern (2015) 42–43; Birley (1988) 124.
71   Herodian (3.7.2–3) referred to the mutual ferocity and courage of the British and Illyrian armies.
72   Dio 76.6.1–5.
73   Dio 76.6.6–7.
74   Hdn. 3.7.3.
75   Dio 76.6.8; Hdn. 3.7.3–4. It is noteworthy that both of our main authors for the period claim that Laetus had intentionally prevaricated, delaying until it was clear who would triumph. His execution for treachery in the following year also does little to reduce the speculation that he may have been waiting in the hope that both commanders would perish; see Birley (1988) 125.

emperor himself arrived in the capital. The tension among the *ordo senatorius* was palpable since, as noted above, many among the order had supported Albinus' claim. Dio provides us with a sense of the atmosphere, stating that 'all pretended to be on the side of Severus, but they were undone the moment that any sudden reports arrived, being unable to conceal the feelings hidden in their hearts.'[76] From surviving epigraphic evidence, it would seem that the senate attempted to forestall Severus' wrath by appointing Caracalla as *Imperator destinatus*, a new position that officially recognised Severus' son as the heir apparent.[77] Regardless, however, our sources agree that the emperor was swift to root out Albinian sympathisers and arrest them, haranguing the senate with letters and other evidence of their betrayal.[78] Severus released thirty-five of his senatorial prisoners, but had a further twenty-nine executed, finely balancing clemency and tyranny in asserting his position.[79]

By the end of the following year, the Severan family was once again on campaign, engaged in a second war against Parthia, whose king, so Dio records, had taken advantage of Rome's civil strife to conquer Mesopotamia, threatening Nisibis.[80] Severus responded with force, launching his campaign in the summer of 197. His offensive was swift and, while he failed to capture the strategically important city of Hatra, he managed to lift the siege of Nisibis, also recapturing Seleucia and Babylon, both of which had been abandoned before he arrived.[81] Ctesiphon fell to Severus' first assault, allowing the emperor to assume a tenth imperatorial title.[82] Despite this rapid victory, Severus chose to celebrate his achievements on 28th January 198, to coincide with the centenary of Trajan's accession.[83] It was during these celebrations that Severus cemented his dynastic ambitions by elevating both of his sons: Caracalla to Augustus, and Geta to Caesar. From this point onwards, the sons of Severus would play an increasingly important role in the dynastic dynamic that would ultimately conclude in Caracalla occupying the imperial throne alone.

---

76 Dio 76.8.5 (tr. Adapted from Cary).
77 For a record of an embassy to the imperial family, see *ILS* 1143.
78 Hdn. 3.8.6–7.
79 Dio 76.8.3–4; Ando (2012) 38; Birley (1988) 127–28.
80 Dio 76.9.1.
81 Dio 76.9.3–4.
82 Ando (2012) 38; Sheldon (2010) 167–69.
83 Southern (2015) 49–50; Potter (2014) 113–14; Ando (2012) 38.

The Sons of Severus

The period following Severus' final consolidation of power in 198 was far from uneventful. The imperial household spent a number of years touring the provinces, notably Egypt and North Africa.[84] In addition, the emperor ensured that significant anniversaries and games were delivered with considerable pomp and ceremony, such as in the case of Severus' *decennalia* in 202 and the Secular Games of 204.[85] The opening decade of the third century was also turbulent for Severus, with an abortive coup d'état by his trusted praetorian prefect, Plautianus, in 205.[86] Arguably the most important aspect of the period 198–211 for understanding Caracalla's later promulgation of the *Constitutio Antoniniana*, however, is the conflict between Caracalla and Geta, a sibling rivalry that was one of the leitmotifs of the early Severan era.

When considering the friction between the sons of Severus, we are required to navigate an obviously problematic source tradition in which ancient authors were eager to draw clear distinctions between the brothers, characterising them as polar opposites of one another.[87] Born in 188, Caracalla is depicted as an aggressive bully, an individual defined by his many personality flaws. Dio, for example, claimed that the eldest son had absorbed all of the negative attributes of his birthplace and family lineage: 'the fickleness, cowardice, and recklessness of Gaul were his, the harshness and cruelty of Africa, and the craftiness of Syria'.[88] The author of the *Historia Augusta* goes even further in his characterisation, claiming that his mode of life was simply evil and brutal, and that there was no resemblance at all between Caracalla and his younger brother.[89]

By contrast, Geta presents us with more of an enigma. While it is clear that he was born less than a year after Caracalla, characterisation of the younger son during his early years is sparse. Dio barely mentions him at all in the course of his *Roman History*, rendering him a figure in the background, a non-entity overshadowed by his more senior relatives.[90] In the *Historia Augusta*, Geta is depicted as a fop, fond of colourful clothing and exuberant living, but a far

---

84 Dio 76.13.1–16.5. The precise itinerary of the journey is a matter of some debate, and Birley (1988) 146–54, in particular, is almost certainly guilty of offering an overly elaborate reconstruction based upon flimsy ancient evidence.
85 Dio 77.1; Hdn. 3.8.9–10; Gorrie (2002) 461–81.
86 Ando (2012) 44–45.
87 Weisser (2011) 8–9.
88 Dio 78.6.1a.
89 HA *Car.* 9.3.
90 Kemmers (2011) 271.

more affable individual, nevertheless.[91] It quickly becomes clear, then, that the literary sources for the period are satisfied to present the fractious fraternal relationship as an uneven struggle, one in which the gentle Geta was dominated by his barbaric older brother. Careful analysis of the rivalry, however, reveals the extent to which such stark characterisation is a wholly literary construct. The siblings were most likely equally recalcitrant and, as their conflict escalated, it became an increasing source of concern for their father.[92]

Initially, the rivalry between Caracalla and Geta manifested in relatively harmless sporting contests and divergent tastes.[93] This inherent sense of competition appears to have been intense from an early stage, and even became physical on occasion, with Dio recording a particularly boisterous chariot race in which the older brother broke his leg.[94] Beneath this potentially innocent, albeit passionate, enmity, however, lay a more sinister struggle that threatened to destabilise the imperial household from the earliest years of the third century.

One detail that underlies the conflict between Caracalla and Geta is that both seem to have had extensive entourages and factions that encouraged the fraternal rivalry.[95] Recently, it has been argued that this factionalism may even have led to an attempt to supplant Severus and Caracalla with Geta between 200 and 202, during which time the young prince's numismatic output appears to exceed his junior position wildly, both in terms of quantity and iconography.[96] In fact, there is even a suggestion that a pro-Getan faction could have been instrumental in engineering the failed coup of 205, with Plautianus acting as part of a larger conspiracy, rather than as a solitary renegade.[97]

In any event, the death of Plautianus represents a defining moment in the princes' fraternal rivalry. In our literary record for the years that follow, little else but the conflict between Caracalla and Geta is covered by either Dio or Herodian until Severus' British expedition.[98] Dio, in particular, considered the removal of Plautianus as the final limitation on the princes' behaviour, stating:

---

91   HA *Geta* 4–5.
92   Southern (2015) 59–60.
93   Hdn. 3.10.3–4.
94   Dio 77.7.2.
95   Hdn. 3.10.4; Dio 77.7.1.
96   Kemmers (2011).
97   Bingham and Imrie (2015).
98   Dio 77.7.1–11.2; Hdn. 3.13; Potter (2014) 120–21. Dio balances his account of the brothers' conflict with a description of the banditry of Bulla Felix.

> The sons of Severus, Antoninus and Geta, feeling that they had got rid of a pedagogue, as it were, in Plautianus, now went to all lengths in their conduct. They outraged women and abused boys, they embezzled money, and made gladiators and charioteers their associates, emulating each other in the similarity of their deeds, but full of strife in their rivalries; for if the one attached himself to a certain faction, the other would be sure to choose the opposite side.[99]

While we must exercise caution in accepting Dio's testimony, given his predilection for criticising the Severan emperors in general, we may still conclude that the conflict between the sons of Severus became increasingly public in nature, and was a source of embarrassment to the imperial household.[100]

Severus was not blind to his sons' unravelling relationship. The evidence suggests that the senior Augustus attempted to reconcile his children through a combination of paternal encouragement on the one hand, and strictly enforcing a public image of familial unity on the other. Herodian, for example, claimed that Severus took pains to remind his sons of the disaster that befell warring brothers in myth and plays, and showed them the extent of the treasuries, with a lesson that they would have ample resources to repel any foreign attack or revolt.[101] While it is tempting to view these tender moments as examples of fiction or retroactive continuity, Severus simultaneously promoted a public image of harmony within the *domus Caesaris* on a massive scale. Caracalla and Geta were made to share the consulship in 205, and imperial coinage for the period is peppered with references to *concordia*.[102] The best example of this contrived amity, however, is arguably seen at the Secular Games in 204, when every member of the imperial household played a prominent role in the celebrations.[103] No suggestion of internal discord was to be allowed to derail Severus' declaration of a new Augustan era.[104]

Despite these efforts by the senior emperor, the acrimony between his sons continued to escalate, to the point that our primary authors agree that Severus' British expedition was at least partially prompted by a desire to remove Caracalla and Geta from the corrupting environment of Rome, in

---

99   Dio 77.7.1–2 (tr. Cary).
100 For a collection of the literary references to this rivalry, see Weisser (2011). Also see Birley (1988) 168.
101 Hdn. 3.13.3–4.
102 For examples of this iconography, see RIC 53, 59–61 *Caracalla*, and RIC 40 *Geta*.
103 Gorrie (2002) 480, n. 100.
104 Bingham and Imrie (2015) 89.

which each son had amassed a considerable entourage who only encouraged the rift.[105] The campaign in Britain was relatively disappointing, the Roman offensive failing to bring the enemy tribes into a decisive battle.[106] More important to the events that would follow, however, was Severus' decision to promote Geta to the rank of Augustus in early 209. Whether this was done for administrative expediency or, as some more recently have posited, in the hope of protecting Geta's life after the ailing Severus' death, it represented a profound change in the power balance within the imperial household, since it meant that his warring sons would be compelled to share the mantle of imperial power as equals.[107]

This arrangement was put to the test sooner rather than later. In the midst of the campaign in early 211, Severus' numerous ailments finally overcame him, and the emperor died at his headquarters in Eboracum on 4th February. According to Dio, Severus spoke to his sons in the hours before his death, exhorting them to rule together and seek an accord with one another: 'Be harmonious, enrich the soldiers, and scorn all other men.'[108] Even if we do not accept the veracity of Dio's account, since he could hardly have been privy to the private conversations of the imperial triad, it is noteworthy that the author draws attention to these elements, further indicating that the rift between Caracalla and Geta was common knowledge, especially among those close to the imperial court.

Our literary sources for the period following Severus' death are characterised predominantly by attacks on Caracalla for executing many of the household's attendants, and exacting revenge on those whom the authors claim resisted his desire to hasten his father's demise.[109] Beyond these allegations, however, it is possible to glean something of the speed with which Caracalla and Geta's shared principate began to unravel. While Dio is silent on the circumstances surrounding the conclusion of the campaign in Britain, Herodian provides a little more information, noting that both brothers hastened towards Rome, Caracalla reaching terms with the British tribes through negotiation.[110] On the one hand, this may be understood in the context of affording Severus appropriate funerary rites. On the other hand, though, there is also a sense

---

105 Dio 77.11.1; Hdn. 3.14.2.
106 Dio 77.13.
107 Hdn. 3.14.9. For modern assessments suggesting a protective urge on the part of Severus, see Southern (2015) 62, and Birley (1988) 186.
108 Dio 77.15.2.
109 Dio 78.1.1–3; Hdn. 3.15.4–5.
110 Hdn. 3.15.6.

that the brothers were increasingly wary of each other. Even before arriving in Rome, the emperors had begun to live apart, apparently from fear of their sibling making an attempt to poison them.[111]

In public, both Caracalla and Geta made an effort to perpetuate the image of familial harmony, earlier presented by Severus. Dio noted that the pair 'pretended to love and commend each other', a sentiment that is borne out in the numismatic record, in which *concordia augustorum* continued to be struck on imperial coinage.[112] Behind the scenes, however, the co-emperors were becoming ever more estranged, gathering large groups of supporters and bodyguards.[113] A potential hint to this rivalry may even be found in the iconography employed on Geta's coinage for the year. In 211, the younger emperor's obverse portraiture was altered to take on a number of physiognomic features reminiscent of his father.[114] While the younger emperor's portrait style had been rapidly evolving since 209, the adoption of such Septimian features as bulging eyes and a tapering beard (neither hitherto associated with Geta) ultimately suggests a political motive in the context of his opposition to Caracalla.

Both Dio and Herodian record poignant episodes to demonstrate the severity of the situation following Severus' death. Dio, continuing his motif of portents and omens, claimed that the senate voted sacrifices to be made to Concord, only for the rite to fail when the priests involved could not locate one another.[115] More temporally, Herodian claimed that the brothers were engaged in a plan to divide the empire itself into two separate realms, with Caracalla based in Rome, Geta in either Alexandria or Antioch.[116] In this episode, only the passionate lament of their mother succeeded in disavowing them of the plan.[117] While almost certainly included for dramatic effect, these accounts nevertheless succeed in suggesting the brewing atmosphere of tension that pervaded the capital in 211. Dio's claim that 'anyone could see that something terrible was bound to result' seems all too likely.[118]

---

111 Hdn. 4.1.1–2.
112 Dio 78.1.4. For examples of this type struck for Geta during this period, see *RIC* 73a–b, 85–86b *Geta*.
113 Hdn. 4.3.1–2, 4.4.1–2.
114 Pangerl (2013) 107–8.
115 Dio 78.1.4–6.
116 Hdn. 4.3.5–9.
117 In this section of the text, it is clear that a number of high ranking officials, such as the praetorian prefect Papinian also worked to encourage cooperation between the brothers during this fraught period. For more on the role of Julia Domna as a peacekeeper, see Levick (2007) 88–89; Imrie (2014) 312–14.
118 Dio 78.1.4.

The gathering storm eventually broke at the end of the year. According to Dio, Caracalla called a meeting with Geta to be held in the presence of their mother Julia, ostensibly to discuss a reconciliation between the brothers. The façade of this conference was quickly revealed, however, when a number of centurions, previously instructed by Caracalla, rushed into the chamber and attacked Geta. The younger emperor, apparently terror-struck, beseeched his mother for protection, but ultimately bled to death in her arms.[119] Herodian's account of Geta's downfall is largely similar, although a lacuna in the text obscures the final act of murder itself.[120] Three interpolations survive to fill this gap, namely those of Politian, John of Antioch and the *Codex Monacensis*. While similar to Dio's version in recounting a meeting held under the pretence of a settlement between the emperors, they diverge when describing the climatic attack. Rather than a group of soldiers bursting in, they attribute the violence to Caracalla himself in graphic fashion.[121]

In the aftermath of the murder, Caracalla is said to have rushed to secure the support of the soldiery, before making a speech to the senate in which he cast Geta as a guilty party in the recent violence and declared him a public enemy.[122] The year 212 thus began with an entirely new order from that of 211. Rather than a co-emperor sharing power with his father and brother, Caracalla found himself as the only ruler of the empire. More than this, however, he was sole emperor through an unprecedented act of political murder. While many opponents or rivals to emperors had been assassinated in the past, this was the first example of one incumbent Augustus murdering another. The implications of such internecine violence within the imperial household were potentially profound, and Caracalla would be required to respond in a number of ways as 212 wore on. As it will become clear, one of the key elements of Caracalla's response was the *Constitutio Antoniniana*.[123]

---

119 Dio 78.2.2–4.
120 Hdn. 4.4.2–3.
121 Whittaker (1969) 391, n. 2. Also see Bingham and Imrie (2015) 80.
122 Dio 78.3; Hdn. 4.4.3–5.7.
123 The ways in which Caracalla asserted his position in the period following Geta's assassination, including the promulgation of the Antonine Constitution, will be discussed in Chapter 5.

The Antonine Constitution in Ancient Literature

The relative absence of evidence relating to the Antonine Constitution is quickly apparent upon examination of the literary sources. The majority of the surviving references to the edict are to be found in sources written long after its introduction. These allusions are relatively brief, and display some confusion regarding the character and provenance of the legislation. The edict is mentioned, for example, in the biography of Septimius Severus contained in the *Historia Augusta*. In this source, the author simply states that the *constitutio* was introduced and that universal enfranchisement was the result.[124] A similarly concise description of the edict can be found in the writing of Sidonius Apollinaris, in which the author declared that only slaves and barbarians did not possess the rights of Roman citizenship.[125] Given the sheer time lapse between the introduction of the *constitutio* and these sources, however, not to mention their literary agendas, it is understandable that we find the Antonine Constitution referred to in such a superficial way here.[126]

More surprising, however, is the level of confusion apparent among other sources of the same period regarding the provenance of the legislation. Aurelius Victor mistakenly credits Marcus Aurelius with the initiative while, in the Justinianic *Novellae*, the *constitutio* is erroneously attributed to Antoninus Pius.[127] On the one hand, this might seem a reasonable mistake to make, owing to the similarity in nomenclature between Caracalla and his predecessors.[128] On the other hand, though, this level of uncertainty surrounding such a supposedly well-known edict raises questions concerning the source tradition surrounding it. While it is tempting to interpret the paltry number of extant references to the *constitutio* as a simple accident of attrition, fundamental misunderstandings concerning the source of the legislation make it more likely that there were simply few authors who devoted extensive attention to it.

The apparent lack of interest in the Antonine Constitution ultimately compels us to consider how revolutionary it was in reality. Did the *constitutio* represent a fundamental constitutional change, or was it merely extending a status marker that carried significantly less relevance than it once had? The relative value of the franchise and its importance compared to other societal

---

124   HA *Sev.* 1.1–2.
125   Sid. Apol. *Ep.* 6.2.
126   The *Historia Augusta* is particularly notorious in this regard. For more on the author's potential literary goal, see Rohrbacher (2016).
127   Aur. Vict. *Caes.* 16.12; *Novellae* 78.5. Also see Ando (2016) 9.
128   Kienast (2011) 162–64.

distinctions, such as the divide between the *honestiores* and *humiliores*, has been a persistent feature of debate regarding the edict's wider significance.[129] The dearth of literary evidence following the promulgation of the *constitutio* thus remains one of the most puzzling aspects of the document's history, with potential repercussions regarding how the ancients perceived its consequences in effect. Despite this, however, it would be imprudent to dismiss the edict's importance on this basis alone.[130] Furthermore, we must also acknowledge that it is unfair to assume that Caracalla would, or even could, have contemplated all of the edict's consequences prior to its introduction.[131]

If the subsequent literary record for the Antonine Constitution is problematic, the contemporary evidence is arguably even more perplexing. Apart from the Giessen papyrus, the only surviving literary source for the period that makes any reference to the edict's introduction is Cassius Dio.[132] On first examination, he appears ideally suited to offer an explanation of the *constitutio*, given his close proximity to the imperial court throughout the majority of the Severan era.[133] Unfortunately, the senator's description of the edict is cursory. The only mention of the legislation in the extant *Roman History* is included as part of a larger critique of Caracalla's fiscal policies and expenditure. Dio claimed that the emperor engaged in an astonishing level of spending and, consequently, required a similarly extraordinary tax yield to sustain it, an obligation which prompted the decision to extend the franchise.

Οὗ ἕνεκα καὶ Ῥωμαίους πάντας τοὺς ἐν τῇ ἀρχῇ αὐτοῦ, λόγῳ μὲν τιμῶν, ἔργῳ δὲ ὅπως πλείω αὐτῷ καὶ ἐκ τοῦ τοιούτου προσίῃ διὰ τὸ τοὺς ξένους τὰ πολλὰ αὐτῶν μὴ συντελεῖν, ἀπέδειξεν.

---

129   Garnsey (2004) 134–40, 155 and (1970) 266; Honoré (2004) 114–15; Hope (2000) 133–50; Nicolet (1980) 20–21. For more on the *honestiores-humiliores* divide, see Rilinger (1988).
130   Hekster (2008) 55.
131   Ando (2012) 56–57; Honoré (2002) 85. Owing to the focus of this study on the emperor's rationale underlying the promulgation of the *constitutio*, however, any additional investigation of this literary silence is currently beyond the scope of this study.
132   Even Herodian's nearly contemporaneous account omits any discussion of the legislation.
133   Davenport (2012) 797, claims that Dio was 'well placed to record the vicissitudes of political life' in the Severan court. For more on the senator's work, see Kemezis (2014) 90–149. Dio himself provides evidence concerning his career. He describes, for example, writing a treatise on the dreams and portents that presaged Severus' rise to power and victory in the civil wars (73.23.1–3). He describes his time as a *comes* in Caracalla's court (78.17.3) and, later, the circumstances of his consulship under Alexander Severus (80.5.1–3).

This was the reason why he made everyone in his realm Romans, he was ostensibly honouring them, but his real purpose was to increase his revenues by this means, since peregrines were not required to pay the majority of these taxes.[134]

The brevity of this account is the least controversial aspect of Dio's work on the subject. This section of the *Roman History* is highly fragmented and largely dependent on the eleventh century epitome of Xiphilinus, said to provide 'not so much a précis of Dio as a rather erratic selection from his material.'[135] The main problem surrounding the senator's account of the *Constitutio Antoniniana*, however, relates to his open loathing of Caracalla. Dio makes several withering attacks on the emperor, characterising him as one of the worst individuals to sit upon the imperial throne.[136] This unrelenting denigration led Millar to describe the senator writing with an 'unabashed hatred' towards his bête-noir.[137]

Dio's unapologetic vilification of Caracalla clearly jeopardises the reliability of his account of the latter's reign, including his assessment of the Antonine Constitution. How far can Dio's testimony regarding the legislation be trusted, then? In his analysis of the senator's account, Ando complained that 'Dio's authority as a contemporary witness has blinded many to the extreme idiocy of his argument.'[138] Similarly, Dio's hatred of Caracalla has also led to his fiscal explanation of the *constitutio* being dismissed or diminished in modern scholarship, considered a motive of secondary importance at best.[139] This seems to be an unfairly absolute position, though.

That the *Roman History* is affected by the author's anti-Caracallan agenda is incontrovertible, and often patently obvious. The fact that Dio is an unsympathetic source for the regime does not mean, however, that his claims are entirely devoid of basis or merit. In fact, just as Ando is correct that we cannot permit Dio's position as an eyewitness blind us to his obvious idiosyncrasies, the hostility of his account should similarly not blind us to the meaning that often underlies his testimony. Rather than dismissing the senator out of hand,

---

134 Dio 78.9.5.
135 Millar (1964) 2. Also see Davenport (2012) 796, who argues contrarily that, despite its obvious issues, we can be relatively confident that the surviving portions of text presented here are the work of Dio, rather than Xiphilinus.
136 For examples, see Dio 78.6.1a; 78.7–8; 79.9.3.
137 Millar (1964) 150.
138 Ando (2000) 375, n. 275.
139 Buraselis (2007) 1–3; Williams (1979) 72.

Dio's account must be set against the wider context of the time and scoured for the historical value that it possesses.[140]

The Role of the Jurists

Cassius Dio's history represents the only surviving contemporary literary reference to the Antonine Constitution, but it is not the only contemporaneous mention to be found. Another reference to the edict, albeit a brief one, can be observed in the legal writing of the jurist Ulpian, whose work was later compiled within the Justinianic *Digest*.[141] His allusion to the *constitutio* is predictably concise, given the juristic medium, and simply states that all persons living within the limits of the empire were granted citizenship by virtue of Caracalla's constitution.[142] This extract is apparently supported by a sentence preserved from the writings of Modestinus, another contemporary jurist, who claimed that Rome represented a common *patria* for all.[143] While the evidence for the *Constitutio Antoniniana* offered by the jurists is sparse, it nevertheless provides an important sense of the edict and, furthermore, alludes to the involvement of these legal intellectuals within the imperial regime of the period.

Professional jurists had become an established element within Roman society by the end of the Republic. The origins of this legal class can be traced to the developments in Roman law that occurred from the second half of the second century BCE. In essence, a formulary system was introduced and developed, the result of which was a more comprehensive legal framework within which to operate, and which afforded 'sharper definition to the basis of claims.'[144] In the late Republic, the role of the jurists was simply to advise on matters of law and custom. This expectation is best seen in Cicero's *De Oratore*, in which the author effectively synopsises the duties of late republican jurists:

---

140 Dio's account and the potentially economic rationale for the Antonine Constitution will be considered in Chapter 2.
141 De Blois (2014) 1014.
142 *Dig.* 1.5.17: *In orbe romano qui sunt ex constitutione imperatori Antonini cives Romani effecti sunt*.
143 *Dig.* 50.1.33. As De Blois (2014) 1014, has remarked, though, this latter sentence is preserved in isolation and is therefore indeterminate in nature.
144 Ibbetson (2015) 28.

> *Sin autem quaereretur, quisnam iurisconsultus vere nominaretur; eum dicerem, qui legum, et consuetudinis eius, qua privati in civitate uterentur, et ad respondendum, et ad agendum, et ad cavendum, peritus esset.*

> If again the question were, who is rightly described as learned in the law, I should say it is the man who is an expert in the statutes, and in the customary law observed by individuals as members of the community, and who is qualified to advise, direct the course of a lawsuit, and safeguard a client.[145]

It is important to note that the jurists of this period, and even into the High Empire, did not represent a single, unified legal caste. They would respond to one another's legal writings, in opposition as much as in agreement, and would often counter their colleagues' work in emphatic terms.[146] This sometimes confrontational structure is arguably best seen in the presence of two large schools, the Proculians and the Sabinians, around the middle of the first century CE. The legal writer Pomponius made comment on these collectives, in writings similarly preserved in the *Digest*, describing the basis for their rivalries and the identities of certain individual jurists within their number.[147] In spite of these academic and methodological differences between the jurists, however, the class as a whole gradually rose further in prominence as the Principate progressed. Writing in the latter half of the second century, Gaius provides a statement on the role of the jurists that highlights their increased importance to the legal procedure of the Roman state:

> *Responsa prudentium sunt sententiae et opiniones eorum, quibus permissum est iura condere. Quorum omnium si in unum sententiae concurrunt, id, quod ita sentiunt, legis vicem optinet; si vero dissentiunt, iudici licet quam velit sententiam sequi; idque rescripto divi Hadriani significatur.*

> The answers of the learned are the decisions and opinions of those who are permitted to establish laws. If the decisions of all are in agreement, what they have decided has the force of law, but if they disagree, the

---

145   Cic. *De Orat.* 1.212.
146   Ibbetson (2015) 37, has highlighted a case in which the jurist Paul criticises Q. Mucius Scaevola, alleging ineptitude. For the original comment, see *Dig.* 41.2.3.23.
147   *Dig.* 1.2.2.48–52.

CONTEXTS   35

> judge may pursue whichever decision he wishes. This is declared by a
> rescript of the divine Hadrian.[148]

This growing legal status is matched by an increased prominence within the imperial government, with jurists occupying significant administrative positions, and even rising to the praetorian prefecture, by the reign of Marcus Aurelius.[149] Far from the knowledgeable but simple consultants of Cicero's time, jurists were now counted among some of the most important and influential officers of the Empire. This process reached its zenith under the Severan emperors, and is consequently regarded as something of a golden age for jurists.[150]

During this relatively short period, three of the most prolific legal experts of the age were active: Ulpian, Paul and Modestinus.[151] In addition, the Severi followed the Antonine precedent of bringing legal experts into the very heart of the imperial court, with Papinian, Ulpian and probably Paul all serving as praetorian prefects.[152] The collapse of the Severan dynasty in 235 also signalled the end of the jurists' prominence and influence within imperial society. When examining the Antonine Constitution and questions of its formulation, then, we must be careful to note that it was produced during a period in which a peculiarly high number of legal authorities were close to the figure of the emperor.

Looking more specifically at the situation under Caracalla's regime, the figure of Ulpian stands out as one of the most feted. For example, he is hailed as 'the most influential writer of the time' by Honoré.[153] Much has been written on the subject of Ulpian's legal philosophy, in particular his desire to set Roman law into a wider conceptual frame, 'demonstrating how the principles and enactments of Roman law can be justified on universal, not just parochial considerations of utility and equity.'[154] This has been taken further by Honoré, who sees Ulpian as a pioneer of human rights expounding law 'as based on the view that all people are born free and equal, and that all possess dignity.'[155] The net result of this cumulative image is a suggestion that the jurist may have been instrumental in the promulgation of the *Constitutio Antoniniana*,

---

148   Gaius *Inst.* 1.7.
149   Roebuck and De Loynes de Fumichon (2004) 25–26.
150   Potter (2014) 157–61; Hekster (2008) 46; Trapp (2007) 481–82.
151   Ibbetson (2015) 38–39.
152   For more on Papinian's oscillating prominence at court, see Bingham and Imrie (2015) 84–85. For an account of Ulpian's unpopularity as prefect, see Dio 80.2.2–3.
153   Honoré (2002) 1.
154   Trapp (2007) 482.
155   Honoré (2002) 80–81.

perhaps even suggesting its creation in the first instance, although this hypothesis remains speculative.[156]

While the precise nature of the relationship between Ulpian and the Antonine Constitution is difficult to identify, the wider role of the jurists in the process of its promulgation must be considered nevertheless, since the legislation was introduced during the heyday of this legal intelligentsia.[157] At the heart of the matter here is a question regarding the fundamental authorship of the *constitutio*: that is to say to what extent the edict should be viewed as a product of juristic influence, rather than a creation of the emperor himself. This is a crucially important distinction, since any conclusions drawn here inevitably bear on how we interpret the nature of the *constitutio* and its underlying motivations.

The question of the emperor's role in formulating legal materials remains complex. It is clear that, despite their theoretical freedom to legislate and dispense summary justice as they pleased, Augusti were at least expected to defer to the advice and counsel of legal experts: they were entitled to make law, but the extent to which they commonly did so remains a matter of debate.[158] Given this traditional reliance on judicially trained civil servants throughout the Principate, the assumption that Ulpian and others were the true architects of the *Constitutio Antoniniana* is a logical one. It would seem inconceivable that the emperor would eschew their advice at the very zenith of juristic influence within the imperial regime.

This interpretation of the Antonine Constitution effectively distances Caracalla from the edict, and renders any attempt to investigate the rationale for its introduction more challenging as a consequence. Other factors must be considered, though. Just as it is unlikely that the imperial household would not have sought advice from top ranking jurists, it is similarly implausible that the emperor himself would have had no input or, even if civil servants actually drafted the document, that jurists were operating independently of their sovereign's directive.[159] In the case of Caracalla specifically, the extant evidence actually provides an image of the emperor as being more independently minded in legal affairs than his predecessors, a feature that ultimately suggests that the decision to introduce the *Constitutio Antoniniana* (and the responsibility for its fundamental content) lay with Caracalla personally.

---

156   Honoré (2002) 85; Birley (1988) 190.
157   Hekster (2008); Trapp (2007) 481.
158   Honoré (1994) 3, 29–30.
159   The same logic has been applied in the past to the similar question of how far emperors involved themselves with official media such as coinage. See Howgego (1995) 70–71.

The image of Caracalla's approach to legal affairs varies depending on the source that records it. In the literary sources, the emperor appears disinterested and easily bored by matters of jurisprudence and procedure.[160] Dio is predictably hostile, complaining that the emperor rarely arbitrated in court, and that he treated his council with contempt, often summoning them only to have them wait for hours to see him.[161] Herodian is less vitriolic, claiming that while Caracalla spent little time in the courts, his decisions were usually swiftly made and incisive.[162] Such depictions appear to result more from the authors' hostility towards the emperor, rather than forming a reflection of a genuine Caracallan disinterest in the legal process. The contemptuous portrait of the emperor found in the ancient literature is in marked contrast to the more attentive impression that can be gleaned from epigraphic sources. Minutes from civil actions found at Dmeir, for example, portray Caracalla in a more positive light.[163] The emperor is depicted as an attentive arbitrator, actively engaging with the trial participants in his role as judge.[164] It is possible, then, to identify an image of Caracalla taking an active interest in judicial matters, even if his behaviour was arguably unorthodox on occasion.

Another important aspect of Caracalla's unconventional relationship with Roman law concerns his proclivity to form decisions that deviated from pre-existing statute. The extant evidence suggests that, of all the third century emperors, Caracalla was the most likely to derogate from written law.[165] Honoré has identified a number of cases in which the emperor's rulings seem motivated more by personal opinion than legal precedent. There are rescripts, for example, which appear to show Caracalla giving excessive favour to soldiers.[166] In another case, the emperor excused an individual from responsibilities relating to tax collection, on the grounds that the claimant approached him personally, rather than any legal basis.[167] Finally, there is an example from the

---

160   Potter (2014) 161.
161   Dio 78.17.3–4. Also see Honoré (1994) 25.
162   Hdn. 4.7.2.
163   For more detail on the detail of this inscription, see Oliver (1974) 289–94.
164   Connolly (2010) 110; Honoré (1994) 25; Williams (1979) 666; Crook (1955) 142–43. Williams (1974) 665, has further suggested that Caracalla might even have selected the counsel for both prosecution and defence in this case, finding their sophistic and rhetorical talents entertaining.
165   Honoré (1994) 26.
166   *Dig.* 48.22.16; *CJ* 1.18.1; 5.16.2.
167   *CJ* 5.41.1.1.

Justinianic *Codex* in which the emperor openly ruled contrary to legal advice in a case regarding inheritance.[168]

The surviving evidence thus provides an indication of Caracalla's intellectual independence in legal affairs. Even in the most hostile of sources, material can be found that proves valuable in analysing the emperor's administration of Roman law. In the midst of Dio's attack on Caracalla for his obsession with Alexander the Great, the author claimed that the emperor became enraged with a lawyer prosecuting a trial against a defendant named Alexander, owing to the way in which the orator referred to 'the bloodthirsty Alexander, the god-detested Alexander'.[169] Caracalla responded by reprimanding the lawyer and threatened him with dismissal. It is self-evident that the purpose of this passage was to highlight the emperor's irrational hero-worship of the Macedonian king, but Dio's account nonetheless provides another example of Caracalla as a ruler actively engaged in dispensing Roman law.

While it remains possible that some of Caracalla's rulings in these cases reflect the influence of the jurist Arrius Menander, since Honoré has shown that many of the more unorthodox rulings can be identified as belonging to his tenure as secretary of the petitions, the fact that the emperor was evidently willing to rule outside of the legally accepted framework on multiple occasions suggests that he was prepared to ignore statute, or at least to interpret it in an unconventional manner to best suit his legal perceptions or agenda.[170] With this in mind, although it is still inconceivable that Caracalla would have promulgated the *Constitutio Antoniniana* without consulting his legal counsel, the hypothesis that the core of the legislation was of his own creation (rather than that of the jurists) remains convincing.

Positioning the emperor, rather than his legal experts, behind the Antonine Constitution has an important implication for this study of the rationale underlying the edict. On this basis, when the potential motives for the legislation are considered throughout this investigation, they will be viewed through the lens of Caracalla's own concerns and desires, rather than through those of the jurists. Caracalla may not have formulated the final draft of the edict alone, but it is probable that he constituted its driving force, and that it was therefore composed and structured to his personal preference and specifications.[171]

---

168 *CJ* 9.23.1.
169 Dio 78.8.3.
170 Honoré (1994) 25–26.
171 The question of how far it is possible to observe the emperor's own hand in the surviving text of the edict will be considered below.

CONTEXTS 39

The Antonine Constitution and the Giessen Papyrus

Given the dearth of surviving evidence described above, *P. Giss.* 40 is of inestimable importance to any study of the Antonine Constitution. Discovered at the opening of the twentieth century, the Giessen papyrus represents the only surviving document thought to contain a copy of the original *constitutio*.[172] Nevertheless, despite its importance, *P. Giss.* 40 is also a controversial source which, as noted in the introduction, has prompted a wealth of debate among modern scholars.[173] Much of the discussion surrounding the Giessen papyrus stems from the severely damaged and fragmentary state of the document in the area containing the text of the edict.

The surviving papyrus measures 27cm × 46cm, and contains the texts of at least three imperial proclamations deriving from the reign of Caracalla.[174] A cursory glance reveals that *P. Giss.* 40 has suffered extensive wear and damage, most notably to the left-hand side of the document, which is unfortunately where the text of the *constitutio* is written. In fact, by comparing the left and (largely complete) right sides of the papyrus, it can be estimated that around one third of the upper left side of the document is missing. The damage in this area is compounded by a large vertical tear in the middle of the surviving papyrus which has obliterated yet more script.

The lower left-hand section of *P. Giss. 40* is even more damaged. The large tear that has destroyed some of the upper left side extends further into the papyrus, meaning that only around thirty characters of text remain. Smaller localised tears and holes in areas suggest that the papyrus has suffered worm-damage, while areas where the top-layer of the document is compromised (more visible on the right side of the papyrus) are the result of damage sustained in the document's afterlife when the museum attempted to glaze it.[175] Finally, there are also a number of dark patches spread over the surface of the papyrus, especially in the upper-right quadrant. This is indicative of water damage sustained in February 1945, when the papyrus was being held in the

---

172 For more information on its discovery and provenance, see Kuhlmann (1994) 1–2; Oliver (1989) 495; Meyer (1910) 25–33.
173 For a brief consideration of the scholarly reactions to the papyrus, see the previous chapter.
174 Heichelheim (1941) 10–22.
175 Kuhlmann (1994) 1.

safe of the Dresdner Bank: the latest tests on this mould, however, have proven that it has become inert, posing no further risk to the artefact.[176]

Despite this severe damage, however, the availability of high-resolution photographs of the papyrus from the *Giessener Papyri- und Ostraka-Datenbank* has facilitated a far more detailed analysis of the text than was ever possible in the past. The text of *P. Giss. 40* is presented in a legible, cursive script of Koine Greek. Meyer claimed that the text was of a 'careful, clerical' nature, while Kuhlmann has concluded that the papyrus is business-like in appearance and that the script is 'regular and aesthetic'.[177] The characters are clear and of a regular size, 0.3–0.4cm wide in the majority of cases, often using capitalised versions of characters and lunate sigmas (c).

In the course of the text, there are larger spaces between the different sections of the documents to allow ease of legibility.[178] This feature permits a more confident estimate regarding the number of missing letters in the various lacunae, while the stylistic features of the script allow the papyrus to be dated to the early third century, possibly even during Caracalla's reign itself.[179] Combining study of previous editions with my own examination of the artefact, then, I have restored the Giessen text in the following manner:[180]

1) [Αὐτοκράτωρ Καῖσαρ Μά]ρκο[ς Α]ὐρή[λιος Σεουῆρος Ἀ]ντωνῖνο[ς] Ε[ὐσεβὴ]ς λέγει
[πάντως εἰς τὸ θεῖον χρὴ] μᾶλλον ἀν[αφέρειν καὶ τὰ]ς αἰτίας κ[α]ὶ [λογι]σμοὺς
[δικαίως δ' ἂν κἀγὼ τοῖς θ]εοῖς τ[οῖ]ς ἀθ[αν]άτοις εὐχαριστήσα[ι]μι ὅτι τῆς τοιαύτη[ς]
[ἐπιβουλῆς γενομένης σῷο]ν ἐμὲ συν[ετ]ήρησαν τοιγαροῦν νομίζω [ο]ὕτω με-
5) [γαλοπρεπῶς καὶ εὐσεβ]ῶς δύ[να]σθαι τῇ μεγαλειότητι αὐτῶν τὸ ἱκανὸν ποι-
[εῖν, εἰ τοὺς ἐν τῇ ἀρχῇ ὁσ]άκις ἐὰν ὑ[πε]ισέλθ[ωσ]ιν εἰς τοὺς ἐμοὺς ἀν[θρ]ώπους
[ὡς Ῥωμαίους εἰς τὰ ἱερὰ τῶν] θεῶν συνει[σ]ενέγ[κοιμ]ι Δίδω[μ]ι τοί[ν]υν ἅπα-
[σι τοῖς κατὰ τὴν Ῥωμαϊκ]ὴν οἰκουμένην π[ολειτ]είαν Ῥωμ[αί]ων [μ]ένοντος

---

176   I am grateful to Olaf Schneider and the staff of the Universitätsbibliothek Gießen Special Collections department for their assistance in arranging a visit for me to view the papyrus, and for sharing their knowledge regarding the storage and recent history of the artefact.
177   Meyer (1910) 25; Kuhlmann (1994) 8–9.
178   *P. Giss.* 40 I, l.7 for example. Also see Kuhlmann (1994) 216.
179   Cavallo and Maehler (2008) 131–32; Kuhlmann (1994) 215–16.
180   For a full commentary and *apparatus criticus* of this edition, see the appendix accompanying this volume.

[τοῦ δικαίου τῶν πολιτευμ]άτων χωρ[ὶς] τῶν [ἀδδ]ειτικίων Ὀ[φ]είλει [γ]ὰρ τὸ
10) [πλῆθος οὐ μόνον τἄλλα συνυπομέ]νειν πάντα ἀ[λλ]ὰ ἤδη κ[α]ὶ τῇ νίκῃ ἐνπεριει–
[λῆφθαι Τοῦτο δὲ τὸ διάτ]αγμα ἐ[ξαπ]λώσει [τὴν] μεγαλειότητα [το]ῦ Ῥωμα[ί]-
[ων δήμου συμβαίνει γὰρ τὴν αὐτὴ]ν περὶ τοὺς [ἄλλο]υς γεγενῆσθα[ι] ἥπερ δ[ι]α–
[πρέπουσιν ἀνέκαθεν Ῥωμαῖοι τιμῇ κα]ταλειφ[θέντων μηδέν]ων τῶ[ν] ἑκάστης
[χώρας ἐν οἰκουμένῃ ἀπολιτεύτων ἢ ἀτιμ]ήτω[ν Ἀπο δὲ τῶν] π[ρ]οσ[όδων τῶν νῦν]
15) [ὑπερχουσῶν συντελούντων, ἅπερ ἐκελεύσ]θη [παρὰ Ῥωμαίων ἀπὸ τοῦ κα ἔτους,]
[ὡς δίκαιον ἐκ τῶν διαταγμάτων καὶ ἐπιστολ]ῶ[ν, ἅ ἐξεδόθη ὑφ' ἡμῶν τε]
[καὶ τῶν ἡμετέρων προγόνων Προετέθη ....]

The Emperor Caesar Marcus Aurelius Severus Antoninus Pius decrees: It is altogether necessary to attribute the causes and reasons [of recent events] to the divine. I, personally, would rightly thank the immortal gods, since although such a conspiracy [as that of Geta] has occurred, they have watched over me and protected me. I think that I am able, both magnificently and piously, to do something fitting to the gods' majesty, if I manage to bring [all] those in the empire, who constitute my people, to the temples of the gods as Romans. I therefore give everyone in the Roman world the Roman citizenship: preserving customary law, without additional privileges. It is necessary for the masses not only to share in our burden, but also to be included in victory. This decree will spread the magnificence of the Roman people. For it now happens that the same greatness has occurred for everyone, by the honour in which the Romans have been preeminent since time immemorial, with no-one from any country in the world being left stateless or without honour. Referring to the taxes that exist at present, all are due to pay those that have been imposed upon the Romans from the beginning of their twenty-first year [of age], as it is the law, according to the edicts and rescripts issued by us and our ancestors. Displayed publically ...

Restoring the text of *P. Giss.* 40 represents only one part of the puzzle, though. The Giessen papyrus also raises a number of questions, the conclusions on which have an impact on our understanding of the edict. Similar to the controversies in the modern scholarly tradition, these points must be noted before any real consideration of Caracalla's motivation for the *constitutio* can begin.

The first of these concerns the precise authorship of the edict. I have argued above that the evidence supports a hypothesis that Caracalla was the guiding architect of the Antonine Constitution, but the issue of how far the emperor can be found in the extant text remains open. This matter is confounded by ambiguity surrounding why the Giessen papyrus itself was compiled. In addition to the *constitutio*, Caracalla's recall of exiles and his later expulsion of ethnic Egyptians from Alexandria are also preserved on the papyrus.[181] It seems probable that the artefact is a copy of official legislation, possibly compiled in advance of a private suit, rather than for archival purposes.[182] To date, however, no one has been able to provide a persuasive explanation for this combination of edicts appearing on the same source.

Such a problem with the Giessen papyrus obviously gives rise to a concern regarding how far we can trust that the text preserved is a faithful copy of the official legislation, be that translated from the original Latin, or simply replicated from a pre-existing Greek copy in Egypt. A way of overcoming some of this doubt, to an extent, can be found in stylistic analysis. Identifying the hand of the emperor in drafting legislation is a notoriously difficult task but, if restricted to general terms, then it is acceptable to suggest that 'the individual personalities of each emperor are revealed in some at least of their official pronouncements.'[183] In the case of the *Constitutio Antoniniana*, attention has been devoted to elements of the language and tone employed by the author to argue that the text preserved on the Giessen papyrus is a record of Caracalla's wording.

Much of the language in the Giessen text emphasises the grandeur and universality of the edict being introduced, a feature which melds not only with other legal documents deriving from the same era, but also with the emperor's well-documented 'passion for vastness' in relation to his building projects and admiration towards Alexander the Great, for example.[184] While this alone does not necessarily preclude another individual composing the edict, further suggestion of Caracalla's involvement can be found if the general tone of the legislation is considered. Rather than a detailed juristic account defining the new edict and its fundamental consequences, as one might expect from a civil servant, the actual terms of the *constitutio* are mentioned only briefly, with more attention devoted to explaining the circumstances that prompted the creation of the edict and its underlying purpose. This led Sherwin-White to declare the Giessen text a 'proclamation of policy', rather than a technical instruction,

---

181   Van Minnen (2016) 205–21; Heichelheim (1941) 10–22.
182   Bryen (2016) 31. The script of the papyrus is regular, but does not exhibit the elongated chancery style of the same period. For more on this, see Cavallo and Maehler (2008) 123.
183   Williams (1979) 67.
184   Williams (1979) has identified a number of other edicts preserved on papyri which contain highly similar modes of expression. Also see Sherwin-White (1973a) 282–83.

though how far this distinction can be thought to represent a genuine difference in the eyes of the emperor is debatable.[185]

However the Giessen papyrus is restored, the reasons offered for the edict in the text all arise from the emperor's personal experience and an unidentified threat from which the gods had preserved him.[186] By combining this focus on Caracalla's person with the personal tone of the edict, and the characteristic use of language emphasising the scale and majesty of his enactment, Williams has concluded that the Latin original of the *Constitutio Antoniniana* was personally composed by the emperor on a rapid timescale, probably dictated for immediate publication.[187] While this is likely an overstatement, once again caricaturing Caracalla as an impulsive and irrational ruler, the idea that the emperor took a personal interest in the text of his great edict remains persuasive.[188] Regardless, then, if the text found on the Giessen papyrus is a complete or abridged copy of the original legislation, the stylistic elements of the decree, paired with the other extant evidence relating to the emperor's administration of Roman law, noted above, suggest that Caracalla himself was the ultimate author of the Antonine Constitution and did not, in this case, defer completely to his jurist counsellors.

If the personal focus of the *constitutio* is one of its defining features, it also raises one of its most significant uncertainties, namely concerning the nature of the events that the emperor was responding to in enacting his reform. In the opening lines of *P. Giss.* 40, the emperor claimed that 'it is altogether necessary to attribute the causes and reasons [of recent events] to the divine.'[189] The events referred to here are never made explicit, though. In fact, Caracalla's explanation of the events is equally enigmatic, with the emperor claiming divine protection from an unnamed danger. The immediate question which must be considered, then, is what was Caracalla claiming that the gods had saved him from?

In typically frustrating fashion, the crucial section of the Giessen papyrus detailing the threat is lost.[190] In response, there have been two restorations of

---

185 Williams (1979) 71–72; Sherwin-White (1973a) 283. For a commentary of *P. Giss.* 40 I, see the appendix to this study.
186 Williams (1979) 71. The nature of the difficulty which Caracalla claimed the gods had preserved him from will be discussed below.
187 Williams (1979) 72, 88.
188 Williams (1979) 72, has suggested, similar to Garnsey (2004) 134–35, that the *constitutio* should be regarded more as a whim of the emperor than a carefully planned policy decision.
189 *P. Giss.* 40 I, ll. 2–3.
190 *P. Giss.* 40 I, l. 4.

the text offered by scholars. One, proposed by Bickermann, refers to a general misfortune (συμφορά) befalling the emperor.[191] The more widely accepted reconstruction of the lacuna, however, is the more pointed ἐπιβουλή, which has a clear inference of a conspiracy and clandestine activity being raised against the emperor.[192] The lack of detail in the *constitutio* itself regarding the events prompting it has led to a number of alternative explanations of the events which motivated Caracalla to advertise his legislation as a grand act of thanksgiving to the gods. It has been suggested, for example, that the emperor made reference to an occasion during which he escaped death or injury during his travels and campaigns: either in battle against the Alamanni or a shipwreck crossing the Hellespont.[193] Neither of these explanations are particularly convincing, however, owing to their impact on the dating of the edict's introduction. The battle in question took place in 213, while the emperor's seaborne difficulties took place the year after, in the context of his entering Asia Minor. These simply cannot be the events referred to in the course of the *Constitutio Antoniniana*, since, as Barnes has shown, there is evidence demonstrating that the edict had already spread to Lydia by March 213, suggesting that the legislation must have been introduced in the middle of 212 at the latest.[194] More recently, Van Minnen has extrapolated a precise date of 11th July 212 from the surviving text of *P. Giss.* 40.[195] With the date of the edict's introduction effectively irrefutable, there remains only one viable explanation for the 'conspiracy' referred to in the course of the edict preserved on the Giessen papyrus, the murder of Geta at the close of 211.[196]

In the aftermath of Geta's assassination, Caracalla moved swiftly to accuse his dead brother of acting treacherously against him, claiming that he was the intended target of a Getan coup. It is noteworthy that, in the course of Dio's account of the night in question, the author also employed ἐπιβουλή in connection with the alleged action:

---

191 Bickermann (1926).
192 See Appendix 1.
193 Millar (1962) 124–31; Letta (1994) 188–90. For an account of the battle in question, see Dio 78.13.6. For more on the alleged shipwreck, which appears to have been exaggerated by the author of the *Historia Augusta*, see Dio 78.16.7; HA *Car.* 5.8.
194 Barnes (2012) 51–52. For a more detailed analysis of this issue, see Hermann (1972) 519–30.
195 Van Minnen (2016) 211.
196 The rivalry between Caracalla and Geta has already been discussed in the historical context section of this chapter.

ὁ δ' Ἀντωνῖνος καίπερ ἑσπέσας οὔσης τὰ στρατόπεδα κατέλαβε, διὰ πάσης τῆς ὁδοῦ κεκραγὼς ὡς ἐπιβεβουλευμένος καὶ κινδυνεύων.

Antoninus, although it was evening, took possession of the legions, after crying out the whole way, as if he had been the object of a plot and his life were in danger.[197]

While we must exercise caution to prevent Dio's prose from influencing our reconstruction of *P. Giss.* 40 retrospectively, it is tempting to imagine that the senator was using language reminiscent of that employed by the emperor when constructing his account. The function and importance of the *Constitutio Antoniniana* to Caracalla's regime in 212 will be considered in detail later in this book, but it remains worth reiterating here that the text of the edict preserved on the Giessen papyrus only really makes sense in connection with the fraternal discord between Caracalla and Geta rather than any other potential misfortune suffered by the emperor.[198]

In addition to the debate regarding the nature of the threat overcome by Caracalla, two other major questions are raised by the *constitutio* as preserved in the Giessen papyrus, both of which derive from the actual gift of *civitas* proclaimed by the emperor between the seventh and ninth lines of the text. The first concerns the impact of the legislation on the legal complexion of the empire. In the course of the *constitutio* text in *P. Giss.* 40, Caracalla declared that his edict extended the franchise to every person living in the Roman realm.[199] Did the Antonine Constitution really herald a significant change in the practical relationship between the Roman state and its subjects, though? Historically, there was a sense that the introduction of Caracalla's edict resulted in an absolute imposition of the Roman *ius civile* across the empire, leading to a rapid equalisation between Greek East and Latin West. This is an attitude exemplified by Sohm, for example, who argued that the *constitutio* resulted in (and was ultimately designed to facilitate) the arrangement of 'one emperor, one state, one law'.[200] The fact remains, however, that this hypothesis is based on an erroneously unitary model of Roman imperial administration, in which

---

197   Dio 78.3.1.
198   For a consideration on the political cachet of the Antonine Constitution, see Chapter 5.
199   *P. Giss.* 40 I, ll. 7–8: Δίδωμι τοίνυν ἅπασι τοῖς κατὰ τὴν Ῥωμαϊκὴν οἰκουμένην.
200   Sohm (1911) 130: *Ein Kaiser, ein Reich, ein Recht*. Also see Hekster (2008) 47; Honoré (2004) 113.

the *ius civile* was applied uniformly across the provinces, for which there is no supporting evidence.[201]

It is apparent that there has been a disconnect in the past between the consideration of the theoretical implications of the *constitutio*, and the practicalities of its implementation. It is fair to conclude, for example, that the introduction of a common legal system would hypothetically result in the simplification and rationalisation of imperial bureaucracy, in which lawyers would no longer be required to navigate 'the differentiations between citizens and many categories of provincial noncitizens that before 212 CE had made lawsuits, inheritances, property transfers, and contracts a nightmare.'[202] Nevertheless, the extant evidence also clearly shows that the imperial regime continued to recognise the *ius gentium* in the period following 212.[203] Caracalla himself declared his respect for customary law; further recognition of its continued relevance can also be found in the legal texts of Ulpian and Modestinus.[204] There is also evidence of emperors beyond the Severan period acknowledging the existence of customary law, such as Diocletian, who appears, in fact, to have legislated to weaken it in relation to the Roman system.[205]

This ambiguity is in contrast to the more obvious process of transformation that has been identified in social terms, particularly in relation to individual self-representation. It is clear, for example, that a vast number of people adopted the imperial name *Aurelius* as their *nomen gentile*, enthusiastically embracing their new citizen identity and following the tradition of including the name of the individual responsible for one's enfranchisement with their own.[206] A similar change can be observed in other media, such as sculptural and

---

201 Ando (2012) 85–99, (2011) 28; Tuori (2007) 39.
202 Mathisen (2006) 1015. See also Honoré (2002) 84–86; Millar (1977) 481. This notion would appear to be strengthened by the writing of Menander Rhetor (*Treatise* I.3.363, ll. 7–14), in which the author claimed that it was impossible to praise cities on the basis of their law, in epideictic literature, since they had all become subject to the Roman framework. Both the later date of his work and his rhetorical objective should be borne in mind, though.
203 For an example of local law in action after 212, see Kantor (2016) 45–62, who discusses the situation in Asia Minor.
204 *P. Giss.* 40 I, ll. 8–9; *Dig.* 1.3.33; 1.3.40. See also Hekster (2008) 52.
205 For more information on the later emperors' responses to customary law, see Amelotti (1995) 211–15; Rees (2007) 105–24.
206 Ando (2012) 57; Hekster (2008) 50; Buraselis (2007) 94–120. This is most easily observed in military epigraphy, with the Dura rosters and the register of praetorians both displaying a rapid increase in *Aurelii*. For more on this, see *P. Dura* 98; *CIL* VI 1058 and 2799; Hekster (2008) 50.

numismatic evidence.²⁰⁷ The Antonine Constitution can thus be recognised to have had a lasting effect on many of the empire's inhabitants, even if these phenomena can only be identified through a variety of both direct and indirect sources and across a long chronological period.²⁰⁸ Part of the difficulty in assessing the legal consequences of the Antonine Constitution is that Roman law itself was a fluid entity, presenting a 'moving target' in which doctrine and procedure underwent continual revision and change, a problem compounded by the dearth of contemporary evidence for the edict.²⁰⁹ Moreover, it is clear that it took time for the *constitutio* to be disseminated, let alone implemented in any meaningful way.²¹⁰ With this in mind, the scholarly emphasis on the long term effects of the legislation into late antiquity and beyond, identified in the introduction to this study, is understandable.²¹¹

The most controversial debate surrounding the Giessen papyrus, and one which does have a direct impact on any consideration of Caracalla's motivation for promulgating the edict, concerns a lacuna in the ninth line of the text. After announcing his extension of the franchise, the emperor made two qualifications to the award. The first of these stated that, while the rights of *civitas* had been bestowed, systems of customary law would remain in force.²¹² The second of these appears to form an exclusionary clause in the legislation, indicated by the prepositional phrase of χωρίς accompanied by a genitive.²¹³ Unfortunately, the genitive in question survives only partially, obfuscated by a hole in the papyrus. The surviving portion, [...]δειτικιῶν, has prompted two alternative reconstructions.

In the *editio princeps* of the papyrus, Meyer restored this word as the Hellenised version of the Latin *dediticii*, referring to a population group who were subject to Roman authority following an act of official surrender.²¹⁴ Such

---

207 The appearance of togate provincial portraits suggests an increasing sense of *Romanitas* even at the peripheries of the empire. See Hekster (2008) 51, 146–47; Simon (1995) 249–50. For more on the numismatic evidence, which includes the famous tri-lingual Tyrian coin, dating to reign of Gordian III, see Howgego (2007) 14.
208 Hekster (2008) 55.
209 Ando (2011) 19.
210 Barnes (2012) 52; Mathisen (2006) 1016; Gilliam (1965) 86–92.
211 Ando (2012) 93–97; Buraselis (2007) 120–57; Tuori (2007) 43.
212 *P. Giss.* 40 I, ll. 8–9: μένοντος τοῦ δικαίου τῶν πολιτευμάτων. The similarity of this construction to the Latin legal formula *salvo iure gentis* will be considered in the second chapter.
213 *P. Giss.* 40 I, l. 9.
214 Meyer (1910). For an ancient legal definition of this group, however, which could also potentially refer to freedmen convicted of crimes during their enslavement, see Gaius, *Inst.* 1.14. The *dediticii* are considered in more detail in Chapter 2.

a reconstruction would mean that the emperor had decided that his legislation should not extend to every free person, in reality, and that the *dediticii* were denied the social promotion afforded to the rest of the populace. This was the generally accepted reconstruction for decades, prompting scholars to debate the extent to which the *dediticii* were excluded from Caracalla's comprehensive extension of *civitas*.[215] The fact remains, however, that the transliteration represents a hapax legomenon and has never been an entirely accepted hypothesis. Sasse, for example, acknowledged the controversy accompanying the *dediticii* by his decision to avoid any discussion of the subject in his monograph on the *constitutio*.[216] The linguistic difficulties that the *dediticii* present have resulted in confusion, leading to an increasing sense that the reconstruction is ultimately unlikely.[217]

The alternative consensus, with which this thesis concurs, has been spearheaded by Kuhlmann, who suggests that the Giessen papyrus makes more sense if interpreted as denying the newly enfranchised any additional honours previously associated with the bestowal of *civitas*. In this version, the problematic lacuna is restored as a transliteration of the Latin *additicia*, an adjectival noun referring to general privileges.[218] The implications of this alternative reconstruction will be considered in connection with the emperor's fiscal and economic agenda, discussed in the next chapter, but it is important to recognise that any conclusions drawn regarding this troublesome passage have a direct impact upon our collective understanding of the effects and consequences of the edict as a whole.

In the absence of further evidence to support the Giessen papyrus and other scanty mentions of the legislation, the *Constitutio Antoniniana* will remain a mysterious and divisive edict in many ways. Not all of the myriad questions surrounding the edict and its evidence can be answered, but we are in a position now to investigate the purpose of the legislation, its function within the Caracallan Empire, and the factors motivating its introduction. While it

---

215 Buraselis (2007) 6–7; Tuori (2007) 42; Zingale (1999) 81; Lukaszewicz (1990a) 97–99; Wolff (1977) 210–38; Sherwin-White (1973a) 382–83, (1973b) 95–97; Oliver (1955) 279–97; Benario (1954) 188–96; Bell (1947) 17–18; Jones (1936) 228–31.

216 Sasse (1958) 17. See also Tuori (2007) 42.

217 Kuhlmann (2012) 48–49; Lukaszewicz (1990a) 97–99. It should be noted, however, that there has been a recent resurgence in those who argue that the text of the Giessen papyrus makes reference to the *dediticii*. For examples, see Moatti (2016) 89–93; Van Minnen (2016) 218–20; Torrent (2011) 141–52; Rocco (2010) 135–35; Hekster (2008) 47.

218 Kuhlmann (2012) 48–50, (1994) 236–37; Oliver (1989) 504. For a more detailed explanation of why the *additicia* hypothesis represents a better explanation of the lacuna, see Chapter 2 and the appendix.

is difficult to identify the extent to which the emperor personally composed the proclamation, the surviving evidence suggests that Caracalla possessed an independent mind in connection with Roman statute and its application, and so certainly took a leading role in the drafting of the Antonine Constitution.

The evidence supports a hypothesis that the legislation was promulgated following the assassination of Geta, with the text of the edict making reference to the violence and presenting the *constitutio* itself as an act of religious thanksgiving for divine intervention. It was introduced at a critical point in the reign of Caracalla, a factor which must always be borne in mind when assessing its purpose. In 212, the emperor faced the prospect of ruling alone for the first time in his life. The Antonine Constitution can thus be seen as a reflection of both his short term concerns regarding his dynastic legitimacy, and his medium to long term military aspirations to expand the empire. The various ways in which these elements are manifest in the *constitutio* will now be considered.

CHAPTER 2

The Fiscal Rationale

The *Roman History* of Cassius Dio is arguably the most valuable literary source surviving for the Severan period. Commencing with Rome's mythical foundation, the author offers a grand vista of history from the regnal period until his own contemporary era. Historically, Dio's opus was criticised for a supposed lack of historiographical originality or even historical perspective. Millar, for example, claimed that the *Roman History* was a work 'whose justification lay in simply being itself'.[1] More recently, however, scholars have been kinder to Dio, penetrating the author's narrative veneer to investigate his sources and perspective in greater detail than ever before.[2] Kemezis, for example, has been pre-eminent in this respect, identifying shifting 'narrative modes' that Dio employed to offer his readers a vision of the Roman past that functioned in opposition to the official narrative released by the imperial household, at least in the contemporary section of his work.[3] It is noteworthy, then, that Cassius Dio makes reference to the introduction of the Antonine Constitution in the course of the *Roman History*. In the midst of criticising Caracalla's economic initiatives, the author remarked that the *constitutio* was a false honour, actually impoverishing the populace in an attempt to fund extravagant spending upon imperial favourites and the emperor's beloved soldiery:

> Οὗ ἕνεκα καὶ Ῥωμαίους πάντας τοὺς ἐν τῇ ἀρχῇ αὐτοῦ, λόγῳ μὲν τιμῶν, ἔργῳ δὲ ὅπως πλείω αὐτῷ καὶ ἐκ τοῦ τοιούτου προσίῃ διὰ τὸ τοὺς ξένους τὰ πολλὰ αὐτῶν μὴ συντελεῖν, ἀπέδειξεν.
>
> This was the reason why he made everyone in his realm Romans, he was ostensibly honouring them, but his real purpose was to increase his revenues by this means, since peregrines were not required to pay the majority of these taxes.[4]

Dio's financial explanation of the *Constitutio Antoniniana* is the only rationale for the legislation offered by any of the contemporary sources. Despite such

---

1 Millar (1964) 118.
2 Lange and Madsen (2016).
3 Kemezis (2014) 90–149.
4 Dio 78.9.5.

explicit testimony from a figure within the imperial court itself, however, the senator's description of the edict has been largely rejected. Some remain convinced that fiscal concerns played a secondary or negligible role in moving the emperor to extend the franchise, and that Dio's account reflects the author's hatred of Caracalla more than the economic reality.[5] Nevertheless, to dismiss the rationale offered by Dio on the basis of his animosity is to ignore other extant evidence relating to the Caracallan economy that we possess. In fact, if Dio's account of the Antonine Constitution is set against a wider economic context, then it becomes possible to argue that, while the senator's rhetoric is clearly designed to denigrate the character of Caracalla, he was at least partly correct to conclude that the emperor was driven to introduce his legislation to augment the level of capital available to the *fiscus*.

My task in this chapter will be to assess the fiscal account offered by Dio against a wider economic backdrop, combining the testimony of the literary sources with numismatic evidence relating to the quality of Caracallan coinage, and papyrological sources regarding the imposition of the tax on inheritances (*vicesima hereditatum*), one of the levies which Dio alleged was doubled by Caracalla, early in his sole reign. By examining this collection of sources, it is possible to observe that the emperor was engaged in a process of manipulating the Roman monetary economy, and that he was concerned with rapidly increasing the physical stock of coinage across the empire. Given this environment, it is appropriate to investigate the Antonine Constitution as form of monetary stimulus, although the rationale for such an initiative will also need to be considered further.

In approaching the *constitutio* from this economic perspective, we should be aware of the difficulties in studying ancient economic history, and must be careful not to present an image of the Roman economy under Caracalla that is devoid of context. This is especially important given the hostile nature of the surviving literary record of the period, in which our sources are consistent in accusing the emperor of excessive spending and financial profligacy.[6] Similar to Roman law, the economy of the Principate presents us with a fluid entity, one that fluctuated as it developed. Before examining the situation under Caracalla specifically, then, it is necessary to consider briefly the development of the Roman economy from the early imperial period onwards. By setting Caracalla's edict and other actions against the longer term economic picture,

---

5 González-Fernández and Fernández Ardanaz (2010) 157–91; Buraselis (2007) 8; Ando (2000) 395, n.275.

6 The image of the Caracallan economy specifically is considered in more detail, later in this chapter.

we are able to assess the emperor's purpose (and that underlying the *constitutio*, by implication) more objectively.

Early Imperial Economic Activity

Far from the apparently desperate financial situation facing Caracalla's regime, the first century of the Empire is characterised by a number of elements that infer both stability and growth.[7] This appears to have been caused to a large extent by a contemporaneous growth in population, a development which created increased demand across the market.[8] Such exigency is also shown by the high nature of slave prices, indicating a high demand for servile labour.[9] In addition, silver production rose to a peak in the first century CE, at one stage rivalling production levels only later achieved in medieval Europe.[10] Furthermore, in the area of seaborne commerce, high numbers of shipwrecks dating to this period suggest an increased level of trade across the Mediterranean basin.[11]

Finally, while the early economy was most likely a subsistence one, evidence suggests that the inhabitants of Italy enjoyed a higher standard of living during this period than in previous decades.[12] This has been hypothesised partly

---

7   Morley (2007) 589; Scheidel (2007a) 322–46.
8   The study of Roman demography is troublesome, owing to a severe lack of dependable evidence on the subject. Information derived from census records is problematic, since the data suggests a meteoric population rise—from the last Republican census recording around 400,000 citizens, to the first imperial censuses recording in excess of four million enfranchised individuals. For a comparative analysis of this data, see Turchin and Scheidel (2009) 17276. Indeed, this disparity has prompted an enduring debate regarding the nature of the individuals recorded in each census and the resulting population estimates. For more information on this, see Scheidel (2008a) 17–70; Lo Cascio (1994) 23–40, and the following edited volumes: Bowman and Wilson (2011); Scheidel (2001).
9   Scheidel (2008b) 105–26; Jongman (2007a) 601.
10 Kehoe (2007) 547.
11 De Callataÿ (2005) 361–72; Parker (1992); Hopkins (1980) 105–6, fig. 1. The precision of these findings has been challenged more recently by Scheidel (2012a) 277–78, and by Wilson (2009) 213–49, who suggest that there was stagnation in such trade under the Early Empire, rather than a peak. However, the period still represents a high-point, since the sheer quantity of dated shipwrecks found in the Mediterranean in the 150-year period from the end of the Republic through the early imperial era still far outnumbers those from any other time under Roman rule.
12 Although Hopkins (1980) 104, has suggested that the monetary economy formed only a thin 'veneer of sophistication, spread over the subsistence economy by the liens of taxes, trade and rent', he also noted the importance of the coinage in circulation, especially after

from a sharp increase in the incidence of animal bone finds across settlement sites both in Italy and in the provinces, as well as human osteological remains suggesting an increased level of physiological health.[13] The nature of the evidence means that it is only possible to theorise in fairly broad strokes, but the combination of these different sources provides at least a general impression of economic development in the early imperial period.

The relative growth and productivity of the early Empire obviously presents a contrast to the reign of Caracalla, in which our authors complain about the exhaustion of the treasury. Such a period of expansion could not be maintained indefinitely, though. In fact, if we continue this examination from this early period into that of the High Empire, there are undeniable symptoms of economic downturn and, as the Antonine era progressed, potentially even crisis. It is therefore imperative that the period from the arrival of the Flavians to the ascendancy of the Severans is considered, since it provides important contextual information in explaining and better understanding the later actions undertaken by Septimius Severus and Caracalla.

Decline and Crisis in the High Empire

Despite the carnage wrought by the Year of the Four Emperors, the beginning of the Flavian dynasty was marked by large-scale building projects spearheaded by Vespasian, funded through a combination of booty seized in the civil conflict, victory in the Jewish War and increased taxation.[14] Such increased public

---

emperors engaged in an increasing level of debasement (a trend that will be discussed in relation to Caracalla, below). The notion that Rome's economy was a subsistence one for long periods has been challenged recently, for example by Jongman (2007b) 183–99. Despite this, however, the idea of a *longue durée* persists. For a more general, comparative discussion of living standards during the early imperial period, see Scheidel (2010) 425–62.

13 Scheidel (2008a) 37–40. For more on animal bone finds, see Jongman (2007a) 613–14; Kron (2002) 53–73; King (1999) 168–202). Also see McKinnon (2004). For a more detailed discussion of human remains, see Kron (2005) 68–83. It must be noted, though, that this increase is a strictly relative one, and that osteological analysis also shows that the overall health of many living in the Roman empire was poor. We must, furthermore, be careful to distinguish physiological health and life expectancy from the question of a quality of life. For more on the general trends, see Scheidel (2012a) 274, 279–81; Walker *et al.* (2009) 109–25.

14 For more on Vespasian's building projects, see Suet. *Vesp.* 8.5–9.1, 17–19. Also see, Frederick (2002) 199–227. Duncan-Jones (1994) 12, has suggested that the cost of these projects

spending was to continue under Domitian, who raised the army wage in addition to funding his own building projects.[15] These initiatives, however, proved far from popular among the propertied classes.[16] In contrast to Domitian's alleged profligacy, the reign of Trajan is marked by evidence of genuine economic vitality, in the form of building projects (his forum, for example), and the expansion of the *alimenta*.[17] Similar to the case of Vespasian, the influx of war spoils and booty from Trajan's Dacian campaign must also be factored into the equation.[18]

It was during the reign of Hadrian, however, that signs of economic downturn began to appear in earnest. That the imperial economy was in a relatively precarious state by the middle of the second century is attested by evidence suggesting that the emperor was compelled to legislate in order to prevent economic instability in the provinces and to preserve liquidity. This can be observed, for example, in Hadrian's *lex Hadriana de rudibus agris*, designed to encourage agricultural expansion, particularly in North Africa.[19] The best known of these initiatives, however, is his moratorium on taxation in Egypt in 136 CE.[20] While on one level this might appear to represent a great act of benevolence, the fact that it was prompted by the populace's inability to pay the annual levy undermines any sense of imperial euergetism.[21] Moratoria were not an uncommon recourse in response to fiscal instability, but this ultimately suggests that Hadrian was required to forego the tax yield of the empire's most productive province in order to prevent its economic collapse during his reign.[22]

---

might have been offset by a reduction in the costs surrounding the Flavian court, as opposed to the lavish Neronian one. For more on the Neronian court, see Mordine (2013) 102–17.

15 Dio 67.3.5; Duncan-Jones (1994) 12, 33–37.
16 The building programme is described by Dio (67.4.5–6) and also by Suetonius (*Dom.* 12.1), who criticised the emperor for resorting to 'every type of robbery' in his attempt to raise capital: *nihil pensi habuit quin praedaretur omni modo*.
17 The *alimenta* is mentioned both by Dio (68.5.4) and the author of the HA (*Hadr.* 7.8). For more on the scheme, thought to have been originally instituted under Nerva, see Carlsen (1999) 273–88; Woolf (1990) 197–228; Garnsey (1968) 367–81; Duncan-Jones (1964) 123–46.
18 For an account of Trajan's campaigns, see Dio 68.8.1–14.5 (Dacia) and 68.17.1–33.3 (eastern provinces).
19 *CIL* VIII 25943. Also see De Vos (2013) 146–50; Kehoe (2006) 58–61.
20 *P. Cairo* 49359 and 49360; *P. Oslo* 78. For a detailed commentary of these papyri, see Oliver (1989) 220–26.
21 Bowman and Wilson (2009b) 20.
22 Hitchner (2009) 285–86, 286 n.7. Caracalla is also known to have similarly absolved the province of Mauretania Tingitana from taxation in 216 CE, a measure considered later in this chapter.

Despite these measures, however, the numismatic evidence suggests that Hadrian's reign was more damaging than profitable. It is under his immediate successor, Antoninus Pius, that the first significant deterioration in silver coinage (the primary trading coin of the empire) occurs, dropping from a 90.5% median fineness at the end of Hadrian's reign to 86.5% by the end of Pius'.[23] Although it is unlikely that this degradation prompted any fiduciary change in real terms, this process can hardly be interpreted as a sign of a vibrant economy.[24] The situation was probably exacerbated by the considerable expenditure devoted to Hadrian's imperial tour, not to mention the traditional gifts distributed upon the emperor's accession. Dio claimed, for example, that he bestowed favour on nearly every city that he visited, devoting specific attention to the largesse and corn dole awarded to Athens.[25] Similar acts of Hadrianic generosity can be found throughout the emperor's biography in the *Historia Augusta*, though with little accompanying detail.[26]

While it is likely that the literary sources exaggerated his euergetism, other extant evidence suggests that Hadrian dramatically increased imperial public spending, with the level of *congiaria* nearly doubling from that observed under Trajan.[27] This increase in public benefaction might seem relatively inconsequential against the wider backdrop of the High Empire, but it is important to remember that, in addition to the difficulties noted above, Hadrian faced a significantly different situation from predecessors such as Vespasian or Trajan, inasmuch as he could not rely on imperial revenues being augmented through a process of expansion. As a consequence, even a reduced level of public spending would likely have represented a considerable drain on the imperial coffers, let alone the increased expenditure associated with Hadrian's reign.[28] This

---

23   Duncan-Jones (1994) 231, Tables 15.7–8.
24   For a larger analysis of silver coinage during this period, see Walker (1977). It should be noted, however, that Walker's figures are based upon a non-destructive analysis of the numismatic material and, therefore, might contain a margin of error of around ten percent, see Gitler and Ponting (2007) 377. It is worth noting that the later, and more significant, debasement undertaken by Septimius Severus does not appear to have upset the fiduciary relationship between coin types (see below). It is therefore unlikely that the initiative undertaken by Pius had such an effect.
25   Dio 69.5.3; 69.16.2.
26   The author mentions the gifts to Athens (*Hadr.* 13.6), but goes on to specify further awards to Campania (9.6), Gaul (10.1), Spain (12.3) and North Africa (13.4).
27   Duncan-Jones (1994) 13, 41 (Table 3.6) has collated papyrological evidence attesting to such an increase. For an example of such a beneficence, see *IGRR* IV 1431.
28   Duncan-Jones (1994) 14. The abandonment of Trajan's eastern conquests may have resulted in some form of a saving in relation to military expenditure, but the damaging nature

trend, though considerably earlier than Caracalla's reign, remains noteworthy. While the general image of the High Empire period is one of expansion, stability and prosperity, the evidence demonstrates that the economy remained potentially volatile, with problems appearing even at the zenith of the Principate.

Another factor which must be considered before assessing the Severan economy and the role of the *constitutio* therein, is the severe decline observed during the Antonine era. The accession of Marcus Aurelius was a costly affair, with Dio claiming that the new emperor distributed gifts of 20,000 *sestertii* per person to the soldiery and men of the praetorian guard.[29] His extended Germanic campaigns also served to deplete the imperial treasury.[30] In addition, there is a suggestion that further economic damage may have been wrought by flooding of the Tiber occurring in 162, disrupting agricultural production and infrastructure in the fertile Italian peninsula.[31] More significant still was the Antonine Plague which, according to extant contemporary

---

of the Bar Kokhba revolt must have represented a significant drain on any favourable financial position that the emperor would have enjoyed at the beginning of his reign. In support of this position, evidence from the HA suggests that Antoninus Pius shied from grand expeditions owing to their financially burdensome nature (*Pius*. 7.11). While evidence from the HA is far from ideal, it makes sense that in the aftermath of the events in Judaea, and Hadrian's costly imperial tour, that Pius would be reluctant to engage further in such expenditure.

29 Dio 78.8.4. The author of the HA is contradictory in his assessment of Marcus, noting the donative (*Marc.* 7.9), only to claim later that the emperor was exceedingly careful in every public expenditure (*Marc.* 11.1). On the one hand, the level of this donative might have been simply exaggerated. On the other hand, however, the high figure could be explained by the fact that Marcus ascended to the throne in a joint principate with Lucius Verus in 161 CE. An interesting possibility is that a high level of donative was required by Marcus since he was not, in fact, the praetorians' primary choice of *princeps*, and that, in addition to sharing rule with their favoured Verus, Marcus was obliged to pay more to assure the guard's loyalty than had previously been required. I am grateful to Christopher Bowling for sharing his thoughts and observations on the accession of Marcus and Verus with me. For more on the donative to the praetorians, see Bingham (2013) 41–42, n.219–220.

30 Rostovtzeff (1957) 414, traditionally associated the beginning of a Roman economic decline with the campaigns of Marcus. More recently, De Blois (2002) 92–94, has associated the Marcomannic campaigns with a rise in plundering and banditry in the northern provinces, a phenomenon which ultimately caused civilian flight from the affected areas and further economic turmoil as a consequence of the resulting agricultural disruption. For more on this, see Whittaker (2002) 204–34; Witschel (1999) 178–210, and Erdkamp (1998) 240.

31 For an account of the floods, see HA *Marc.* 8.4–5.

sources, caused utter devastation to the imperial state.[32] It is important to include the Antonine Plague in any consideration of the economic recession of this period, since the sudden reduction in the population caused by the disease would have had a lasting effect on basic levels of economic activity such as production and revenue sourced through taxation.

The scale of the epidemic is still a matter of debate.[33] It was previously believed, for example, that the disease represented a watershed moment in Roman history. Niebuhr claimed that the empire never truly recovered from its effects, while Seeck argued that the plague claimed over fifty percent of the total population, prompting the settlement of Germans within imperial borders and fundamentally changing the ethnic makeup of the empire.[34] More recently, however, there have been attempts to offer a more conservative image of the epidemic. Bruun, for example, has sought to sever any perceived connection between the disease and the crisis of the third century, let alone the downfall of the western empire.[35] Gilliam, moreover, has argued that the plague cannot have claimed more than two percent of the empire's population, though his assessment appears to be based more on responding to the hyperbolic literature than on other datasets.[36] Among these extreme positions, it is more likely that Littman and Littman are correct in their assessment of a mortality rate between seven and ten percent.[37] This figure rests more comfortably with the sense of localised devastation observed in the non-literary evidence, noted below, while not inferring the cataclysmic scenario envisaged by earlier scholars.

The economic implications of this epidemic might initially seem difficult to identify, but if extant evidence from Roman Egypt is considered, then the disease can be shown to cause severe disruption to agricultural production and tax

---

32   Ael. Ar. *Or.* 48.38–44; Galen 19.17–18 (Kühn) recorded the flight of the emperors from Aquileia when the disease struck the Roman forces stationed there. For later sources on the pestilence, see Amm. Marc. 23.6.24; Eutrop. 8.12.2; Jerome 206 (Helm); Lucian, *Alex.* 36 and Oros. 7.15.5–7, 27.7. The outbreak of the plague is given a predictably fanciful treatment by the author of the HA, who claimed that the disease was released from a mysterious golden casket by Roman forces in the east, and thus unleashed on the entire world, see HA *Ver.* 8.1–2.

33   Gilliam (1961) 247.

34   Niebuhr (1849) 251; Seeck (1910) 398–405.

35   Bruun (2007) 201–17.

36   Gilliam (1961) 225–51. For more on this argument and criticism thereof, see Scheidel (2012a) 285–88; Jongman (2007b) 195.

37   Littman and Littman (1973) 252–55.

collection by causing a significant population decline in areas.[38] Papyrological evidence suggests that there was a severe population contraction when the plague was virulent. In some areas, a decline of anywhere between thirty and ninety percent can be observed.[39] It is possible that this shift was the result of *anachoresis*, but the numbers involved make it more likely that the plague was to blame for the rapid decline.[40] In addition to the drop in population, it should also be noted that the production of Egyptian tetradrachms collapsed around 171 and did not recover for nearly six years.[41] Again, while it is possible that this interruption was the result of more mundane factors, it is striking that the most significant disruption to the minting process in around two generations occurred precisely at the time when plague was prevalent across the empire. The economic damage wrought by the epidemic was not a fleeting phenomenon. In fact, some communities were still struggling to honour quotas for taxation in kind as long as twenty years after the outbreak.[42] In

---

38   Given the unique position of Egypt within the imperial state, we must exercise caution before assuming that certain trends would have been replicated across the empire, but it has already been established that the phenomenon of population contraction can be observed in other provinces at around the same time. For more on this, see Jongman (2007b).

39   Population drops of 33–47% are recorded in areas of the Fayum, see *P. Mich.* 223–25 and *P. Ryl.* 594 for examples. Similarly, *P. Thoumis* I. 104.10–18 record that taxes for the village of Kerbenouphis had been struck off by the local *komogrammateus* owing to the number of tax-paying men that had perished from the plague. Duncan-Jones (1996) 121, Table 1, has also shown that the Delta region experienced a population decrease of up to 93% in some villages as the plague took hold.

40   Referring to a process of flight or retreat, equivalent to the Latin *recessus*, the term *anachoresis* is often used in connection to individuals illegally fleeing from their homes and towns an attempt to avoid taxation or liturgical duties. Also see Kelly (2011) 204–8. For more role of the plague in this population decline, see Scheidel (2012a); Duncan-Jones (1996) 121. In support of this hypothesis, similar evidence of death and population decline can be observed in other regions. In Dacia, for example, an inscription records the dissolution of a funerary club which may have been compromised by members fleeing from the spread of the disease, see *ILS* 7215a. Papyrological evidence shows that Athens was affected by the pestilence, to the extent that the emperor was required to extend the eligibility criteria for membership of the Council of the Areopagus to maintain consistent numbers, see *Oliver* 84, pp. 366–88. Further, more general disruption can be identified if the number of military diplomas and local government papyri issued in Egypt are compared for the plague period to the years on either side of the outbreak, see Duncan-Jones (1996) 124–25, Figs. 6 and 7.

41   Duncan-Jones (1996) 124–25, Figs. 6 and 7.

42   *P. Oxy.* LXV 4527; Van Minnen (2001) 175–77, *contra* Bagnall (2000) 288–92.

order to assess the fiscal explanation for the Antonine Constitution, then, it is necessary to acknowledge that, rather than simple profligacy on the part of Caracalla, there were a number of factors, like the plague, that played a significant role in negatively shaping the Roman economy before the Severans had even seized power.

The Severan Recovery

The image of the economy in the immediate prelude to Caracalla's sole reign is one of contradictory evidence. On the one hand, Commodus' reign and the consequent civil wars following the death of Pertinax had been economically ruinous. Dio alleged that there was scarcely a million *sestertii* in the imperial coffers by the end of 192.[43] While he was careful to state that Severus never murdered individuals for their estates, Dio also claimed that the emperor was required to raise money from every avenue in order to meet his financial obligations.[44] This literary image is supported by evidence suggesting that the imperial currency was manipulated during the reign of Severus, the *denarius* being restored to its traditional weight, but with its silver content being simultaneously reduced by around one third.[45] Indeed, the depreciation of the primary trading token of the empire can hardly be seen as anything other than a symptom of stress.[46]

On the other hand, however, there is also evidence to contradict the hypothesis of further economic downturn under Caracalla's immediate predecessor. The early Severan period represents a high watermark in relation to public building projects in Rome and across the empire, for example. These ranged from the restoration of buildings destroyed by the fire of 191, such as

---

43   Dio 74.5.4. While this precise figure is likely an exaggeration, the unpopular policy of economic austerity pursued by Pertinax' short-lived regime supports the notion that the state's position was hardly a favourable one.

44   Dio 77.16.2. It was also into this context that Dio (77.10.1–7) described the campaign of robberies committed by Bulla Felix. While the character of Bulla is probably apocryphal, it is likely that the senator had constructed a literary archetype in response to a wider problem of banditry at the time, further suggesting economic instability and lack of imperial control. For more on this, see Fuhrmann (2012) 134–35; Riess (2001) 170; Grünewald (1999) 157–95, and Shaw (1984) 43–52.

45   Duncan-Jones (1994) 227, Table 15.6. Also see Bowman *et al.* (2005) 332–33.

46   Greene (1986) 60–61. Also see Gitler and Ponting (2007) 375–97, who claim that this debasement represents a key step in pushing the Roman economy towards the monetary chaos observed in the course of the later third century CE.

the temples of Peace and Vesta, through to the construction of new edifices such as the camp of the *equites singulares Augusti*, the Arch of Severus and the *Septizodium*.[47] Arguably the most famous result of this programme was actually completed between 211–17, although was probably commenced under Severus: the Baths of Caracalla. This imposing structure was designed on an epic scale and carried a similarly massive construction cost. It is difficult to establish an exact figure, but DeLaine has sought to offer a general impression through extrapolating a figure using the later *Edict on Maximum Prices* introduced by Diocletian in 301. DeLaine has estimated that the bath complex would have cost around 12 million *kastrenses modii* (KM), equating to a monetary figure in excess of 1.2 billion *denarii*.[48] Even accounting for inflation between the Severan period and the beginning of the fourth century, the Baths of Caracalla would certainly have cost hundreds of millions of *denarii*—an astronomical figure. The scale of this building alone, let alone the other construction and restoration projects, hardly creates the image of an emperor suffering from a lack of funds, or an empire gripped by economic anxiety.

The emperor's manipulation of the currency is also open to interpretation. Severus was the first Roman ruler to raise the army wage since Domitian.[49] It is interesting to note, then, that a change in the nature of Roman silver coinage has also been recently identified to this period. In her analysis of numismatic find sites in the north-western provinces of the empire, Kemmers has shown that there is a significant rise in coin finds across sites of all natures, though predominantly in military ones. She has argued that this increase ultimately supports the hypothesis that Severus' army pay rise required a vast amount of new coinage to be produced.[50] While debasement can never be interpreted as a financially positive initiative, the connection here between the process and the Roman army does not suggest a generalised economic decline. Rather, the monetary economy would not have been prepared for such a marked increase in demand for physical coinage and, as a consequence, the act of debasement is better interpreted as a measure dedicated to addressing an immediate problem of liquidity, rather than systemic instability.

---

47 Dio 77.16.1–4; Lusnia (2004) 517–44; Gorrie (2002) 461–81; DeLaine (1997) 197.
48 DeLaine (1997) 207–20. The KM are a grain standard, employed here owing to the relative stability in the cost of wheat and labour during the tumultuous third century.
49 While the precise nature of the pay rise is difficult to identify, owing to the poor state of the surviving evidence, the raise itself was significant nonetheless. For a detailed breakdown of Severus' military reforms, see Smith (1972) 481–500.
50 Kemmers (2009) 143–58.

Further complicating the image of the pre-Caracallan economy is the impression of the sheer wealth left behind by Severus. Indeed, all of our main literary sources for the period claim that the emperor was able to leave the imperial treasury with a fortune far greater than any other, though it is impossible to test the veracity of such a claim.[51] It is worth remembering, however, that, unlike his immediate predecessors, Severus was able to capture considerable sums through expropriations from his political rivals, as well as his lucrative campaign against Parthia.[52] It seems clear that the image of the Roman economy on the eve of Caracalla's sole reign is more complex than might initially be assumed. Even during the relative stability of the High Empire, the economy was affected by a variety of factors which represented a significant drain on the imperial treasury. The decades prior to Caracalla's accession were characterised by warfare and disease, and yet the emperor's own father appears to have stalled terminal decline, albeit temporarily. The quality and fineness of imperial silver coinage was significantly inferior compared to earlier periods, but it seems unlikely that this is indicative of any major financial or economic problem. Rather than basing an economic explanation of the *Constitutio Antoniniana* on the emperor's temperament and cronyism, as Dio does, we must view the initiatives introduced under Caracalla, including the edict, as a continuation of a longer process.

The Economy under Caracalla

Dio claimed that Caracalla was responsible for raising a number of taxes. Among the levies described by Dio were doubling of tax on the emancipation of slaves and an increase in inheritance duties from five to ten percent.[53] He explained that Caracalla changed the law regarding legacies and had abolished rights of succession, with their accompanying tax exemption, for close relatives of the deceased.[54] Most galling to the senator, however, was the emperor's repeated demands for the *aurum coronarium*, Dio accusing Caracalla

---

51   Dio 77.16.4; Hdn. 3.15.3; HA *Sev.* 12.3.
52   For an account of the expropriations against Albinus' supporters, see Dio 76.8.3–9.1. For more on the Parthian campaign, see Dio 75.9.4; Hdn. 3.9.9–11. I am grateful to Charmaine Gorrie for her assistance and advice on this subject.
53   Dio 78.9.4.
54   Dio 78.9.4–5.

of inventing a number of military victories in order to levy the charge.[55] Even accounting for a degree of hyperbole in Dio's testimony, since increased taxation would never be popular with any echelon of society, let alone the *ordo senatorius*, it seems that the imperial government was engaged in a process of trying to augment levels of capital from the outset of Caracalla's sole reign.[56]

Dio also accused Caracalla of debasing precious metal coinage in circulation within the empire, alleging that the emperor bought peace with tribes on the frontiers using high quality gold coinage, while circulating devalued currency among his actual citizenry.[57] While it is tempting to dismiss Dio's account here as little more than speculative melodrama, numismatic data suggests that Caracalla was, in fact, manipulating imperial coinage at the time. Three general trends can be observed: a decline in the fineness of silver coinage, a reduction in the weight of coin output (resulting in a higher number of coins struck per pound of metal) and, finally, a fiduciary pricing of coin types over their intrinsic value. If this data is considered, then Dio was ultimately correct to identify a process of numismatic debasement, even if he did so in a facetious and factually inaccurate manner. The evidence suggests that the emperor was anxious to increase rapidly the number of coins in circulation across the empire, even if this meant devaluing his precious metal coinage to achieve the goal.[58] Metallurgical analysis of *denarii* from Augustus to Alexander Severus clearly demonstrates that the Severan period formed a nadir in relation to the overall fineness of Roman silver coinage.[59]

Diminution in precious metal fineness was accompanied by a simultaneous reduction in the weight of both gold and silver coinage. The target weight of *aurei* under Caracalla appears to have been *c.* 6.46 grams, equating to fifty coins per pound of gold. The target weight of *denarii*, by contrast, was *c.* 3.23 grams, resulting in an average of 192 coins per pound of silver.[60] This represents an increase of over twenty coins per pound from coins of the same denomination

---

55   Dio 79.92–3. For more on the history of the *aurum coronarium*, originally a levy in connection with triumphs or anniversaries during the Principate, see Klauser 1944 (1948) 129–53.

56   Marasco (1994) 508–11, has argued that Caracalla's exploitation of the *aurum coronarium* was one of his most damaging policies, with regards to the propertied class.

57   Dio 78.14.4.

58   Langenegger (2010) 171–76.

59   Duncan-Jones (1994) 225, 232, Tables 15.5 and 15.9. Under Augustus, the median silver fineness of *denarii* was 98% but, by Caracalla's reign, that figure had dropped to 50.5%. For more on the fluctuation in quality of silver coinage for the later period, from Severus to Aemilianus, see Langenegger (2010) 179–81.

60   Duncan-Jones (1994) 217, 225, Tables 15.3 and 15.5.

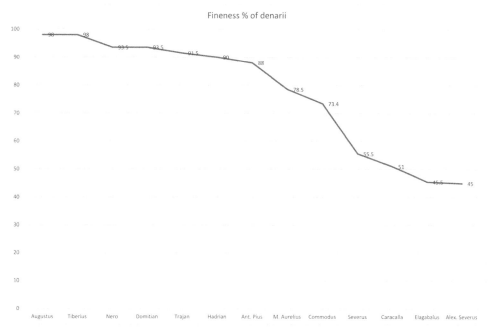

FIGURE 1   *Graph illustrating the decline in median fineness of* denarii.
Note: Data based on analysis from Duncan-Jones (1994) 225.

struck under Septimius Severus, and nearly forty more than even the disastrous closing period of Commodus' reign, 187–92 CE.[61]

Caracalla's most famous numismatic innovation, however, was the introduction of the *antoninianus* coin type in 215. Characterised by a radiate obverse bust of the emperor, the circulation of this denomination is widely regarded to have been a terrible economic move on Caracalla's part.[62] The primary problem with this coin type is the relationship between its precious metal content and the face value at which it was tariffed. While metallurgical analysis confirms that they contained a silver content roughly equivalent to 1.5

---

61   Although it should be noted that the weight of Commodian coinage was slightly lower than Severan issues. See Fig. 2, below.

62   Sutherland (1974) 218, considers its circulation to be 'the first great overt act of depreciation in the currency of the Roman empire.' Similarly, Greene (1986) 61, claimed that the new coin only worsened a deepening economic crisis, while Harl (1996) 128, argued that its introduction was a disastrous policy which undermined the system of price and exchange across the empire, and that Elagabalus' decision to scrap it was wholly correct. Also see Gitler and Ponting (2007) 375–76.

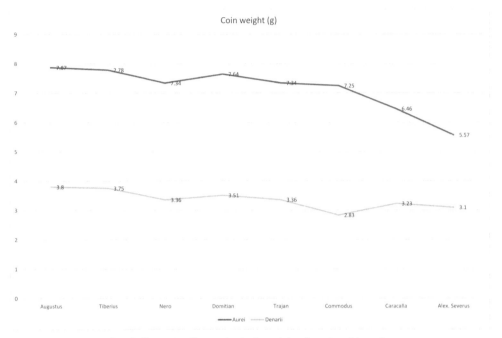

FIGURE 2 *Graph illustrating fluctuation in the weight of* aurei *and* denarii.
Note: Data adapted from Duncan-Jones (1994) 215, 225.

denarii, there is no explicit evidence for the fiduciary value placed upon *antoniniani* by the emperor.[63] If, for example, the coin was valued at 1.25 *denarii*, this would represent a positive revaluation of the silver currency, though such a hypothesis contrasts with Caracalla's wider policy of debasement, rendering it ultimately unpersuasive.[64] It is more likely that the *antoninianus* was tariffed at two *denarii*.

This hypothesis is further supported by the coins' obverse iconography. The radiate crown depicted on the emperor's bust is a feature usually associated with the *dupondius*, tariffed at double the face value of an *as*, even if not containing double the weight of orichalcum.[65] The creation of an underweighted double-*denarius* represents a significant change to the Roman monetary economy of the period, devaluing the regular *denarius* by twenty-five percent.[66] It

---

63 Depeyrot and Hollard (1987) 57–85.
64 Lo Cascio (1984) 133–201.
65 Duncan-Jones (1994) 138, 222 n.39. Also see BMCRE V, p. xviii.
66 Greene (1986) 60–61; Bowman *et al.* (2005) 339–40.

must be stressed, however, that even this seemingly destructive initiative did not destabilise the economy until the later crisis of the third century.[67]

The Economic Function of the Antonine Constitution

Given the context of rising taxation and monetary debasement, it is appropriate to consider further Dio's testimony regarding the nature of the Antonine Constitution. As previously noted, Dio's hostility towards Caracalla is well-known, and there can be little question that the author perceived the introduction of the *constitutio* as another opportunity to criticise the emperor, but this does not mean that we ought to dismiss the senator's account entirely. Rather than focusing solely on the credibility of Dio as a source, it is further necessary to return to the Giessen papyrus and to consider the legislation itself. Indeed, if the text of *P. Giss.* 40 is examined closely, it can be shown that the evidence supports the hypothesis that economic factors did play a role in motivating Caracalla to introduce his edict.

Examination of the Giessen text reveals that there are two areas where possible allusions to edict's economic purpose can be identified. The first is based upon a reconstruction of the severely damaged final lines of the decree. Of the many attempts to study and restore the *constitutio*, only Heichelheim has offered any substantial edition of these lines.[68]

Ἄπο δὲ τῶν] π[ρ]οσ[όδων τῶν νῦν] | [ὑπερχουσῶν συντελούντων, ἅπερ ἐκελεύσ]θη [παρὰ Ῥωμαίων ἀπὸ τοῦ κα ἔτους,] | [ὡς δίκαιον ἐκ τῶν διαταγμάτων καὶ ἐπιστολ]ῶ[ν, ἃ ἐξεδόθη ὑφ' ἡμῶν τε] | [καὶ τῶν ἡμετέρων προγόνων Προετέθη ....]

Referring to the taxes that exist at present, all are due to pay those that have been imposed upon the Romans from the beginning of their twenty-first year [of age], as it is the law, according to the edicts and rescripts issued by us and our ancestors. Displayed publically ...[69]

---

67 Langenegger (2010) 176–81. During the reign of Elagabalus, production of *antoniniani* was halted, and only resumed in 238, under Balbinus and Pupienus. The denomination was further debased by Gordian III, a process which contributed to a destabilisation of the currency and monetary economy at large.

68 For an apparatus and commentary of the text, see the accompanying appendix.

69 *P. Giss.* 40 I, ll. 14–17. Originally, Heichelheim was unable to conclude how the mention of a 'twenty first year' fit into the text, but this is easily overcome if the use of the genitive is

When restored in this manner, these lines form an explicit directive that all of the newly enfranchised Romans were immediately liable to pay all taxes levied against the citizen body.[70] If it is accepted that the final detail of the *constitutio* text was to remind new *cives* of the fiscal obligations accompanying their new status, this would certainly lend credence to Dio's claim that Caracalla's primary intention in promulgating the Antonine Constitution was to raise capital through direct taxation. The heavily damaged nature of the papyrus means, however, that the reconstruction offered by Heichelheim is ultimately conjectural, and hence cannot be accepted in isolation as confirmation of a Caracallan fiscal motive underlying the edict. This is not the only potential reference to fiscal matters in the course of *P. Giss.* 40, though.

The second area in which it is possible to identify an economic rationale is better preserved but even more controversial, since it surrounds the ninth line of the text, in which the terms of the *constitutio* were outlined. This section proves problematic owing to a lacuna in the papyrus obscuring a key word in the construction:

Δίδω[μ]ι τοί[ν]υν ἄπα– | [σι τοῖς κατὰ τὴν Ῥωμαϊκ]ὴν οἰκουμένην π[ολειτ] είαν Ῥωμ[αί]ων [μ]ένοντος | [τοῦ δικαίου τῶν πολιτευμ]άτων χωρ[ὶς] τῶν [...] ειτικίων.

I therefore give everyone in the Roman world the Roman citizenship: respecting customary law, except/without ...[71]

Traditionally, the exclusionary clause contained in the ninth line was thought to make reference to the *dediticii*, with the lacuna being restored to read as δεδειτκίων.[72] With this reconstruction, the edict is thus assumed to make reference to one of two potential groups. The first were freedmen found guilty of crimes during their servitude, with the result that they could never attain the rights of the franchise, despite their free status.[73] Alternatively, the term could

---

in reference to the citizens' age of eligibility, an issue separate from the question of one's age of majority in Roman Egypt. For more on the age of majority, see Hagedorn (1996) 224–26; Lewis (1979) 117–20.

70 Heichelheim (1941) 12.
71 *P. Giss.* 40 I, ll. 7–9.
72 Meyer (1920); Bickermann (1926), Schönbauer (1931) 277–335; Stroux (1933) 272–95; Wilhelm (1934) 178–80; Heichelheim (1941) 10–22. An alternative spelling of δηδειτικίων was proposed later, see Weissert (1963) 239–50. For a recent defence of the restoration, see Rocco (2010) 131–32.
73 Gaius, *Inst.* 1.13–15.

be used in reference to newly conquered barbarians who, following their surrender (*deditio*), experienced a period of complete subjugation to Rome before being slowly inducted into the empire and being able to attain greater status. In either case, if the restoration of δεδειτικίων was correct, the clause was designed to prevent at least one socially undesirable group from enjoying the emperor's otherwise universal grant.[74] The most recent attempts to identify the *dediticii* have emphasised the military exigency for maintaining a manpower pool of barbarian *numeri* constantly available.[75]

The *dediticii* hypothesis is far from assured, however, despite such historical support. In fact, the restoration has been completely rejected in what is arguably the most authoritative modern study of the text.[76] Analysis of the Giessen papyrus has shown that the inclusion of *dediticii* is syntactically and semantically problematic and awkward.[77] Furthermore, the clause has always been historically challenging, owing to the fact that none of the other sources who mention the *constitutio* in the course of their works, such as Dio or Ulpian, ever refer to any exceptions to the wide-reaching nature of Caracalla's edict.[78] Such an omission is troubling. It would seem uncharacteristically careless of a jurist of Ulpian's character, an individual hailed by Honoré as one of the most influential writers of the Severan age, to neglect such a crucial detail in the course of his legal texts.[79] Indeed, while it is possible that Ulpian's original text was adapted and altered in the course of inclusion in the *Digest*, this argument does not explain the silence of other sources, contemporary or secondary, on the matter. This has led to further scepticism regarding any connection between the *constitutio* and the *dediticii*.[80]

Owing to the well-established process of assimilating communities into the empire by this point in imperial history, the number of *dediticii* living in Caracalla's realm must have represented a statistically insignificant portion of the empire's total population.[81] Furthermore, if Gaius was correct that the

---

74 Lukaszewicz (1990a) 93–101.
75 Van Minnen (2016) 219–20; Rocco (2010) 145–55. The potential military application of the Antonine Constitution will be considered in the next chapter.
76 Kuhlmann (2012) 47, (1994) 236. Kuhlmann's own opinion regarding the lacuna will be considered later in this chapter.
77 Kuhlmann (1994) 236.
78 Dio 77.9.5–6; *Dig.* 1.5.17.
79 Honoré (2002) 1.
80 Benario (1954) 188.
81 Sherwin-White (1973a) 272, refers to the process of including communities into the Roman body politic as taking on an increasingly mechanical character even by the end of the Flavian period.

dediticii were a class of people who had lost all political identity and could never hope of attaining the rights of Roman citizenship under any circumstance, then there would have been no need to stipulate or emphasise their ineligibility in the course of the text now preserved on the Giessen papyrus.[82] It is logical to conclude that if the *dediticii* were indeed social pariahs, then their absence from the terms of the *constitutio* would be automatically assumed and entirely non-negotiable. In fact, there would have been as little requirement to specify their exclusion as there would have been for slaves. This conclusion renders any attempt to restore the lacuna in *P. Giss.* 40 to read as δεδειτικίων almost untenable.

How, then, ought we reconstruct the controversial gap in the Giessen text? The publication of materials relating to the Antonine *Tabula Banasitana* has fundamentally altered the nature of this debate. The *tabula* is a record of a grant of citizenship being bestowed to a member of the Mauretanian provincial elite, Julianus, and his descendants, during the reign of Marcus Aurelius and Commodus.[83] While much of the grant is predictably formulaic, a pair of caveats at the end of the document forms the primary point of interest. Following the notice that citizenship was to be conferred upon Julianus and his family, the emperors declared that the grant was to be bestowed *salvo iure gentis* and *sine diminutione tributorum et vectigalium populi et fisci*.[84] The first of these clauses was designed to ensure that the newly enfranchised individual could continue to function in the midst of a largely peregrine population, by clarifying that the grant of Roman *civitas* did not exclude the recipient from access to their customary legal framework, an arrangement which also protected any claim of the parent community over the services of the new citizen.[85] The second clause served to clarify the fiscal responsibilities inherent on the individual in question. Unlike the citizens of the earliest years of the Principate who enjoyed the fiscal *immunitas rerum omnium*, the newly enfranchised would be liable to pay Roman taxation in addition to pre-existing local levies.[86]

---

82 Gaius, *Inst.* 1.13–15. Also see Buraselis (2007) 7.

83 *IAM* 2.1, 94 = *AE* 1961, 142. For an annotated edition of the *tabula*, see Oliver (1972) 336–40.

84 *IAM* 2.1, 94, ll. 11–12; 37–38. The *salvo iure gentis* clause features both in reference to Julianus himself and his descendants, whilst the *sine* clause is presented in connection with the extension of the franchise to his descendants later in the same text.

85 Kuhlmann (1994) 231–32; Oliver (1989) 504.

86 Sherwin-White (1973b) 86–98.

A similarity between the grammatical structure of the Latin *tabula* and the Greek edict on *P. Giss.* 40 was noted by Sasse, who observed that the papyrus appears to contain a comparably formulaic grammatical construction, despite the difference in language. In fact, the μένοντος participle is a relatively common one, in connection with Greek legal texts, and Sasse has identified forty seven other cases in which the construction is identical to the Giessen papyrus, employing a participle of μένειν followed by a genitive absolute.[87] In the past, this led Sherwin-White to conclude that the *dediticii* were therefore not excluded from the franchise itself, but rather some other, unspoken subsidiary grant.[88] This position is tenuous, however, both on linguistic grounds and for the reasons outlined above regarding the fundamental fragility of any connection between the *dediticii* and the Antonine Constitution.[89] An alternative has to be found which is reminiscent of the *Tabula Banasitana*, as per Sasse's observations, but which also contains no reference to the erroneously included *dediticii*. With these considerations in mind, I would argue that it is preferable to restore the critical eighth and ninth lines of the *constitutio* text in the following manner: [μ]ένοντος [τοῦ δικαίου τῶν πολιτευμ]άτων χωρ[ὶς] τῶν [ἀδδ]ειτικίων.[90] In this reconstruction, the Greek χωρίς is translated in its form meaning 'without' rather than the 'except' favoured when thought to make reference to the *dediticii*.[91] The adjectival noun ἀδδειτικίων, transliterated from the Latin adjective *additicius* and meaning 'additional', is becoming increasingly favoured as a more realistic alternative to the *dediticii* hypothesis, one which fits more comfortably with the ancient literary sources who make no reference to a disbarred population group.[92]

Rather than proclaiming a universal extension of the franchise, only then to specify the ineligibility of an insignificant population group, the μένοντος clause should be interpreted as a Greek equivalent to the formulaic Latin *salvo*

---

87 Sasse (1958) 48–58.
88 Sherwin-White (1973a) 381–83; (1973b) 95–97.
89 Lukaszewicz (1990a) 98–99.
90 *P. Giss.* 40 I, ll. 8–9.
91 Indeed, the possibility that χωρίς might mean 'without' at this juncture has proven problematic to those desiring to maintain a link the *dediticii*, see Lukaszewicz (1990a) 99.
92 Kuhlmann (2012) 48–50. It is true that the word is a *hapax legomenon*, but it must be remembered that the transliteration δεδειτικίων (or any variant thereof) is also unique. In this sense, the revised wording is no more difficult to accept than a reference to the *dediticii* and, more importantly, forms a better fit in relation to the formulaic nature of Greek legal texts noted by Sasse, see above, and with its Latin counterpart, the *Tabula Banasitana*, see Oliver (1989) 504.

iure gentis, safeguarding the pre-existing relationship between the recipient of the franchise and their parent community. It follows, then, that the χωρίς + genitive construction makes sense if interpreted as roughly equivalent to the Latin *sine* prepositional phrase found in the *Tabula Banasitana*, making reference to privileges that the newly enfranchised might expect.[93] The controversial seventh to ninth lines of the *constitutio* should therefore be translated to read: 'I therefore give everyone in the Roman world the Roman citizenship, respecting customary law, without additional privileges.'[94] This restoration and translation, while preferable to any mention of the *dediticii*, does not end the debate on how the wording of Caracalla's edict should be understood, though. In his assessment of the Giessen text, Oliver concluded that the similarities between the *constitutio* and the *Tabula Banasitana* were so pronounced that the two documents should be considered identical in terms of the conditions set upon the grants:

> Since the reference to citizenship in both and even the order is the same, the conclusion is inescapable that the reservations with no intervening conjunction are identical, even if a short phrase, namely "without the *additicia*" replaces the "*sine diminutione tributorum et vectigalium populi Romani*" of the *Tabula Banasitana*.[95]

Such a conclusion would strongly suggest that Caracalla's edict was promulgated with a clearly economic or financial motive in mind. More recently, however, this absolute connection between the two documents has been questioned. While he agrees that the reconstruction of *additicia* has some palaeographical basis, since it features in a similar fashion in Latin sources, Kuhlmann disagrees that the χωρὶς τῶν ἀδδειτικίων clause represents a direct transliteration of *sine diminutione tributorum et vectigalium populi et fisci*, inasmuch as he doubts that it refers to fiscal immunity alone, preferring a more general reference to assorted privileges.[96] He questions how far the sentiment from the Latin construction can be inferred from one word alone, arguing that if Oliver

---

93 Wolff (1977) 99–102.
94 *P. Giss.* 40 I, ll. 7–9.
95 Oliver (1989) 504. The precise language of the exclusionary clause clearly does not meld flawlessly with the Latin of the *Tabula Banasitana*. Oliver is content, however, that this is owing to the difficulties in replicating the precise Latin terminology in Greek, rather than any other issue.
96 Kuhlmann (1994) 237. For examples of the term in the Latin corpus which Kuhlmann identifies, see *Dig.* 50.16.98.1 and Tert. *Resurr.* 52.

THE FISCAL RATIONALE 71

was correct in his assumption regarding the focus of *additicia*, then it must represent a hitherto unrecognised Greek *terminus technicus*.[97] This clearly presents an issue since, in the event that *additicia* was a commonly used legal term, we would expect to find more examples of its usage.[98]

While Oliver has overstated the grammatical similarity between the *constitutio* and the *tabula*, this does not necessarily weaken the hypothesis that economic or financial concerns were high priorities for the emperor. In fact, of the innumerable benefits that the Giessen papyrus might theoretically make reference to in the controversial clause, fiscal privileges were among the foremost concerns of both Caracalla and his newly enfranchised populace. To illustrate this, it is necessary to return to the account offered by Dio. Perhaps the question that should be asked is why Dio chose to criticise the emperor's edict on the basis of economy specifically. The author's account of Caracalla's reign is filled with a variety of personal attacks and insults on a number of subjects, from the emperor's adoration of Alexander the Great through to his fundamental personality and ethnicity.[99] Considering the visible thread of 'hatred and mockery' running through the senator's prose, it seems unlikely that Dio would have neglected any opportunity to demolish the character of his bête-noir.[100] As a member of the senatorial class, it would be arguably more logical for Dio to criticise Caracalla for diluting the prestige of the franchise, since this would form an obvious point of concern for a social group already in possession of the rights of Roman citizenship.[101] He does nothing of the sort, though.

On the one hand, this omission could be the result of Xiphilinus' later epitomising of Dio's original work at this juncture.[102] On the other hand, however, it should be noted that despite Dio's obvious hatred of the emperor, the author's fierce criticism of Caracalla's financial drives does appear to contain

---

97   Kuhlmann (1994) 236–37. Also see Van Minnen (2016) 219.
98   Kuhlmann (1994) 237.
99   Dio 78.6.1a; Millar (1964) 150–51; Davenport (2012) 797–98.
100 Millar (1964) 151. A similar idea was espoused by Benario (1954) 188, for example, who argued that the *dediticii* could not have been mentioned in the course of the *constitutio* since Dio did not mention them: 'if a significant portion of the population had been barred from the enjoyment of the emperor's gift, Dio would, in all likelihood, not have failed to mention it, since he was a bitter enemy of the ruler.' Whilst Benario overstates the case here and underestimates the level of self-interest ingrained in Dio's work, he is fundamentally correct to highlight the level of criticism levelled at the emperor by the author.
101 Garnsey (1970) 270–71.
102 Millar (1964) 155, for example, has concluded that Xiphilinus' work is 'exceptionally poor' in relation to Caracalla's principate.

an accurate knowledge of the initiatives, once the hostile rhetoric has been stripped away.[103] A similar logic can also be applied to the senator's relationship with the *Constitutio Antoniniana*. It is entirely understandable that Dio would attempt to underplay the majesty of the edict promoted by Caracalla. It would be imprudent to assume, however, that Dio had simply fictionalised its fiscal implications rather than choosing to exploit a genuine facet of the *constitutio* in the course of condemning the emperor's unrestrained spending on his favourites.

Dio did not fabricate economic concerns or otherwise simply settle on this criticism from among a variety of potential slights; his account is certainly not an exercise in 'extreme idiocy', as Ando would claim.[104] Instead, Dio must have considered the fiscal implications of the *constitutio* to be a factor that was public knowledge and, furthermore, an aspect that would have impacted upon many of his intended audience. While there is little firm evidence to suggest that Dio's history was published in any meaningful way in antiquity, it is still possible to conclude that Dio believed that his attack of Caracalla's edict on economic grounds would have carried the most resonance with his readers, real or intended.[105]

The Vicesima Hereditatum

This leads us to another objection to the fiscal hypothesis that must be challenged. In an attempt to undermine Dio's credibility regarding the economic rationale for the edict, scholars have tried to argue that any desire on Caracalla's part to reap an increased tax yield must have been a secondary concern, at best. To substantiate this argument, they point out that the majority of the wealthiest inhabitants of the empire were most likely already citizens, and therefore subject to the emperor's taxes, meaning that the increased yield resulting from the expanded franchise cannot have been considerable.[106] This position, however, ignores other available financial evidence from the period which suggests that Caracalla was eager to increase exponentially his tax yield in a short period of time by raising money from estates across a variety of social strata. Returning to Dio's text once more, it was noted earlier in this

---

103   Millar (1964) 154–55.
104   Ando (2000) 395, n. 275.
105   For more on the composition of Dio's history, see Millar (1964) 28–72.
106   Buraselis (2007) 8–9; Sherwin-White (1973a) 281.

THE FISCAL RATIONALE   73

chapter that one of the taxes that Dio explicitly mentions in connection with Caracalla's fiscal reform is that on inheritances and legacies, claiming that the emperor had doubled the rate from five to ten percent.[107] Upon close examination, the evidence supports the theory that this taxation was levied on estates far smaller than was once thought. In fact, the connection between this citizen tax and the expansion of the franchise by Caracalla further substantiates Dio's fiscal explanation of the edict, demonstrating that the emperor was eager to raise capital from all corners of his realm, and shows that he did not focus merely on the social elite to achieve this objective.

Introduced by Augustus in 6 CE, the *vicesima hereditatum* was an inheritance duty levied upon estates over a certain value.[108] While there appears to be good evidence for the collection of this tax, the lack of precise information offered by ancient authors means that the exact level of exemption from this tax remains unknown. Evidence gleaned from Pliny the Younger suggests that the charge could be raised against estates of varying sizes.[109] The only other source to mention inheritance duty explicitly is Dio again, who claimed that only the smallest and most modest estates were exempt from the charge.[110] Neither Dio nor Pliny ever provide any numerical figures in support of their claims.

Despite the hints offered by ancient authors, however, there has been a trend among modern scholars to accept an exemption level for the *vicesima* of estates valued at 100,000 *sestertii* and above, obviously leading to a perception that it was a tax only levied against the propertied classes and the wealthy.[111] It is difficult to establish from where this figure has actually derived, since its extrapolation seems to be founded less on examination of the extant evidence and more on baseless speculation. I argue that it is the acceptance of this groundless figure that is clearly to blame for the outmoded scholarly

---

107 Dio 78.9.4.
108 Gilliam (1952) 397; Perez (2009) 211–13.
109 Plin. *Pan.* 39.5–40.1. In this source, Pliny commends Trajan for his generosity in alleviating the terms of the levy from those of the Flavian period, in which very few estates seem to have been exempt. Whilst it is frustrating that Pliny gives no precise figures, despite serving as a *praefectus aerarii militaris* (magistrate in charge of the military treasury, into which the funds from the *vicesima* were channelled) it must be remembered that he was writing to glorify the emperor rather than offer a detailed account of the tax itself, see Gilliam (1952) 398. The significance of the connection between the *vicesima* and the military treasury will be considered in the next chapter.
110 Dio 55.25.5.
111 Gilliam (1952) 398–99. Also see Sherwin-White (1973a) 221–22; Cagnat (1882) 226, n. 4.

consensus that a fiscal rationale could not have prompted the Antonine Constitution, since 'the majority of the great fortunes of the empire were already in the fold'.[112] Such a conjectural position regarding the terms of the *vicesima hereditatum* can, however, be easily dismantled by examining material evidence available in the form of papyri. Contrary to the notion that the *vicesima* was a tax on the propertied classes alone, papyrological evidence can be found which suggests that the threshold for exemption from the levy was far lower than previously believed, and thus impacted upon the majority of the empire's enfranchised inhabitants.

Thought by some to form different parts of the same document, *P. Mich.* 435 and 440 are military texts which record a number of inheritances and payments to the *vicesima* made by soldiers of the legions *II Traiana* and *III Cyrenaica*.[113] The texts are poorly preserved and blighted by a number of lacunae, but it is still possible to identify that a number of troops of varying ranks seem to have paid their tax contributions on the same day.[114] It is the varying size of the legacies involved in these soldiers' transactions that is particularly striking when assessing the potential fiscal reach of the *Constitutio Antoniniana*. In the third entry contained on *P. Mich.* 435, the estate was calculated at c. 5360 *drachmae*, with the *vicesima* deducting 265 of that amount. Even more surprising is the partially damaged second entry on the same papyrus, which recorded the contribution to the *vicesima* at 95 *drachmae*, a figure that would derive from an estate total of only around 1900 *drachmae*.[115] This is clearly far below the 100,000 *sestertii* figure so confidently mooted by scholars in the past. As Gilliam has observed, it would be patently ridiculous to assume that each of the soldiers stationed at Nicopolis could ever bequeath an estate approaching one hundred thousand *sestertii*, meaning that the previous assessment of the levy is incorrect and that a conclusion that the *vicesima* was collected from much smaller estates is incontrovertible.[116]

Sherwin-White's observation that the largest estates of the empire were probably all owned by individuals who had been enfranchised for some time

---

112   Sherwin-White (1973a) 221–22.
113   The papyri are thought to have derived from the legionary camp at Nicopolis. The appearance of these two legions together suggests a possible date range of the papyri of 109–19 CE, see Gilliam (1952) 402; Arangio-Ruiz (1949) 257–59; Wallace (1938) 324.
114   Three of the better preserved entries on *P. Mich.* 435 carry the date *IV Nonas Iulias*, as does the first readable entry on *P. Mich.* 440.
115   Gilliam (1952) 403–4.
116   Gilliam (1952) 404.

by 212 is technically correct, but it assumes that Caracalla was only interested in harvesting tax income from the largest estates in the wealthiest echelons of Roman society and, furthermore, that these prosperous individuals alone would have provided sufficient capital to bankroll the imperial administration.[117] While there is no suggestion that the emperor was uninterested in the estates of the elite, the fact remains that the vast majority of the empire's inhabitants did not possess estates in excess of 100,000 *sestertii*. Even though the level of tax raised on an individual basis would undoubtedly be smaller, there is no reason to accept the claim of Buraselis that the cumulative taxation raised across the empire from smaller estates would have been insignificant or of little consequence.[118] In fact, if the number of eligible tax payers was vastly multiplied through legislation such as the *constitutio*, the resulting increase in tax yield must have been considerable, even accounting for inefficiencies within the physical process of tax collection.[119] Consequently, this evidence, when combined with that of Dio and the Giessen papyrus, ultimately supports the hypothesis that the *Constitutio Antoniniana* had a fiscal purpose and that, among Caracalla's different motivations for the edict, an economic agenda was prominent. Despite the many scholarly attempts to claim otherwise, it would seem that Millar was correct to observe that by expanding the franchise as Caracalla did, the emperor 'will have included most people who were worth taxing'.[120]

The Purpose of Caracallan Fiscal Innovation

The evidence supports the notion that the Antonine Constitution contained a significant fiscal dimension, but the question of its purpose remains open. If the ancient authors are correct that Septimius Severus was able to leave the imperial coffers with higher revenues than had been observed under any of his predecessors, Caracalla must have engaged in an unprecedented level of spending to result in a situation where he was compelled to raise capital on the scale suggested by Dio. However, it has been shown above that Dio's

---

117 Sherwin-White (1973a) 221–22.
118 Buraselis (2007) 8–9. While it is difficult to assess the urban population, Kron (2008) 97–110, has argued that the agricultural peasants were often more productive has been assumed. This notion ultimately supports a hypothesis that the state could profit from extending a tax to encompass smaller scale estates.
119 For the complexity of tax collection, see Duncan-Jones (1994) 56–63.
120 Millar (1964) 153.

accusations of flagrant favouritism and cronyism, are unconvincing. Two factors warrant consideration. Firstly, Davenport has shown that Dio's criticism probably results more from his own bitterness at not being one of the emperor's favoured senators.[121] Secondly, even accounting for increases in *congiaria* and donatives to the military, these gifts would need to have been titanic in nature to exhaust the imperial finances and warrant such a far-reaching fiscal response. Furthermore, it should be remembered that financial profligacy is not a charge unique to Caracalla and is often a negative trait associated with allegedly bad rulers by hostile sources.[122]

An alternative explanation might be that, in recording the end of Severus' reign, the ancient writers have presented an inaccurate or even false image regarding the level of wealth left behind by the dying emperor. Some evidence suggests that, rather than inheriting the empire in a healthy financial position, Caracalla was forced to respond to economic uncertainty during his period as sole ruler. An example of the emperor reacting to an economic depression can be observed in the epigraphic corpus, in which he publicised his imperial *indulgentia* towards the province of Mauretania Tingitana.

1)   ] *Imp(erator) Caes(ar) divi Severi Pii Arab(ici) Adiab(enici) Parth(ici) Max(imi) Brit(annici) Max(imi) filius divi M(arci) Antonini Germ(anici) Sarm(atici) nepos divi Antonini Pii pronepos*
   [*divi H*]*adria*[*ni divi Traiani Parth(ici) et di*]*v*[*i*] *Nervae adnepos Marcus Aurelius Antoninus Pius Aug(ustus) Part(hicus) Max(imus) Brit(annicus) Max(imus) Germ(anicus) Max(imus) Pont(ifex) Max(imus) Trib(uniciae) potestatis*
5)   *XVIIII Imp(erator) III co(n)s(ul) IIII p(ater) p(atriae) proco(n)s(ul) dicit obsequium et fidem vestram remunerans omnia quaecumque sunt debita fiscalia frumentaria sive pecuniaria pendentium quoque causarum concedo*
   vobis exceptis de quibus pronuntiatum est provocatione non secuta et hoc amplius eas quoq(ue) causas at beneficium meum profiteor ipse pertinere in
10) *quibus appellationem interpositam probatum fuerit etiam si non sit admissa*
   certum habens quod indulgentiam meam obsequio sitis remuneraturi cum

---

121 Davenport (2012) 797–803.
122 Suetonius was particularly quick to level this type of accusation, for example. For instances of 'bad' emperors behaving in a financially extravagant manner, see his accounts of Caligula (*Cal.* 37), Nero (*Nero* 30–31) and Domitian (*Domit.* 12).

THE FISCAL RATIONALE

    vicor(um) et provinciarum bene de re p(ublica) merentium non tantum viris fortibus
    in omni ordine spectatissimis castrensium adque civilium officiorum ve-
    rum etiam silvis quoque ipsis caelestium fertilibus animalium meritum
15) *aput me conlocaveritis hoc beneficio meo praesumo omnes de cetero an-*
    nuas pensitationes sive in frumento seu in pecunia eo promptius datu-
    ros quo me reputabitis non expectasse quin ultro offerrem neque petenti-
    bus vobis neque sperantibus nova remedia et magnificam indulgentiam
    curantibus L(ucio) Ant(onio) Sosibiano et Aulo Pompeio Cassiano
20) *d(u)umviris*

Emperor Caesar Marcus Aurelius Antoninus Pius Augustus, *Parthicus Maximus, Britannicus Maximus, Germanicus Maximus*, pontifex maximus, holder of the tribunician power for the nineteenth time, *imperator* for the third time, consul for the fourth time, *pater patriae*, proconsul; son of the divine Severus Pius *Arabicus, Adiabenicus, Parthicus Maximus, Britannicus Maximus*; grandson of the divine Marcus Antoninus *Germanicus, Sarmaticus*; great-grandson of the divine Antoninus Pius; great-great grandson of the divine Hadrian; great-great-great grandson of the divine Trajan *Parthicus*; and great-great-great-great grandson of the divine Nerva, proclaims: In rewarding your allegiance and loyalty, I remit any debts that you owe the *fiscus* in either grain or money, and also the claims in suits pending, except those where a judgment has been given and no appeal has been lodged. Furthermore, I proclaim that my generosity also extends to suits in which proof can be offered that an appeal has been lodged, even if it has not been yet granted, since I am confident that you will repay my indulgence with zeal when you have gained credit with me from this favour, not only by the service of the finest of brave men from the towns and countryside, who are highly regarded by all in civil and military positions, but also by contributing from your forests, which are known for their abundance of celestial beasts. As for the future, I expect that annual taxes in grain and money will be paid more promptly, when you remember that you never expected that I would voluntarily offer unprecedented relief and unstinting indulgence without your request. This bronze was engraved under the order of the *duumviri* Lucius Antonius Sosibianus and Aulus Pompeius Cassianus.[123]

---

123   *AE* 1946, 109. Translation adapted from Johnson *et al.* (2003).

The inscription shows that the emperor released an order in 216 that remitted debt across the province, both in money and in kind. Caracalla's desire to promote himself as *indulgentissimus* means that it should come as no surprise to find him stressing this quality by drawing attention to the 'great indulgence' (*magnificam indulgentiam*) that he had bestowed upon the Mauretanian populace.[124] What might seem unusual, in the context of Caracalla's sole rule, is that the emperor should excuse the province of its debts at precisely the same time as he increased taxation across the rest of his empire, according to Dio.

It is tempting to draw a comparison between this proclamation and the earlier moratorium issued by Hadrian in Egypt.[125] It might appear that the Caracallan document is, in real terms, nothing more than a temporary remission of taxes, a pragmatic response to economic stress in Mauretania and designed to allow the province time to recover whilst not destabilising the region at large.[126] Indeed, Buraselis is correct to observe that, in genuine cases of economic distress, the generosity of the Augusti could be even more useful than in times of prosperity, and the text of the inscription makes it clear that the emperor expected the province to pay their tax contributions promptly, after the duration of the remission had expired.[127] If interpreted in this manner, the Banasa tablet would appear to suggest that Caracalla faced the unenviable prospect of accepting a short term economic deficit in his tax yield in order to preserve the long term liquidity of the provinces, a conclusion that might lead one to consider that the *Constitutio Antoniniana* was a reactive edict, designed to ensure some form of taxation reached the imperial coffers during an otherwise troubled time. This is not the entire picture, though.

Objections can be raised against the theory that economic depression was the primary motivation behind the promulgation of the *constitutio*. Firstly, economic difficulties prompting a provincial-scale remission were isolated in nature: there is no evidence to suggest that Caracalla was obliged to offer similar fiscal relief to any other provinces during his sole reign. This means that the Mauretanian case above ought to be viewed as exceptional during the 212–17 period. Secondly, the intensive building programme undertaken by Severus and Caracalla should be remembered since, even though we cannot

---

124 *AE* 1946, 109, l. 18. The emperor's emphasis on his own *indulgentia* will be considered in Chapter 5.
125 *P. Cairo* 49359, 49360; *P. Oslo* 78.
126 Buraselis (2007) 67–68.
127 Buraselis (2007) 69–70; *AE* 1946, 109, ll. 16–18.

infer a modern sense of economic rationality in the emperors, it is very unlikely that they would have engaged in construction upon such a large scale if the economy of the empire at large was in the doldrums; the inactivity of their predecessors Commodus, Pertinax and Didius Julianus only serves to strengthen this hypothesis.[128] While it remains possible that the ancient authors may have exaggerated the scale of the wealth left behind by Septimius Severus, it does not appear as if the empire was in economic decline or immediate peril during the sole reign of Caracalla. Another explanation is required, then, one that does not infer economic meltdown on an imperial scale, but which also required the emperor to mint an extraordinary number of new coins, to the extent that he debased the currency and introduced the over-valued *antoninianus* into circulation.

Returning to Caracalla's monetary reform, the most striking feature of this phenomenon is the similarity that it bears to the currency manipulation carried out by Septimius Severus, noted above. In fact, given the period of shared rule between the men between 198 and 211, it is probably more appropriate to view the Caracallan programme as a direct continuation of that executed by his father, rather than an entirely separate initiative. This suggests that the problem remained one of liquidity, a trend that, as already discussed, was prompted by a requirement to support a higher number of soldiers at an increased rate of pay. The extra demands placed upon the Mauretanians by Caracalla in the Banasa inscription thus merit additional attention. In the course of his proclamation, the emperor declared that he was certain that the province would repay his indulgence and generosity by furnishing him with men for both the Roman army and civil service, in addition to the enigmatic 'celestial beasts' (*caelestium animalium*).[129] While there is no suggestion that the Caracallan *tabula* of Banasa was specifically designed to guarantee manpower for the army and civilian administration, it is noteworthy that such a demand was issued in 216, in the period leading to Caracalla's planned offensive against the Parthian Empire.

The similarity between Severan and Caracallan monetary reforms, combined with the appeal for manpower from the Mauretanians in 216, suggests that there should be a connection made between the emperor's fiscal and military reforms and, therefore, between the Antonine Constitution and Caracallan military policy, by extension. Such a hypothesis offers a rational

---

128   Gorrie (2002) 461–81.
129   *AE* 1946, 109, ll. 11–15. There has been much debate on the nature of the animals requested. For more on this, see Guey (1947) 248–73; (1948) 128–30; Picard (1948) 134–35.

explanation for Caracalla's decision to debase the silver coinage while, at the same time, raising a number of taxes and exponentially expanding the number of Roman citizens in his empire. With this in mind, then, it is now necessary to assess exactly how far a link between the *Constitutio Antoniniana* and the Roman army can be identified, and to what extent the edict was motivated by an imperial need to support the military apparatus.

CHAPTER 3

The Military Rationale

Military expenditure was a key pillar of Severan rule from the outset. Septimius Severus' bid for power had rested on the size and strength of the forces at his disposal and, as noted in the previous chapter, the evidence suggests that emperor was keen to reinforce this powerbase through a programme of reforms and an increase in basic pay. Indeed, the essential nature of the army to the Severan regime is observed in the final words reportedly shared between Severus and his children, as he lay on his deathbed: 'be harmonious, enrich the troops, and scorn all other men.'[1] This advice was taken seriously by Severus' eldest son, according to our main sources for the period. Herodian, for example, criticised Caracalla for allowing his soldiers free-rein in looting temples and treasuries, a move that effectively wiped out the mass of wealth accrued by Severus.[2] Similar claims can be found in the *Historia Augusta*, in which the author described Caracalla buying the support of the army through massive donatives.[3] Finally, Dio alleges that the emperor engaged in excessive spending on the military, going so far as to accuse Caracalla of seeking out war simply to maintain his soldiers' favour:

> Οὗτος οὖν ὁ φιλαλεξανδρότατος Ἀντωνῖνος ἐς μὲν τοὺς στρατιώτας, οὓς πάνυ πολλοὺς ἀμφ' αὑτὸν εἶχε, προφάσεις ἐκ προφάσεων καὶ πολέμους ἐκ πολέμων σκηπτόμενος, φιλαναλωτὴς ἦν.

> Now this great admirer of Alexander, Antoninus, was fond of spending money upon the soldiers, great numbers of whom he kept in attendance upon him, offering excuse after excuse and one war after another.[4]

---

1 Dio 77.15.2: ὁμονοεῖτε, *τοὺς στρατιώτας πλουτίζετε*, τῶν ἄλλων πάντων καταφρονεῖτε (emphasis added).
2 Hdn. 4.4.7–5.1.
3 HA *Car.* 2.7–8. In this account, the author alleged that the emperor was required to offer considerable sums to the troops of the *legio II Parthica*, in particular, owing to the soldiers' initially displayed loyalty to the murdered Geta in the aftermath of the assassination. The author further claimed that the legionaries actually prevented Caracalla from entering their camp at Albanum until they had been won over by the promise of payment.
4 Dio 78.9.1.

At the close of the previous chapter, I noted that there is some evidence to suggest that a link should be made between the economic and military reforms undertaken by Caracalla. If Dio's account on the matter is accepted, the connection would appear to be one of simple cronyism, in which the emperor lavished money on his troops in order to ensure their continued loyalty and support. While it is evident that the image of the soldier-emperor was a central facet of Caracalla's self-representation as an emperor, the notion that he sought to rapidly increase his tax revenue and coin stock for the sole reason of indulging his favourites is clearly the result of Dio's desire to depict Caracalla as a tyrant and is, therefore, unconvincing.[5]

Just as it is important to engage with Dio's assessment of the fiscal significance underlying the Antonine Constitution, it is necessary to look beyond the inflammatory rhetoric employed by the senator, and investigate whether the military application of Caracalla's edict contained another purpose that is not elucidated by any of our hostile extant sources. In recent years, an attempt has been made to examine the military significance of the *constitutio*, in which Rocco placed martial concerns at the heart of the emperor's decision to extend the franchise, arguing that the edict was designed to address a perennial shortage of legionary recruits across the empire.[6] While his argument approaches the legislation solely through the lens of the military and, furthermore, accepts the questionable inclusion of the *dediticii* in *P. Giss.* 40, it highlights an important potential facet of the *Constitutio Antoniniana*, nonetheless. This chapter will therefore build on the research undertaken by Rocco in assessing the military application of Caracalla's edict.

As with the investigation of the economic importance of the *constitutio*, we must recognise that the military application of the edict was not a reaction to an unexpected or even sudden turn of events. In fact, it can be argued that Caracalla was responding to a trend of inadequate recruitment that had been a problem for the imperial administration from the early years of the Principate. At the outset of this chapter, then, I will consider the factors that resulted in a low level of legionary volunteers, specifically the restrictive nature of selection criteria for service, combined with the socially and financially unappealing nature of service in the legions compared to other branches of auxiliary forces. By setting Caracalla's reign against this wider context, the Antonine Constitution can be seen to address the emperor's military agenda in two distinct ways. In one respect, it overcame one of the most significant obstacles to recruiting

---

5 The emperor is depicted sharing in the toils of the soldiery, marching and dining with them, and leading from the front. See Dio 78.13.1.
6 Van Minnen (2016) 218–20; Rocco (2010) 131–55.

men for the legions, namely that they had to be fully enfranchised. Moreover, the fiscal consequences of the *Constitutio Antoniniana* also ensured that there was increased revenue for the military treasury, meaning that Caracalla could reform the army pay scale in a similar fashion to his father and also plan expenditure on offensives on the northern and eastern frontiers.

Obstacles to Legionary Recruitment

The Roman army was a vast organisation. Although forming less than one percent of the empire's population, it has been calculated that around 400,000 men were serving within its ranks by the reign of Severus and, by 215, that the organisation cost the Roman state c. 1130–1190 million *sestertii*, a financial drain representing around three quarters of the imperial government's total annual expenditure.[7] Despite its prominence, however, it appears that there were simply too few men enrolling in the legions by the time of Caracalla's principate. Assessing the number of recruits needed by the army on an annual basis is a challenging exercise. Scholars have been conservative in the past, with Le Bohec, for example, claiming that manpower levels could have been maintained with an intake of around 18,000 men.[8] Haynes was similarly cautious in his study of the *auxilia*, suggesting that auxiliary branches would only have needed around 10,500 men annually to maintain their levels at c. 215,000 during the first two centuries of the Principate.[9] While it is fair to conclude that the army would not have required hundreds of thousands of recruits to sustain an acceptable fighting strength, the figures postulated by Le Bohec and Haynes still seem artificially low. The primary issue with these conservative estimates is that they are based upon absolutely consistent numbers of men enlisting and demobilising in every year, and thus do not reflect the realities of military service, such as operational losses.[10] Whatever the reality of this requirement, the literary evidence suggests that the Roman government was often unable to fill the legions completely, even during the Julio-Claudian period. Tiberius, for

---

[7] Erdkamp (2002) 5–7.
[8] Le Bohec (2000) 71. Also see Forni (1953) 30, who arrives at a similarly low figure by calculating an annual requirement of only 240 men per legion (6000 in total), and estimating a similar number to fill the auxiliary levy.
[9] Haynes (2001) 62–63.
[10] It is, however, admittedly impossible to recreate a truly reflective model but, in failing to offer even an estimate of such attrition, these figures remain improbably low.

example, is alleged by Tacitus to have complained about the shortage of men volunteering:

> *Multitudinem veteranorum praetexebat imperator et dilectibus supplendos exercitus: nam voluntarium militem deesse, ac si suppeditet, non eadem virtute ac modestia agree, quia plerumque inopes ac vagi sponte militiam sumant.*

> The emperor referred to the number of veterans [who had completed their term of service and were waiting to be finally discharged] and the need of fresh levies to maintain the strength of the armies. He said there was a shortage of volunteers and, even when they were forthcoming, they failed to display the same courage and discipline, since it was often the penniless and vagrant who enlisted willingly.[11]

It is of interest that Tacitus refers to the levies as *dilecti*, a description which, as Mann notes, is open to interpretation.[12] It is important, however, that we consider briefly the nature of this term, since the phrase has a bearing on how we perceive the process of recruitment during the imperial era. Surviving evidence suggests that *dilectus* was employed in reference to both voluntary enlistment and reassignment, as well as conscription. Tacitus offers two examples of willing enrolment, for example, using *dilectus* in connection with Vitellius' reassignment of legionary soldiers to urban and praetorian cohorts, and also in reference to the inhabitants of Rome begging the same emperor to be armed against the advancing armies of Vespasian.[13] On the contrary, however, Tacitus also employs the term when describing the earlier expulsion of the Neronian official, Paedius Blaesus, from the senate in response to accusations of corruption:

> *Motu senatu et Paedius Blaesus, accusantibus Cyrenensibus violatum ab eo thesaurum Aesculapii dilectumque militarem pretio et ambitione corruptum.*

> Paedius Blaesus was also expelled from the senate on the accusation of the people of Cyrene, that he had violated the temple of Aesculapius and interfered with a military levy through bribery and corruption.[14]

---

11   Tac. *Ann.* 4.4 (tr. adapted from Jackson).
12   Mann (1983) 49–50.
13   Tac. *Hist.* 2.93–94; 3.58. Also see Mann (1983) 49.
14   Tac. *Ann.* 14.18.1.

The inference that Blaesus had accepted bribes to excuse men from military service confirms that levies raised by conscription were an accepted practice and a core component of the *dilectus* during the imperial period. Further evidence to this effect can be found in legal writing, which suggests there was a traditional liability on the part of the citizen body to undertake military service.[15] This is a significant point, since it demonstrates that, while the emperors appear to have been reluctant to introduce an extensive programme of conscription, the state was unable to meet the manpower requirement of the legions through voluntary enlistment alone, and was therefore often required to resort to a compulsory draft.[16] In fact, the severity of this problem was so pronounced at times that a *dilectus* was required across a large geographical expanse: occurring, for example, in Africa and Asia, in addition to Italy and Narbonese Gaul, when raising men for the Illyrian legions created by Nero.[17] In times of military crisis, there is even evidence to suggest that the army resorted to enrolling individuals usually ineligible for legionary service, such as sailors or even freedmen, leading to a distinction being made between the traditionally levied *iustae legiones*, and those raised from men of other branches of service.[18]

The extant evidence relating to recruitment demonstrates that the legions were often understrength and depended on unorthodox or irregular sources of manpower to bolster their numbers.[19] Even at the height of imperial expansion under Trajan and Hadrian, the emperors were required to deploy vexillations from one legion to another, in order to address acute shortages.[20] Given the nearly continual warfare on the northern frontier during the Antonine period,

---

15   *Dig.* 49.16.4.10. In the legal treatise *On Military Matters*, Arrius Menander noted the traditional punishments, including reduction to servitude and even execution, levelled at 'traitors to liberty' who were found to have avoided such service.
16   Forni (1953) 19–20.
17   Tac. *Ann.* 16.13.
18   Forni (1953) 103. For examples of freedmen being enlisted during the early imperial period, see Dio 55.31.1–2; 56.23.1–3. Also see Forni (1953) 105–7, 115, and Mann (1983) 53, who discusses the composition of the *legio I Adiutrix* levied under Nero, which included a high number of men previously serving in the Roman navy. This practice is also seen around the same time, with Vitellius and Vespasian drafting men from the fleets to fight in their legions during the Year of the Four Emperors. For more on this, see Tac. *Hist.* 3.55. For epigraphic and papyrological evidence recording sailors or auxiliaries being employed to augment legionary strength, see *ILS* 9095; *P. Mich.* VII 432; *PSI* 1026.
19   Veg. 1.2–7; Mann (1983) 50–55; Forni (1953) 103.
20   Mann (1983) 55, Tables 1 and 25a. Also see Eck (1999) 76–89. For an example of one such vexillations being deployed during the Bar Kokhba revolt, see *CIL* VI 3505.

paired with the civil wars following the death of Commodus, this phenomenon has profound implications for the military situation that Caracalla faced as the sole emperor in 212. As a ruler who presented himself as a soldier-emperor, it is unsurprising that Caracalla would devote substantial sums to the maintenance of his army. The almost perennial difficulty experienced by the Augusti in filling legionary levies, however, means that we must hesitate before accepting Dio's suggestion that the emperor's military spending was the result of simple favouritism. Instead, we are faced with the possibility that Caracalla's extravagant expenditure and reforms (including the *Constitutio Antoniniana*) were designed to improve the state of the Roman army that he had inherited from his father.

It is first necessary to consider briefly the question of why the imperial state was unable to ensure a satisfactory level of manpower within the legions. While external conflict represents an obvious drain, the pattern of insufficient recruitment is more significant and appears to have been largely a problem of the government's own making. According to Vegetius, entrance criteria for legionary soldiers were severe.[21] The author claimed, for example, that there were a selection of moralistic standards required of legionaries, further arguing that a variety of professions, from fishermen to textile workers, should be disbarred from service.[22] This somewhat sanctimonious position was not unique to Vegetius, moreover, with similar prohibitions preserved in the *Digest* and the *Theodosian Code*.[23] These conditions appear to have been largely inflexible, even in the aftermath of military disaster, such as the catastrophic Roman defeat at Adrianople in 378.[24] In fact, the penalties for anyone caught enlisting under false pretence were severe; Pliny the Younger even mentions capital punishment being employed in some cases.[25]

Even more basic requirements served to reduce further the pool of available manpower. There was a minimum height restriction, for example, with no one under 1.72 metres tall being classed as eligible for service.[26] Arguably the best known obstacle to prospective legionaries, however, was that every soldier had

---

21 It should be noted that, although Vegetius was writing significantly after the High Empire period and the Severi, he borrowed heavily from a variety of earlier treatises on the military. He thus created a 'scissors and paste mosaic' of such writing and expanded sections to fit his own literary design. For more on this, see Milner (1993) xvi–xvii.
22 Veg. 1.2–7.
23 *Dig.* 49.16.2.1; 49.16.6; *CTh.* 7.13.8 (380 CE).
24 Speidel (2012) 177–78.
25 Plin. *Ep.* 10.29–30.
26 Junkelmann (1986) 106–7. Also see Speidel (2012) 177–78; Rocco (2010) 139, and Forni (1953) 25–26.

to be a fully enfranchised citizen.[27] This criterion has obvious implications for the available recruitment pool. Firstly, it reduced the potential number of recruits considerably since it has been established that *cives* represented a clear minority of the empire's population, even in the immediate prelude to the Antonine Constitution.[28] Furthermore, a reliance on the already enfranchised populace would have resulted in the burden of legionary service being unevenly distributed across the empire, with the more heavily Romanised provinces bearing the brunt of the *dilectus*.[29]

Another factor in the military situation pre-212 is that the evidence suggests that the very prospect of legionary service became increasingly unpopular among the minority of individuals eligible to enlist therein. At the heart of the problem appears to have been that the basic conditions of service were progressively more unpalatable to the citizen population: 'service was long, pay became more and more insufficient, and the meagre grants made to veterans were no recompense for these sacrifices.'[30] The average length of legionary engagement was between twenty five and twenty six years.[31] While this was the same as the lesser branches of service, the duties appear to have been more arduous, and the meagre wages of little recompense.[32] Further to these practical considerations, it is also worth noting the social impact of legionary enlistment, although this is more difficult to define. Recruits enlisting from the Romanised heartlands of the empire could be posted anywhere among the provinces, meaning that there was a significant chance that they would never see their families and relatives again. It is unsurprising, then, that individuals were prepared to bribe officials in order to escape the *dilectus*.

This problem was compounded by the fact that there were other routes to military careers also open to fully enfranchised citizens. They could apply to enlist, for example, within the urban cohorts of Rome, Lyon and Carthage. Unlike their legionary counterparts, the men of these formations enjoyed both shorter lengths of service and a better pay scale and grant structure for veterans.[33] In addition, service in the urban cohorts was guaranteed to be restricted

---

27 Forni (1953) 103.
28 Lavan (2016) 3–46; Garnsey (2004) 135.
29 Haynes (2001) 63.
30 Mann (1983) 49.
31 Aug. *Res gest.* 16; Dio 54.2.6, 55.23, 57.6.5; Tac. *Ann.* 1.17.2, also see Forni (1953) 142–44; Le Roux (1982) 263.
32 For more on legionary pay and benefits, see Tac. *Ann.* 1.17, 78.2; Suet. *Nero.* 32.1. How legionary service differed from that of the *auxilia*, in particular, will be discussed below.
33 Le Bohec (2000) 20–21, 100; Mann (1983) 49.

to the locale of the formation in question. As a result, this option proved a more popular choice for *cives*, particularly from the Italian peninsula, and the *urbaniciani* never encountered a shortage of volunteers from which to fill its ranks.[34] Service in the *auxilia* also presented a potentially more attractive alternative to the legions. In late antiquity, Vegetius noted that ever increasing numbers of men were enrolling with the auxiliaries, writing with some scorn that he believed those who enlisted in this fashion were actively seeking a softer and more comfortable alternative to service in the legions:

> *Est et alia causa, cur adtenuatae sint legiones: magnus in illis labor est militandi, graviora arma, plura munera, severior disciplina. Quod vitantes plerique in auxiliis festinant militiae sacramenta praecipere, ubi et minor sudor et maturiora sunt praemia.*

> There is also another reason why the legions have become diminished, the labour of serving in them is great, the arms heavier, the duties more frequent, the discipline more severe. To avoid this, many flock the *auxilia* to take their oaths of service, where the sweat is less and the rewards come sooner.[35]

Far from empty hyperbole on the part of Vegetius, the arduous nature of the *plura munera* found in the legions is also noted by Ammianus Marcellinus.[36] More compelling evidence for a shift in the backgrounds of auxiliary recruits can be found in the epigraphic corpus. In his study of epitaphs belonging to named infantrymen and cavalrymen of the *auxilia* found in the Rhine region, Kraft demonstrated a visible change in the nature of the troops from the time of the Julio-Claudians to the end of the second century, with high numbers of fully enfranchised citizens found in both the auxiliary cohorts and *alae*.[37]

---

34   Mann (1983) 49.
35   Veg. 2.3 (tr. adapted from Milner). It has been suggested by some that Vegetius might have been referring to the later formation of the *auxilia palatina*, see Formisano and Petrocelli (2003) 131; Milner (1993) 33. It has been acknowledged by these same scholars, however, that Vegetius' source in this case was an older one, making reference to the traditional auxiliary organisation found under the Early-High Empire period.
36   Amm. Marc. 18.2.6.
37   Kraft (1951) 79–81, 140–99. The cavalry *alae* had their own physical entrance criteria, namely a minimum height requirement. Those ineligible for service in these squadrons could still join the *equites cohortis*, who do not appear to have been regarded differently from the *alae*, except in terms of their armament. For more on the distinction between the two formations, see Ureche (2009) 331.

TABLE 1   *Table illustrating the changing legal status among auxiliaries*[a]

	Alae		*Cohortes*	
	Peregrini	Cives	Peregrini	Cives
Julio-Claudian	48	7	44	0
Flavian-Trajan	32	19	27	17
Hadrian-c.170 CE	13	10	13	17
2nd–3rd Century	0	38	3	43

a   Le Bohec (2000) 98, after Kraft (1951) 140–99. This pattern of increasing citizen enlistment is not unique to the Rhine, and can also be seen in other areas, such as the auxiliary cohorts of Dura Europos, for example. For more on this, see Gilliam (1965) 82–84.

Haynes has suggested that this trend might be explained by the growth in military families, with sons following their fathers into the ranks.[38] It is equally possible that this data also reflects the natural expansion of the franchise observed during the Principate. Even with the potential impact of these two elements, though, the shift in the legal status of the soldiery across this 200-year period and beyond remains striking. In fact, this process appears to have prompted a change in the *auxilia* as a whole, with auxiliary and legionary units increasingly resembling one another in terms of basic equipment and tactical deployment.[39]

The relative appeal of joining a static auxiliary unit is understandable in that the recruit would be enlisting in a formation whose members were likely already known locally and, like the urban cohorts, the location in which the troops would pass their engagement was predictable. Furthermore, the difference in the pay scale between the legionaries and auxiliaries, a source of academic contention for decades, is now thought to have been almost negligible, with soldiers in the auxiliary infantry earning 5/6 of the legionary wage.[40] It seems an insignificant difference considering the socially preferable terms of

---

38   Haynes (2001) 67–68.
39   Rocco (2010) 140; Strobel (2007) 267–78; Speidel (2009a) 283–304. For more on arms and general deployment, see Gascarino (2008).
40   Speidel 1992 (2009) 349–80, particularly 370–78. Also see Jahn (1984) 53–74 and Speidel 2000 (2009) 407–37, *contra* Alston (1994) 113–23, who argued that there was, in fact, no real distinction at all between the pay scales of the *auxilia* and the legions. Auxiliary

service demanded by the *auxilia*.[41] Indeed the differential must have seemed increasingly negligible during the second century, with the legionary rate of pay set under Domitian remaining static in the face of increasing inflation.[42]

A final point worth noting here is Vegetius' observation that the rewards of service in the *auxilia* were more rapid and forthcoming than for those in legionary units.[43] Although legionaries could theoretically be advanced to the staff of provincial governors and even the emperor, membership of the *singulares* was primarily composed of men from among the auxiliary cohorts and *alae*.[44] In a similar fashion to the praetorian guard, the soldiers of the *singulares* enjoyed a close proximity to officials (including the emperor himself, in the case of the *equites singulares Augusti*) and were responsible for their safety; the importance of these units is clear.[45] Even more so than regular mounted divisions, the evidence suggests that the designation of *singularis* carried a level of social prestige simply unattainable in standard legionary service.[46] In fact, soldiers in the *singulares* could achieve promotion to the position of centurion or decurion after only three years of service, compared to around fifteen years for a legionary soldier that did not possess equestrian status.[47]

The evidence relating to military enlistment in the pre-212 era demonstrates that legionary service was an unpopular choice among the citizen body. The availability of more attractive alternatives means that the hypothesis that many would opt against becoming a *miles legionis* is persuasive. Indeed, this has led Rocco to the conclusion that there were 'recurring crises in the recruitment of native-born citizens joining the legions'.[48] While this is perhaps a slight overstatement of the situation, inasmuch as there is no evidence to suggest that the legions lost their fighting capacity completely, Rocco is correct to identify that the trend was both persistent and would have been problematic

---

cavalrymen similarly enjoyed a wage commensurate with their legionary counterparts. For more on this, see Speidel 1992 (2009) 357–58, (1994) 45, 56–59; Rocco (2010) 142–43.

41   Le Bohec (2000) 25–29.
42   Kemmers (2009) 143–58; Smith (1972) 481–500.
43   Veg. 2.3.
44   Speidel (1978) 6–11, also see Speidel (1994) 61–78.
45   Speidel (1994) 61–63, also see Bingham (2013) 40–41.
46   Rocco (2010) 144; Speidel (1994) 63–64; Speidel (1978) 36. The pride which accompanied service in the *singulares* can be observed in the wealth of epigraphic evidence commissioned by these soldiers (or their families) upon which the designation appears. For selected examples, see *AE* 2003, 1221; *AE* 2004, 319; *CIL* III 1160; *CIL* III 3472, and *CIL* III 14693.
47   Speidel (1978) 36; Forni (1953) 47–48.
48   Rocco (2010) 144.

for an emperor with any military ambitions like Caracalla. This is the context that must be borne in mind when evaluating the military significance of the *Constitutio Antoniniana*.

The Severan Reforms

I suggested in the previous chapter that, in order to understand the actions of Caracalla better, it is necessary to consider those of his father. Similar to the impression of an economic recovery, the military situation appears to improve under Severus who, in addition to securing his dynasty's grip on power by armed force, was able to raise three new legions, the *I*, *II* and *III Parthicae*, and wage extended campaigns in Parthia and Britain, the former of which was such a success that Mesopotamia was added to the empire.[49] The reality behind these well-known victories, however, was that Severus was required introduce a variety of reforms to the army, and to devote a vast amount of revenue to incentivising service in the legions and restoring an army that had been wracked by civil war.[50]

As I have already shown, there is evidence to suggest that the debasement of silver coinage that occurred under Severus should be associated with his augmentation of the army wage rather than an economic malaise.[51] As the first emperor to raise the soldiers' pay since Domitian, Severus increased the military wage by 100%.[52] The hostile nature of the ancient writers towards the army is well-known and, consequently, caution must be exercised when assessing the underlying rationale of the emperor's initiative. On the one hand, it seems unfair to condemn the policy as a reward for loyalty in the civil war, or as an obsequious bribe to ensure the army's support of the family's claim to power. On the other hand, it also seems unlikely that the pay increase was a wholly selfless or compensatory act, designed to correct an historical injustice regarding the stagnation of the legionary wage. In the context of an ongoing

---

49 For more on Severus' new legions, see Mann (1983) 63 and Balty (1988) 91–104. For accounts of Severus' military exploits, see Dio 75.9.4, 76.9–12; Hdn. 3.9.1–12; HA *Sev.* 15.1–16.3.
50 De Blois (2002) 95; Develin (1971) 687–95.
51 See Chapter 2.
52 Alston (1994) 115, has suggested that the wage reform only constituted a 50% pay rise, but the consensus supports the notion that Severus in fact doubled the Domitianic rate, see Speidel 1992 (2009) 349–50, 366–71; De Blois (2002) 95–96. Again, however, we must concede that the extant papyrological evidence in general is unclear on the matter. I am grateful to Graham Andrews for sharing his thoughts on the military pay rise with me.

struggle to recruit legionary volunteers, it seems likely that the Severan pay increase should be interpreted as an incentive to make the prospect of legionary service more appealing than it had previously been. This hypothesis is strengthened by the marked increase in silver coinage dating to the period and onwards found in military sites identified by Kemmers.[53] As De Blois has noted, however, despite the large amount of capital seized in the aftermath of the Wars of Succession and Parthian campaign, the pay rise was not an initiative that the emperor could afford within the pre-existing monetary system: he lacked the plate but also, more importantly, the tax income to fund the wage increase without devaluing the denarius.[54] It is doubly noteworthy then, that we can observe an intensification in the *annona militaris* under Severus, since such payment in kind represented a convenient way to ensure that the soldiery was well provisioned without exacerbating the issue of liquidity facing the imperial government.[55]

The army was a key factor in assuring the success of Severan rule, during the Wars of Succession and beyond. It is therefore unsurprising that Septimius Severus engaged in a programme of reforms designed to ameliorate conditions of service and thereby encourage greater numbers to enlist from the outset of his reign. These initiatives do not represent a successful end in themselves, though, and should rather be considered the beginning of a process of strengthening the Severan military apparatus. This was a particularly important requirement for Caracalla during the period of his sole reign, considering the significance of militaristic imagery in the emperor's self-representation and the emphasis he placed on the army to the security of his rule in the aftermath of Geta's assassination.[56]

---

53 Kemmers (2009) 148–49, especially Fig. 1. From a survey of 3827 coins discovered as site finds in a military context, 93% of this figure is comprised of precious metal coinage. This has led the author to remark that it seems likely that Severus' wage reform probably altered the way in which the soldiery was paid, their salaries being distributed nearly exclusively in silver coinage.
54 De Blois (2002) 95.
55 For more on the *annona*, see Strobel (2007) 280; Lo Cascio (2005a) 153; Corbier (2005) 381; Speidel 1992 (2009); Develin (1971) 693–95.
56 Dio 78.3.1–2. The actions of Caracalla in the aftermath of Geta's assassination will be covered in more detail in Chapter 5.

The Military Application of the Antonine Constitution

The evidence suggests, then, that Caracalla inherited a military apparatus that had been somewhat stabilised by his father, but was far from a dynamic organisation. While the programme of reform undertaken by Severus was partly effective in improving legionary enlistment, its success was far from complete. Papyrological evidence confirms that Caracalla chose to raise the basic rate of pay for the legions by a further fifty percent beyond the level set by his predecessor.[57] Owing to the rapid nature of the army wage increase, one-hundred and fifty percent in less than twenty years, it is unsurprising that we find Dio depicting Caracalla as ruler obsessed with lavishing gifts on the military, alleging that the emperor declared that the continued security of Severan rule depended on the army, and that he intended to enrich the soldiery at the expense of all others: 'Nobody in the world should have money but me; and I want to bestow it upon the soldiers.'[58] It should also be noted, however, that there is evidence to suggest that the emperor was not alone in perceiving the army to be a crucial element in ensuring the continued survival of the imperial state. Ironically, some of the best material on this subject can be found in the midst of Dio's highly critical work.

Set in the context of the end of the Republic, Dio constructs a lengthy debate between Maecenas and Agrippa, ostensibly to inform Octavian regarding the mode of government that Rome should adopt.[59] Rather than a faithful, or even simply hypothetical, rendition of a historical discussion between Agrippa and Maecenas, the debate is thought to outline many of the author's own political views and attitudes, carefully positioned in the Augustan period to avoid making overt comments regarding his own political milieu.[60] In the course of

---

57 Speidel 1992 (2009) 367–68. Speidel has employed papyrological evidence to demonstrate that, during the Severan period and its aftermath, pay rises took place under Septimius Severus, Caracalla and Maximinus Thrax. For selected examples, see *ChLA* 446, 495, and *P. Panop.* 292. If the pay records for this period are analysed and divided into individual soldiers' wages, it can be shown that Severus raised the Domitianic rate by one-hundred percent, Caracalla raised the Severan rate by fifty percent, with Maximinus Thrax later doubling the Caracallan rate during his short reign.

58 Dio 78.10.4: οὐδένα ἀνθρώπων πλὴν ἐμοῦ ἀργύριον ἔχειν δεῖ, ἵνα αὐτὸ τοῖς στρατιώταις χαρίζωμαι. In this same passage, Dio claimed that Julia Domna reproached her son for such extravagant spending, to which Caracalla replied by inferring that the dynasty would never run short of money when the army was loyal to it.

59 Dio 52.1–41.

60 Adler (2012) 477–520; Hose (2007) 461–67.

the dialogue, Dio emphasises the importance of the army to the survival of the Roman state and the need for money to keep the soldiery in place:

> Πόθεν οὖν χρήματα καὶ ἐς τούτους καὶ ἐς τὰ ἄλλα τὰ ἀναγκαίως ἀναλωθησόμενα ἔσται; ἐγὼ καὶ τοῦτο διδάξω, σμικρὸν ἐκεῖνο ὑπειπών, ὅτι κἂν δημοκρατηθῶμεν, πάντως που χρημάτων δεησόμεθα· οὐ γὰρ οἷόν τε οὔτ' ἄνευ στρατιωτῶν ἡμᾶς σώζεσθαι οὔτ' ἀμισθί τινας στρατεύεσθαι.

> From where, then, is the money to be provided for these soldiers and for the other expenses that will be incurred by virtue of necessity? I will explain this point also, prefacing it with a brief reminder that even if we have democracy, we shall in any case need money, of course. For we cannot survive without the soldiers, and men will not serve as soldiers without payment.[61]

Two points should be noted here. The first relates to the assertion that the Empire could not survive without the army. While Dio also had the characters discuss potential reforms of the military, and despite his vehement dislike of the military, he was ultimately forced to concede that it was nevertheless a necessity.[62] The second point relates to the observation that the army would not be able to function without sufficient pay.[63] The concepts of the military apparatus, finances and state survival are inextricably linked.[64] While he was openly critical of Caracalla's spending on the army, even Dio reluctantly realised that a significant level of expenditure was necessary to ensure its loyalty, and to encourage men to enlist at all. This is seen powerfully, later in his work, when Dio described a letter to the senate written by Macrinus, in which the usurper emperor bemoaned the predicament he faced of being unable to pay the troops the wages and donatives pledged to them by his predecessors, but realising that it was politically impossible to refuse the soldiery the sums that they expected.[65]

Dio's hostile account of Caracallan spending, then, masks the military reality that existed in 212. State expenditure on the army was regarded to form

---

61 Dio 52.28.1 (tr. adapted from Cary).
62 De Blois (2002) 91–92. For the section on the proposed restructuring of the army, see Dio 52.27.
63 In fact, in the following section (52.29), Dio had Maecenas and Agrippa progress to discuss finances more generally.
64 Hose (2007) 466.
65 Dio 79.17–18.

a necessary investment to maintain the security of the empire, and yet was becoming an increasingly severe drain on the economy. The troops' wages may have been improved, but the resulting shortage of coinage had prompted a process of currency debasement.[66] Moreover, the restrictive nature of the selection criteria based on the possession of the Roman franchise remained in effect, limiting the areas from which legionaries could be recruited. In this context, the *Constitutio Antoniniana* may be interpreted as an imperial response to the continuing dilemmas associated with the military apparatus. In fact, if the primary consequences of the edict are considered, it can be seen to address the problems outlined above in two distinct ways. Firstly, it circumnavigated the fundamental impediment to increasing the manpower pool from which to draw legionaries, namely that they had to be *cives* prior to their enlistment. While it is clear that a number of minor prerequisites for service still remained, the military application of the Antonine Constitution here seems an uncomplicated one; as Rocco concludes:

> The *constitutio Antoniniana* eliminated, *de facto*, with one single sweep, whatever legal obstacles (except the requirement of *ingenuitas*) that could jeopardize legionary service and practically abolished the need to recur to expedients such as the *ad hoc* concession of citizenship to *peregrini* every time that there was a scarcity of recruits.[67]

While it is true that the process of conceding citizenship on an individual basis cannot have been an overly arduous process, since no emperor prior to Caracalla seems to have been motivated to reform the system, the value of the *constitutio* in achieving greater efficiency, as well as exponentially increasing the available number of potential recruits, is irrefutable. The social aspect of this legislation must also be considered at this juncture. Another valuable dimension to the edict here is that, in expanding the franchise across the entire empire, the Roman state would not be reliant on the heartland provinces for their levies.[68] Extant evidence relating to the *origo* of legionaries in the subsequent period suggests that the newly enfranchised population were not as sensitive to the perceived hardships of legionary service as communities that had enjoyed the rights of *civitas* for a considerable time, and were thus more inclined to enlist in the legions rather than seeking alternatives or trying to

---

66   The debasement of coinage that occurred under Severus and Caracalla has been noted above in Chapter 2.
67   Rocco (2010) 145.
68   Rocco (2010) 144.

evade conscription.[69] This phenomenon is supported, for example, in the marked increase of provincials from the Thracian and Pannonian areas found serving in the Danubian legions during the course of the third century.[70]

The other potential military application of the Antonine Constitution is linked to the fiscal significance of the edict considered in the previous chapter, namely the process whereby the *vicesima hereditatum* was doubled from five to ten percent and, furthermore, the knowledge that it was levied against estates of varying sizes, even very modest ones. While a connection between this taxation and the army reforms of Caracalla might seem obscure initially, the significance of the levy to the emperor's military apparatus quickly becomes clear when the traditional purpose of the *vicesima* is taken into account. Indeed, the evidence suggests that the tax on inheritances was originally designed to support the requirements of the military treasury, the *aerarium militare*.[71]

From the surviving literary record, it is clear that one of the key functions of this reserve was to fund the payment of discharge bonuses due to army veterans.[72] The extent to which the treasury was used to fund basic army pay, however, is a more contentious subject. At the core of this controversy is the fact that there is a difference here between many modern assumptions regarding the purpose of the military treasury and what the ancient evidence actually suggests. It has been claimed, for example, that salaries were not paid from the assets of the *aerarium militare*, and that this treasury was only used to fund discharge bounties, once the soldiers had completed their required period of service.[73] The ancient writers, however, are far more open in their description of the connection between the *vicesima*, the military treasury and the Roman army pay structure. Suetonius claimed that Augustus introduced the taxation so that he would have 'funds ready at all times without difficulty for maintaining the soldiers and paying the rewards due to them.'[74] Dio also recorded that the levy was brought forth in order to assure the maintenance of troops, as well as their bonuses.[75] Contrary to the modern notion that the *aerarium militare* was only utilised for discharge payments, the clear

---

69 Rocco (2010) 145.

70 Forni (1953) 187–212.

71 Rocco (2010) 136; Corbier (1977) 197–234; De Martino (1975) 897.

72 It is mentioned in connection with this purpose in a number of ancient sources, see Aug. *Res gest.* 17.2; Tac. *Ann.* 1.78.2; Suet. *Aug.* 49.4; Dio 55.25.2. For a modern association between the payment of bonuses and the *vicesima*, see Hassall (1987) 165–84.

73 Corbier (1977) 198–99.

74 Suet. *Aug.* 49.2: *Utque perpetuo ac sine difficultate sumptus ad tuendos eos prosequendosque suppeteret,* **aerarium militare cum vectigalibus novis constituit** (emphasis added).

75 Dio 55.24.9.

suggestion by both of these ancient writers is that the military treasury was also employed in the payment of the basic army *stipendia*.

This combination of evidence has significant implications when considering the factors that prompted the emperor to introduce the Antonine Constitution. In addition to overcoming the primary legal obstacle preventing greater recruitment into the legions, the military purpose of the edict also explains Caracalla's apparent desire to increase vastly his taxation revenue, a phenomenon that, until now, has lacked an explanation beyond the hostile allegations of financial irresponsibility and favouritism espoused by Cassius Dio. The simultaneous increase in the number of citizen tax-payers and the doubling of a levy associated with the military treasury allows for a theory that, in introducing the *Constitutio Antoniniana*, Caracalla was not only encouraging greater recruitment into the legions, but was also legislating to ensure that the government would have the necessary capital to maintain and pay the newly enlarged soldiery. In this sense, the *constitutio* represents an unexpectedly elegant solution to the military-economic dilemma that had become more apparent as the Empire progressed. It is the inextricably linked nature of the military and fiscal elements of Caracalla's legislation that has led Rocco to the conclusion that the edict 'probably disguised aims primarily connected to the needs of the empire's defence system.'[76] While the position is generally correct, I would argue that even this understates the emperor's intentions in passing the *constitutio*, since it understates Caracalla's evident military ambitions to extend the empire in the north and wage an offensive campaign against the Parthian Empire.[77]

In summary, then, if the martial concerns facing Caracalla in 212 are paired with the economic implications of the edict considered in the previous chapter, the hypothesis that reforming the pre-existing military apparatus was a motivating factor in the emperor's decision to promulgate the *constitutio* in 212 becomes more convincing. As an emperor for whom identification and popularity with the army was a key foundation of his reign, it is entirely logical that Caracalla should continue the programme of reforms undertaken by his father and should attempt to address problems in the military apparatus that had become perennial by the time of his accession. There is no suggestion that the emperor was able to remedy completely the persistent issues facing the Roman army of the Principate. In fact, the eventual success or failure of

---

76   Rocco (2010) 135.
77   A campaign that appears to have been inextricably linked to Caracalla's self-association with Alexander the Great. The question of the emperor's Alexander-mania, and its potential bearing on the Antonine Constitution, will be covered in the next chapter.

Caracalla's initiative here is arguably beside the point, for our purposes. The evidence supports the hypothesis that the emperor had his military apparatus in mind when promulgating the *Constitutio Antoniniana*.[78]

At the outset of his reign, Caracalla decreed that every free person in the empire should enjoy the rights of the franchise via the *constitutio*. At the same time, however, the emperor carefully worded the grant to ensure that new *cives* were fully liable for taxes levied against the citizen body. One of the major taxes affecting citizens was the charge on inheritance and estates, the *vicesima hereditatum*, a levy that was associated with the military treasury from its inception and was significant enough for Dio to mention by name in the course of describing the most unpopular fiscal reforms introduced by the emperor between 212 and 217. Once again, the senator's account must be re-evaluated. It is clear that Dio's rhetoric is the result of bitterness regarding his own position and lack of favour shown by the early Severan emperors.[79] However, if we attempt to look beyond the hostile tone of his work, it is possible to identify both the economic and military elements which motivated Caracalla to introduce the Antonine Constitution.

So far, this study has shown that it is possible to view the *Constitutio Antoniniana* as an imperial response to issues that were affecting the empire on a systemic level and, moreover, transcended the life and reign of any one individual emperor across the span of the Principate. While the interlocked fiscal-military explanation of the legislation appears to be the result of an imperial programme of reform in these spheres, the fact remains that, in the opening lines of his edict, Caracalla made an explicit reference to his contemporary context, and cast the Antonine Constitution as a reaction to recent events that had threatened his position of authority. It is therefore imperative that we focus our attention towards the emperor on a more individual level. The following chapters will therefore be dedicated to an investigation of the personal factors and events that may have prompted Caracalla to promulgate his edict. Just as it is imprudent to remove the Antonine Constitution from its contemporary milieu, it would be severely misguided to conduct a study of the 212 edict without assessing the motives specific to its ultimate architect.

---

78 Rocco (2010) 136.
79 Davenport (2012) 814–15; Meckler (1999); Millar (1964) 150–55.

CHAPTER 4

Alexander Imitatio

When Caracalla was assassinated in in 217, he was in the process of leading a Roman army on campaign against the Parthian Empire.[1] Dio recounts that war had been declared following the Parthian king's refusal to allow Caracalla to marry his daughter, though the author regarded the proposal as a ruse on the part of the emperor to swiftly annex his enemy's territory.[2] Regardless of the historicity of the alleged events that prefigured the campaign, one constant feature of this episode is that the ill-fated offensive has been interpreted as a final attempt by Caracalla to mimic his lifelong idol, Alexander the Great.[3] Even a cursory glance at the ancient literature shows that Caracalla was believed to have harboured a veritable mania for anything relating to the Macedonian king.[4] This is an image that has endured into the modern era, with Birley, for example, classing the emperor's interest as a pathological obsession, while Baharal has declared that 'no one questions the fact that Caracalla modelled his day-to-day conduct and actions on those of Alexander'.[5] More recently, however, it has been acknowledged that there was more to the emperor's admiration of the conqueror than superficial affectations, and that he probably fostered a public connection with Alexander for political effect.[6]

My aim in this chapter is to consider the extent to which the *Constitutio Antoniniana* functioned as an ideological grant promoting an association between Caracalla and Alexander the Great, and whether the edict should be viewed as a politically astute initiative that exploited Alexandrian rhetoric and imagery, or rather as a simple act of *imitatio*. I will begin by examining the text of the Giessen papyrus, once again, and setting it against literary evidence for Alexander's attitude towards his imperial subjects, following the argument advanced by Baharal that the *constitutio* was inspired by an Alexandrian attempt to achieve universal harmony amongst his peoples.[7] This is a difficult hypothesis to assess, owing to the problem of establishing the intentions of

---

1 Cowan (2002) 154–55.
2 Dio 79.1.1. Also see Hdn. 4.10.1–2.
3 Sheldon (2010) 171.
4 For a summary of his obsession, see Dio 78.7.1.
5 Birley (1988) 194; Baharal (2003) 27.
6 Buraselis (2007) 33; Rowan (2012) 152.
7 Baharal (1996) 70.

Alexander himself from the surviving authors. By examining the text of *P. Giss.* 40 in conjunction with other literary sources, then, I will argue that while there is a link to be made between Caracalla and Alexander through the Antonine Constitution, the relationship is not as pronounced as some might suggest.[8] In fact, it is impossible to link the historical Alexander with the *constitutio*. If the scope and terminology of the Giessen text are examined closely however, it does become possible to identify a potentially Alexandrian inspiration among the words and rhetoric of Caracalla's edict.

The emperor's tone and expression in drafting the Antonine Constitution were inspired by the romanticised, legendary image of the king relayed through later writers, such as Plutarch, with whose work it seems clear that the emperor came into contact. This chapter will therefore conclude by considering to what extent this phenomenon was the result of Caracalla's well-attested hero worship of Alexander, or was a connection that was deliberately engineered for political effect. In this question, we are plagued by the often dubious reliability of the evidence relating to Caracalla offered by the main literary sources but, if the text of the Giessen papyrus is combined with other bodies of literary and material evidence, then it becomes possible to see that Alexander imagery formed one facet of a wider revolution in Caracalla's imperial self-image that occurred from the outset of his sole principate.

Alexandrian Influences in the Antonine Constitution

The theory that Caracalla was attempting to forge 'universal harmony' by extending the franchise to all corners of the empire seems to have some basis if the text of the Giessen papyrus is studied closely.[9] In addition to the fundamental act of inducting nearly every free person to the rights of *civitas*, the emperor's statements following the announcement of the grant appear to promote social inclusion at all levels of society: 'it is necessary for the masses not only to share in our burden, but also to be included in victory.'[10] On initial examination, this rhetoric would appear to bear a degree of similarity to the banquet held by Alexander at Opis, in which he espoused a similar sentiment:

---

8 For a recent example of scholarship emphasising an Alexandrian link, see González-Fernández and Fernández Ardanaz (2010).

9 Baharal (1996) 70.

10 *P. Giss.* 40 I, ll. 9–11: Ὀφείλει γὰρ τὸ πλῆθος οὐ μόνον τἆλλα συνυπομένειν πάντα ἀλλὰ ἤδη καὶ τῇ νίκῃ ἐνπεριειλῆφθαι.

> Then Alexander, interrupting him, said: "But all of you without exception I consider my kinsmen, and so from this time I shall call you."[11]

This has led, in the past, to a discussion of Alexander's desire for a brotherhood of man, in which the king would unite all of the races of mankind into a single empire, whose inhabitants would be partners, rather than simply subject peoples. It is clear that this is from where Baharal has found her evidence for Caracalla's later plan to achieve a single, united world empire. There are fundamental problems in reaching such a conclusion, though. Much of the concept of Alexander's brotherhood of man derives from the work of one scholar, and their interpretation of the events at Opis. Tarn considered the banquet scene to represent the conclusion of a peace following the *de facto* mutiny of Alexander's Macedonian troops, claiming that Alexander shared wine with everybody from his *krater*, in a symbolic gesture showing his commitment to universal harmony.[12] The problem with this hypothesis is that even a cursory examination of the *Anabasis* shows that Tarn has misread the content of the episode entirely. If Arrian's text is examined, it quickly becomes clear that the author was depicting Alexander responding specifically to jealousy among his Macedonian soldiers and officers, who were concerned that their king honoured Persian and other non-Hellenic peoples excessively.[13] In fact, there is no real evidence that Alexander, even through the lens of Arrian, ever desired a brotherhood of man in the fashion postulated by Tarn.[14] Even the assertion that Alexander shared from his *krater* has been proven to be an inept rendition of the original.[15] With Tarn accused of 'mistranslation in the crucial passage, misdirection in its setting, free imaginative interpretation where its restrictions and precision are irksome, and vague use of words charged with emotion', the hypothesis that Alexander the Great yearned for a brotherhood of man has been completely discredited.[16]

This has serious consequences for any potential association between the Antonine Constitution and Caracalla's emulation of Alexander, the first implication being that Baharal's hypothesis regarding the emperor's intentions must be rejected immediately. This does not mean, however, that it is impossible to observe an Alexandrian inspiration within the text of the *constitutio* in another

---

11   Arr. *Anab.* 7.11 (tr. Chinnock).
12   Tarn (1948) 400, 440.
13   Arr. *Anab.* 7.6–8.
14   Bosworth (1980) 1–21; Brunt (1965) 203–15.
15   Badian (1958) 428–29.
16   Badian (1958) 432.

way. Rather than trying to identify a link between Caracalla and the historical Alexander, it is more profitable to examine the literary presentation of the king. If we analyse the tone of the Antonine Constitution further, we observe that the evidence supports the hypothesis that Caracalla was influenced by the heroic image of Alexander presented by later authors, particularly Plutarch.

Of particular interest here is a section of Plutarch's *De Fortuna Alexandri* located in the course of the *Moralia*. In this text, the author contemplates what might have been realised if Alexander had lived for longer and been able to accomplish his imperial ambitions. Rather than an empire unified on the basis of a homogenous race or culture, there is a clear inference that the Plutarchan Alexander would have achieved unity through the imposition of a common system of law and justice:

> ἀλλ' ἑνὸς ὑπήκοα λόγου τὰ ἐπὶ γῆς καὶ μιᾶς πολιτείας, ἕνα δῆμον ἀνθρώπους ἅπαντας ἀποφῆναι βουλόμενος, οὕτως ἑαυτὸν ἐσχημάτιζεν· εἰ δὲ μὴ ταχέως ὁ δεῦρο καταπέμψας τὴν Ἀλεξάνδρου ψυχὴν ἀνεκαλέσατο δαίμων, εἷς ἂν νόμος ἅπαντας ἀνθρώπους διῳκεῖτο καὶ πρὸς ἓν δίκαιον ὡς πρὸς κοινὸν ἐπέβλεπον φῶς. νῦν δὲ τῆς γῆς ἀνήλιον μέρος ἔμεινεν, ὅσον Ἀλέξανδρον οὐκ εἶδεν.

> But Alexander desired to render all upon earth subject to one law of reason and one form of government and to reveal all men as one people, and to this purpose he made himself conform. But if the deity that sent down Alexander's soul into this world of ours had not recalled him quickly, one law would govern all mankind, and they all would look toward one rule of justice as though toward a common source of light. But as it is, that part of the world which has not looked upon Alexander has remained without sunlight.[17]

Unlike the problematic notion of an appeal to universal harmony, the concept of an empire united by its legal system can clearly be recognised in the text of the Antonine Constitution. While the guarantee, preserved in the Giessen text, that customary law was to be respected might appear contrary to this notion, the very inclusion of the clause in the text only draws attention to the fact that local systems were, in reality, being superseded by the Roman one, as Ando notes: 'it is important to recognize that the Antonine Constitution had foreclosed the very means for validating local practice … For the extension of Roman citizenship—and the eradication of alien communities as autonomous political entities—had necessarily also invalidated local codes

---

17   Plut. *Moralia* 330d–e (tr. Babbit).

of law.'[18] The assimilation and homogenisation of the empire's myriad population groups is further emphasised towards the end of the Giessen text, where Caracalla declared that by the terms of his edict, no one would be left without a state and everyone would share in the glory of Rome:

> Τοῦτο δὲ τὸ διάταγμα ἐξαπλώσει τὴν μεγαλειότητα τοῦ Ῥωμαίων δήμου συμβαίνει γὰρ τὴν αὐτὴν περὶ τοὺς ἄλλους γεγενῆσθαι ἥπερ διαπρέπουσιν ἀνέκαθεν Ῥωμαῖοι τιμῇ καταλειφθέντων μηδένων τῶν ἑκάστης χώρας ἐν οἰκουμένῃ ἀπολιτεύτων ἢ ἀτιμήτων.

> This decree will spread the magnificence of the Roman people. For it now happens that the same greatness has occurred for everyone, by the honour in which the Romans have been preeminent since time immemorial, with no-one from any country in the world being left stateless or without honour.[19]

If the legal dimension of the *Constitutio Antoniniana* is compared to the unrealised promise of Alexander presented by Plutarch, an association between the two leaders can be drawn. When seeking to gauge the influence of Alexander the Great on the terms of the edict, then, it is necessary to concentrate on the literary, rather than historical Alexander. Indeed, this emphasis has already been made in the past, with Brunt arguing that the idealised king presented in such works represented an inspiration to Roman leaders who were themselves eager to construct an expansive and enduring empire:

> Neither Alexander nor anyone else realized the objective [of a completely unified empire spanning east and west], and it may be doubted if in his own mind it was so clearly defined as in Plutarch's ideal description. But his work tended in this direction and helped to inspire not only perhaps Stoic philosophers but the Romans, who were also to transcend national differences and to conceive that Italy had been marked out to unite scattered empires.[20]

We know that legendary figures such as Alexander the Great probably featured prominently in the education of elite young Romans, in the form of historical

---

18   Ando (2012) 98 *passim*. Also see Ando (2011) 19–27. For the section of the *constitutio* addressing customary law, see *P. Giss.* 40 I, ll. 8–9.
19   *P. Giss.* 40 I, ll. 11–14.
20   Brunt (1965) 215.

exempla in the study of both history and rhetoric.[21] There is further evidence to support the hypothesis that the idealised image of Rome as representing a common fatherland for the empire and beyond had infiltrated the elite mind-set, with Pliny the Elder claiming that Italy was the 'fatherland for all the nations of the world.'[22] Given this cultural and educational context, it is to be expected that the Augusti, including Caracalla, would be familiar with the example of Alexander's kingdom presented by later authors, and that it is plausible that this influenced both their perception of the Empire and, indeed, how they then interpreted and presented their own imperial power through official documents, such as the Antonine Constitution.[23]

Returning to Caracalla, then, we are faced with the question of why the emperor chose to employ rhetoric reminiscent of Alexander the Great in the course of the *Constitutio Antoniniana*. I would argue that there are two potential explanations. The first is based upon the overwhelming volume of ancient evidence which suggests that the emperor was an obsessive admirer of Alexander, and that he was therefore simply inspired to emulate the grandeur that he associated with the king. The alternative explanation depicts Caracalla in a more active light. Far from mimicking Alexander to indulge in an irrational fantasy, there is sufficient evidence to suggest that the emperor opted to promote an association with the conqueror in particular ways for political gain, but that this process was only one facet of a wider shift in his self-representation that was to occur from the outset of 212 onwards.

Alexander Iconography in the Caracallan Empire

When describing Caracalla's adoration for Alexander the Great, the author of the *Historia Augusta* claimed that the emperor rarely ceased referring to his idol, and suggested that Caracalla might have felt an irrational compulsion to behave like the king.[24] While these accusations might seem innocuous, they are nonetheless indicative of a significant problem we face when attempting to assess the extent to which the emperor was inspired by the legend of Alexander. A cursory glance at our main literary sources for the period reveals that they are littered with a variety of unusual anecdotes regarding the ways

---

21   Bonner (1977) 67–75. Also see Baharal (2003) 31.
22   Plin. *HN*. 3.39: *una cunctarum gentium in toto pro orbe patria*.
23   For a general overview of Alexandrian influence on the Roman state, see Heuss (1954) and Kühnen (2008).
24   HA *Car*. 2.1–2.

in which Caracalla is alleged to have exhibited his admiration for the king. These range from the relatively innocent, if eccentric, such as dressing in the Macedonian style, through to the more serious accusation that the emperor believed himself to be Alexander reborn.[25]

An obvious problem encountered when considering these allegations is that they derive from an overwhelmingly hostile literary tradition, in which the sources, particularly Dio, were eager to denigrate the emperor. This can be seen, for example, in the author's claim that Caracalla was obsessed with acquiring and using items believed to have once belonged to the king.[26] Dio's image of the emperor is immediately reminiscent of Caligula's alleged proclivity for wearing a breastplate that he had previously removed from the tomb of the king, a comparison that can only have reflected badly on Caracalla.[27] The result of this is that it becomes difficult to separate genuine examples of Alexander *imitatio* performed by the emperor from the hyperbolic or even fictitious creations of the ancient authors. This becomes even more problematic when it is noted that the literary image of Caracalla fixating over the king is not supported by evidence produced through official media of the period.

For an emperor so apparently obsessed with Alexander the Great, there is a surprising dearth of Alexandrian iconography to be found in Caracalla's official media, across both the sculptural and epigraphic corpora as well as among numismatic artefacts. Baharal has conducted a study of imperial portraiture and concluded that, far from any notion that the emperor sought to forge an artistic assimilation between himself and his idol, there is actually a significant degree of divergence in Caracallan sculpture from anything that could be considered Alexandrian.[28] The emperor's portraits are not executed in an idealised, Hellenistic style; they often depict considerable detail of his facial features, for example, including his famed furrowed brow.[29] The gaze of the statuary, furthermore, fails to conform to the Alexandrian style, exhibiting a downward glance towards the viewer, rather than the gaze into infinity. Even the emperor's hairstyle is different, with Caracalla's close-cut military hairstyle presenting a stark contrast to the flowing, leonine hair of his idol. In fact, only

---

25   For the example of Caracalla adopting Macedonian dress, see Hdn. 4.8.2. For the idea that Caracalla claimed to be the reincarnation of the king, see Dio 78.7.2.
26   Dio 78.7.1.
27   Suet. *Cal.* 52. Also see Spencer (2002) 93.
28   Baharal (1996) 73–76.
29   Hannestad (1984) 284. Also see Jucker (1981) 667–725. For the allegation of Caracalla's increasing severity, ostensibly in imitation of Alexander, see HA *Car.* 2.1.

one statue has ever been found which might depict Caracalla with Alexandrian features, although the identification of the figure remains in doubt.[30]

Similarly problematic is the fact that there is a notable absence of any reference to Caracalla as Alexander found in the epigraphic sources. This can hardly be blamed upon a lack of sufficient source material since the early third century has been shown to represent a peak in the Roman epigraphic habit for the imperial period.[31] These remains suggest that, rather than associating himself with Alexander through this medium, the emperor focused more on promoting traditional themes and virtues.[32] The numismatic corpus provides equally little evidence of Caracalla exploiting the memory of Alexander the Great for propagandistic effect. While there is a small selection of coin types which initially appear to refer to Alexander, each of these specimens can be questioned or explained in alternative terms, upon closer examination. It is tempting, for example, to connect appearances of Hercules on coinage of the period with the emperor's fascination, since Alexander was reputed to have been able to trace his ancestry back to the demigod.[33] Reverse iconography depicting Hercules can be found among the variety of deities struck on Caracallan coinage during the 212–17 period.[34] The precise purpose of this imagery, however, is far less distinct. Hercules was commonly revered throughout the imperial period, proving particularly popular with Commodus, for example.[35] The demigod was, furthermore, closely associated with the Severan dynasty as a whole, owing to his role as the patron deity to the family's *patria* of Lepcis Magna.[36] Herculean allusions on Caracallan coinage, then, may refer to a number of aspects important to the emperor, be they Alexandrian, Antonine, or even simply a declaration of piety.[37]

---

30 This is now thought more likely to represent one of the *Dioscuri*. For more on this debate and modern identification, see Hijmans (1994) 165–74.

31 Bodel (2001) 6–15.

32 Caracalla's promotion of *indulgentia*, for example, will be considered in Chapter 5.

33 Diod. Sic. 17.1.5; Plut. *Alex.* 2.1–2.

34 For example, RIC 192. The wider implications of Caracalla's religiously themed coinage will be considered in the next chapter.

35 Dio 77.7.2. See also Beard *et al.* (1998) 90.

36 Beard *et al.* (1998) 255. Severus honoured Hercules, for example, by constructing him a temple on the Quirinal hill in Rome; see Dio 77.16.3, who claims that the building was dedicated to Hercules and another deity associated with both Alexander and Lepcis Magna, Bacchus/Dionysus. For more on the links between these gods and the Severi, see Rowan (2012) 158–59; Lichtenberger (2011) 42–43, and Baharal (1996) 78.

37 Indeed, there is little reason why this reverse type need have been designed to evoke one particular propagandistic thread, alone.

There is, in fact, only one coin type that has been linked to Caracalla's reign which makes a direct reference to Alexander the Great and that cannot be interpreted in a more general manner. The coin is a small golden type, referred to simply as one of Caracalla's bracteates by Mattingly.[38] It has been attributed to Caracalla's period of sole rule, but this link is highly tenuous. The coin depicts a right facing bust of Alexander in a typical style, with flowing hair and wearing a diadem. There is no accompanying legend, however, to explain further the nature or purpose of this type. The absence of such crucial supporting data, paired with the enormous stylistic difference between the depiction of Alexander's coin portrait with that of the emperor, whose obverse busts follow the more severe style of portraiture observed in his statuary, means that the coin simply cannot be dated with any confidence or even associated with Caracalla with any degree of certainty.[39]

The Political Significance of Alexander Iconography

Given the absence of imperial evidence to suggest that Caracalla publicly linked himself with Alexander the Great, we might be forgiven for assuming that the obsession alleged of the emperor by our ancient authors is the result of literary hyperbole at best, complete fiction at worst. Despite the disappointing lack of evidence for Caracalla's Alexander-mania through official media, though, there are other phenomena which suggest that the emperor's fascination was a public one and did contain a political dimension. In fact, evidence found dating to after Caracalla's assassination proves that the emperor's association with Alexander the Great was an important aspect of Caracallan self-representation and, furthermore, carried a political significance.

During the 220s, there was an increase in Macedonian coinage bearing Alexandrian motifs; there is furthermore an increase in epigraphic attestations to games being held in the hero's honour, the *Alexandreia*, although it seems clear that the games themselves probably started under Caracalla himself.[40] Dahmen has attributed this upsurge in Alexander iconography to the reign of

---

38   BMCRE V 202.

39   Baharal (1996) 79, has suggested that Caracalla might have distributed this coin type throughout the eastern provinces prior to his advance, doing so to establish how popularity. This theory is unpersuasive, however, given the likely negligible impact that a small series of high value coins could have had on the provincial population. For more on this, see Noreña (2011) 196–97.

40   Dahmen (2007) 32–33.

Elagabalus, under whom the images begin to appear on Macedonian *koina*.[41] Given the lengths that the Severan faction went to, to ensure that Elagabalus was accepted as the legitimate heir to Caracalla during the brief civil war against Macrinus, it is logical to conclude that this promotion of Alexandrian themes was chosen owing to its well-known link to Caracalla.[42] The political element to this process of *veneratio* was even more assertive under the final Severan emperor, whose imperial name was chosen to evoke a link to Caracalla via the Macedonian.[43] Under Alexander Severus, further games were held in the name of Alexander the Great.[44] Furthermore, in the young emperor's commemorative series of coinage, Caracalla was assigned the epithet *magnus*.[45] The repetition of Alexandrian iconography during a time at which the emperor's legitimacy was most uncertain (both Elagabalus and Alexander Severus rose to power through the murder of their predecessor) suggests not only the inherent potency of Alexander the Great's legacy as a propagandistic image, but also that it was widely associated with the sole reign of Caracalla.

Similar to the later numismatic evidence, there are clear examples of coins bearing Alexandrian iconography among the civic coinage struck by eastern cities during the reign of Caracalla. Specimens from a number of cities in the provinces have been identified: Alexandria at the Issus; Gerasa; Caesarea in Cappadocia and Heliopolis in Syria, to give some examples.[46] The exact purpose of this output has been debated, with Dahmen asserting that the coins represent an attempt by the communities in question to stress their fidelity to the emperor, while Noreña has argued that they form evidence of the cities attempting to secure imperial patronage or, alternatively, expressing their thanks for it.[47] Whatever the rationale for the provincial coinage, and there is no reason why it cannot be a synthesis of the aforementioned ideas, the fact remains that this iconography would only have made an impact with the emperor if it made reference to a theme that contained a contemporary relevance.[48]

---

41 Dahmen (2007) 33.
42 Hdn. 5.3.10; Icks (2011) 10–18; Arrizabalaga y Prado (2010) 202–6.
43 Icks (2011) 37, 107.
44 Rowan (2012) 154.
45 RIC 717–20 *Alexander Severus*.
46 Dahmen (2007) 22, 29, 34.
47 Dahmen (2007) 5; Noreña (2011) 270–71.
48 The Aboukir Medallions form a very striking example of this, with portraits of both Caracalla and Alexander featuring in the series. Rowan (2012) 154, has suggested that they were, in effect, interchangeable. For more on the medallions and the question of their dating in the early third century, see Dahmen (2008) 493–546. Dahmen claims that the artefacts might date from the period following Caracalla's death but, even if this is the

A good example of an attempt by a provincial community to simultaneously impress Caracalla and also exploit Alexander iconography for the city's own benefit can be found in the case of Philippopolis in Thrace. Amongst the wider numismatic output for this city, there are coins struck in commemoration of the Pythian Games held there during Caracalla's sole reign.[49] As Rowan has noted, there are two factors that are particularly significant in analysing this coinage. Firstly, Philippopolis could only have staged the games on the permission of the emperor himself, meaning that the city either petitioned Caracalla or received them as an imperial benefaction.[50] Secondly, the games were traditionally named after the emperor or deity responsible for the grant to hold them.[51] Since Alexander was not a name that featured in Caracalla's imperial nomenclature, this ultimately raises the question of what the inhabitants of Philippopolis were trying to achieve by labelling their Pythian Games as *Alexandreia*. Rowan argues that it is unclear whether the city was directly honouring the emperor, the king or a 'happy confusion' of the pair.[52] While she is correct that the lack of any definitive information regarding the content of the games prevents an absolute conclusion from being drawn, I would argue that this phenomenon fits easily into the wider trend of cities reflecting the emperor's public association of Alexander the Great.

With this evidence in mind, we must move away from the superficial connections between Caracalla and Alexander and consider how the emperor might have exploited an association with the king for political gain. As I noted at the outset of this chapter, this has become the accepted hypothesis regarding the relationship between the two men, with Buraselis arguing that Caracalla's identification with Alexander represents 'nothing less than the assumption of a wholly political ideology.'[53] While the connection need not be quite as absolute as Buraselis claims, it is important to note that there is substantial evidence to suggest that Caracalla's exploitation of the king's mythos was not without precedent. In fact, association with Alexander appears to have been an accepted practice for Roman emperors.

---

case, they are still useful in demonstrating the persistence of the link between the two rulers even after the emperor's assassination in 217.
49 For an example, see *GIC* III 1474.
50 Rowan (2012) 154.
51 Rowan (2012) 156.
52 Rowan (2012) 157.
53 Buraselis (2007) 33. Also see Rowan (2012) 152, who claims that Caracalla 'cultivated an alignment' with the king.

The act of engaging with, or even appropriating, the image of Alexander became a powerful tool of kingship from almost immediately after the monarch's death in 323 BCE. Many Hellenistic rulers, including the *diadochoi* themselves, sought to associate with Alexander or even to assume facets of his identity in an attempt to strengthen and legitimise their positions of power within the network of successor kingdoms.[54] The relationship between Alexander and the Roman audience in the context of the late Republic was understandably more problematic, given the Macedonian's absolute monarchy, with sources such as Livy using the character of the king as a vehicle for a discussion on the nature of the newly founded Principate.[55] As the imperial regime was consolidated, however, we can observe a more concentrated use of Alexander imagery once again, with a number of emperors from Augustus through to Julian showing themselves eager to replicate his considerable military success.[56]

If viewed within the wider context of the Principate, then, it is evident that much of the alleged *veneratio* and *imitatio* alleged of Caracalla was far from exceptional. A number of emperors visited the tomb of Alexander and honoured his corpse.[57] Augustus was said to have sealed his official communications with a stamp bearing a bust of Alexander.[58] Trajan made reference to the luck of Alexander in being able to explore India during his own war against Parthia. According to Dio, the emperor then falsely claimed that he had, in fact, exceeded Alexander's empire in his campaign of expansion.[59] Even Caracalla's alleged levying of a military unit inspired by Alexander has a Neronian precedent.[60] The trend of imperial identification with the Macedonian appears most commonly in connection with the eastern empire, or in the context of war with Parthia (or later Sassanid Persia).[61] This is certainly the case with

---

54   For examples of the exploitation of Alexander's likeness during the Hellenistic period, see Stewart (1993).
55   Livy 9.18.1–7. For more on the difficulties presented by Alexander *Rex* for a Roman audience, see Spencer (2002) 39–82.
56   Spencer (2002) 41.
57   Spencer (2002) 41; Athanassiadi (1992) 193–94. Also see Croisille (1990).
58   Suet. *Aug.* 50.1.
59   For more on the luck of Alexander, see Dio 68.29.1. For Trajan's imperial expansion, see Dio 68.29.2. The emperor is also placed by Dio (68.30.1) in Babylon during this period, stemming from a desire by Trajan to sacrifice at the deathbed of the king.
60   For Caracalla's phalanx named in honour of Alexander, see Dio 78.7.1–2. For more on Nero's military homage to the king, see Suet. *Nero.* 19.
61   Athanassiadi (1992) 193, claims that 'any expansion eastwards in which political motives were mingled with civilising pretensions was bound to be conceived in terms of the

Caracalla's advance, since it appears that the route of his travel throughout the eastern empire and eventual offensive against Parthia were modelled extensively on that taken by Alexander, even including a visit to Ilium.[62]

Based on the above evidence, it stands to reason that, in addition to reflecting the idealised image of Alexander found in the ancient literature, Caracalla's use of imagery associating him with Alexander was part of a generally accepted *topos* inferring military strength and *virtus*, with a particular emphasis on being the champion of the east. A final observation must be made, however, in reference to Caracalla's own relationship with the king and his legacy. The Alexander legend played a prominent role in the civil war between Septimius Severus and Pescennius Niger, with the pretender to the throne accepting the epithet of a 'new Alexander' from his supporters in the eastern provinces.[63] In the aftermath of the Wars of Succession, Septimius Severus visited Alexandria with his family as part of their imperial tour.[64] During his time in the city, the emperor took the unusual move of closing the tomb of Alexander and removing some its contents, so that 'no one in future should either view Alexander's body or read what was written in the above mentioned books [tomes reputedly containing secret lore].'[65] Severus had appreciated the propagandistic value that the legend of Alexander could generate. By closing the tomb and preventing any access, the emperor must have hoped to minimise the opportunity for any others to claim that they were the successors to the king's legacy in a similar fashion to Pescennius Niger.[66] In Caracalla's youth, then, as the heir apparent and even before he rose to share the mantle of power with his father, he would have been able to witness to the significant political cachet connected to the mythos surrounding Alexander. Given the potentially Alexandrian inspiration underlying the rhetoric of the *Constitutio Antoniniana*, in addition to the other examples of *imitatio*, it would appear that he did not forget this important lesson.

Even accounting for the hostile literary source tradition criticising the emperor, it is clear that the imagery and legacy of Alexander the Great had a

---

heroic exploits of Alexander the Great, whose life-story had already passed into the realm of folklore.'

62 For studies devoted to Caracalla's circuitous route of travel and its similarity to that taken by his idol, see Boteva (1999) 181–88; Johnston (1983) 58–76, and Levick (1969) 426–46.
63 Dio 75.6.2a; Buraselis (2007) 28; Birley (1988) 135–36.
64 Dio 76.18; Birley (1988) 136.
65 Dio 76.13.2: ἵνα μηδεὶς ἔτι μήτε τὸ τούτου σῶμα ἴδῃ μήτε τὰ ἐν ἐκείνοις γεγραμμένα ἀναλέξηται.
66 Buraselis (2007) 29.

considerable bearing on elements of Caracalla's life and rule. It would be incorrect to accept that this was a simple case of obsessive hero worship, though.

The evidence suggests that the emperor was acting within a pre-established tradition of Augusti invoking the memory of the conqueror for their own political agenda, specifically promoting military virtue and success. It is into this context of imperial propaganda that we must interpret the Antonine Constitution. While the tone and rhetoric of the edict cannot be linked conclusively to the historical Alexander, since the source tradition is too unreliable, it is possible to identify a similarity in the text and the idealised version of the king presented in Plutarch's *De Fortuna Alexandri*. The extent to which Caracalla would have drawn a distinction, however, is debatable. That Caracalla was potentially emulating Alexander the Great through his expression in the Antonine Constitution seems plausible. There is no suggestion here, however, that this was the primary intention of the emperor in introducing the edict. In fact, if other evidence for Caracalla's reign is consulted, it is patently evident that his use of Alexander iconography formed only one facet of a wider propagandistic revolution, in which Caracalla sought to redefine the character of the Severan dynasty, following the demise of his brother Geta. It is now necessary, then, to move beyond the emperor's exploitation of Alexandrian imagery and to focus on the wider context of Caracalla's sole rule. By examining the different ways in which Caracalla sought to consolidate his position as emperor, it will become clear that the Antonine Constitution was of critical importance to the emperor's new regime.

CHAPTER 5

Securing the Caracallan Empire

The transition from a principate shared between the sons of Severus in early 211 to the sole rule of Caracalla, by the close of the same year, had been marked by some of the worst internecine violence ever to be witnessed within the imperial household. Our main literary sources for the period, Dio and Herodian, differ in points of detail regarding the ways in which the rivalry between Caracalla and Geta was made manifest, but they agree that the final clash between the Augusti was brutal, the younger brother stabbed to death while clinging to his mother.[1] While the enmity between both men appears to have been public knowledge, the death of Geta represented a watershed moment in the history of the Empire, nonetheless; emperors had been murdered in the past, but never before had the assassin been someone who already possessed a share of the imperial throne.[2] After eliminating his co-emperor in such an open and ferocious manner, the extant evidence suggests that Caracalla felt vulnerable and was concerned about the public legitimacy of his own principate.[3] Indeed, given Severus' nearly continual promotion of his sons as a guarantee of imperial harmony and continuity, Caracalla's position at the outset of 212 must have seemed worryingly precarious.[4]

From the moment of Geta's death, Caracalla was compelled to offer a public re-evaluation of recent events, including the assassination of his brother.[5] It has already been noted that the emperor made reference to the murder of Geta in the course of the Antonine Constitution, and so it is imperative that the edict is considered as a component part of this wider process. My task in this chapter, then, will be to assess the political significance of the *Constitutio Antoniniana* in consolidating Caracalla's position as the sole emperor at a time when his rule seemed fragile. This examination will begin with a consideration of the *aequitas* promoted in the Giessen text, noting that, while scholars such as Mennen and Honoré are partially correct to view the legislation in the context of a wider social change, the social levelling embodied in the edict also contains a more immediate political application when set against the

---

1   Dio 78.2.3; Hdn. 4.1.3.
2   For an allusion to the brothers' divergent personalities, see Dio 78.1.4.
3   The economic aspect of army pay and donatives has been discussed in Chapters 2 and 3.
4   Rowan (2012) 93.
5   Kemezis (2014) 31–32.

background of a strained relationship between the imperial household and senatorial elite.[6]

Following this, I will then outline how the Antonine Constitution can be seen to promote and consolidate the Caracallan regime in three distinct ways. Firstly, the religious ideology present in the text will be examined, since this served the dual purpose of promoting an image of personal piety on the part of the emperor, while also allowing him to control the narrative of the events surrounding Geta's demise. Secondly, Caracalla's promotion of his own imperial *indulgentia* will be discussed. The general importance of this virtue to the Augusti will be observed briefly, since the promotion of generosity was far from unique to Caracalla, before the value of such a display in the context of 212 is noted. Finally, the extent to which the *constitutio* can be deemed a social contract between the emperor and his citizens will be considered. I will argue that if the legislation is examined through the lens of the patron-client relationship, a theory that Caracalla was attempting to forge a personal tie of loyalty between himself and the new *cives* becomes persuasive. This combination of factors ultimately supports the hypothesis that the *Constitutio Antoniniana* was a key element of Caracallan propaganda in the aftermath of Geta's assassination, in which the emperor endeavoured to redefine the character of the Severan dynasty.

The Drive for Aequitas

The jurist Paul, a contemporary of the Severi, recorded the general principle that 'in all matters, especially the law, equity (*aequitas*) must be considered.'[7] Similarly, the drive for equity appears to have been an ideological concern that occupied the earlier Severan emperors. Both Septimius Severus and Caracalla can be observed arbitrating cases, for example, and emphasising how their perception of *aequitas* had moved them to reach their final conclusions and judgments.[8] It is tempting to view this phenomenon in the context of a

---

6   Mennen (2011) 22–23; Honoré (2004) 114.
7   *Dig.* 50.17.90: *in omnibus quidem, maxime tamen in iurem* **aequitas** *spectanda est* (emphasis added).
8   For an example of this under Septimius Severus, see *Dig.* 36(34).1.76.1. For an example from the reign of Caracalla, see *CJ* 2.1.4. It should be noted, however, that this was not a guarantee of complete legal equality (social distinctions were maintained, for example), but rather an assurance of equitable treatment in the spirit of the written law. For more on this, see Buraselis (2007) 60–65.

changing philosophy of imperial government, in which there was a growing belief that the Principate should be concerned with the benefit of its people, rather than the personal gain of the emperors themselves. This attitude is found in a selection of documents from the period, including the *Meditations* of Marcus Aurelius, and in the decree of Alexander Severus cancelling the demands of the *aurum coronarium*.[9] On first examination, the *Constitutio Antoniniana* can be interpreted as a significant piece of legislation in this vein. Indeed, if the Giessen text is examined, there would appear to be hints that Caracalla adhered to this ideology, prompting him to enact a benevolent and inclusive initiative:

> Ὀφείλει γὰρ τὸ πλῆθος οὐ μόνον τἄλλα συνυπομένειν πάντα ἀλλὰ ἤδη καὶ τῇ νίκῃ ἐνπεριειλῆφθαι. Τοῦτο δὲ τὸ διάταγμα ἐξαπλώσει τὴν μεγαλειότητα τοῦ Ῥωμαίων δήμου συμβαίνει γὰρ τὴν αὐτὴν περὶ τοὺς ἄλλους γεγενῆσθαι ἤπερ διαπρέπουσιν ἀνέκαθεν Ῥωμαῖοι τιμῇ καταλειφθέντων μηδένων τῶν ἑκάστης χώρας ἐν οἰκουμένῃ ἀπολιτεύτων ἢ ἀτιμήτων.

> It is necessary for the masses not only to share in our burden, but also to be included in victory. This decree will spread the magnificence of the Roman people. For it now happens that the same greatness has transpired for everyone, by the honour in which the Romans have been pre-eminent since time immemorial, with no-one from any country in the world being left stateless or without honour.[10]

By advancing nearly every free person in his empire to the rights of *civitas*, Caracalla thus assured that they would have enjoyed legal parity, to the extent that they all had access to the Roman legal system.[11] In this context, Buraselis has argued that the Antonine Constitution should be viewed as a step in a larger process of legal and social levelling occurring during the imperial period, one in which provincial subjects were viewed as active participants in the empire, rather than simply tributaries for the Italian heartland.[12] On its own, however, this is too simplistic an impression of the phenomenon: other factors

---

9   M. Aur. *Meditations* 1.14; *Oliver* 275 (= *P. Fay.* 20). For more detail on Alexander Severus' decree, see Oliver (1978) 474–85; Buraselis (2007) 22–23.

10 *P. Giss.* 40 I, ll. 9–14.

11 As noted in Chapter 1, however, other social distinctions, such as the divide between the *honestiores* and *humiliores* remained. For more, see Rilinger (1988) 13–33; Garnsey (1970) 261–80.

12 Buraselis (2007) 12, 86.

must also be taken into consideration. Firstly, the process of social levelling was, to an extent, the natural result of a development in which there was a general shift in power from the imperial centre to the provinces.[13] At its most basic, this can be seen in the gradual extension of *civitas* and other lesser rights that occurred in the pre-212 era.[14] This development can also be observed in the increasing prominence awarded to individuals of equestrian status over those of the *ordo senatorius*. It is difficult to identify a 'full-scope' rise in the *ordo equester*, since it was far from a homogenous group, but a number of individual advances can nevertheless be identified in relation to provincial governorships, the military and the imperial bureaucracy.[15]

The Severan period forms a high watermark in relation to this process, with a high number of equestrians serving across the civil service and the army, not to mention the rise of the jurists that were to flourish until the military crisis of the third century.[16] As above, this can be explained by a natural shift in the priorities of government. With an expanding bureaucracy and an increasing dependence on the army, it is understandable that the Roman state would rely upon, and eventually promote, capable equestrians rather than selecting officials from the traditional elite only.[17] Another factor that must be considered, however, is the political friction between the senatorial order and the Severan emperors. It is clear from our literary sources, for example, that Septimius Severus was not the senate's preferred choice to succeed Didius Julianus. Dio alleged that the senators harboured secret hopes against Severus in in the war against Clodius Albinus, while Herodian claimed that some actively encouraged and supported the governor of Britain to march on Rome while the Severan armies were engaged against Pescennius Niger:

> πολλούς τε, μάλιστα τοὺς ἐξέχοντας τῆς συγκλήτου βουλῆς, ἰδίᾳ καὶ κρύβδην ἐπιστέλλοντας αὐτῷ, ἔς τε τὴν Ῥώμην ἐλθεῖν πείθοντας ἀπόντος καὶ ἀσχολουμένου τοῦ Σεβήρου. ἡροῦντο γὰρ οἱ εὐπατρίδαι ἐκεῖνον μᾶλλον ἄρχοντα, ἅτε ἐκ προγόνων εὖ γεγονότα καὶ χρηστὸν τὸ ἦθος εἶναι λεγόμενον.

---

13   Mennen (2011) 40.
14   For more on the extension of the franchise in the period before 212, see Sherwin-White (1973a).
15   Mennen (2011) 135.
16   Mennen (2011) 151–56; Buraselis (2007) 55–57. For more on the rise of the jurists, see Chapter 1. This trend can be seen most markedly in connection with the army. Mennen (2011) 193–240, has shown that, while Septimius Severus maintained a senatorial presence in his officer corps, this diminished rapidly under Caracalla and had all but disappeared by the reign of Gallienus.
17   Mennen (2011) 44.

Many people, particularly the more distinguished senators, were sending personal, private letters urging him to come to Rome while Severus was occupied in the East. The nobles preferred to have him as emperor because he traced his noble birth back to a long line of ancestors and was said to be good natured.[18]

The consequent acrimony resulted in the emperor punishing a number of senators for their actions during the war, and leads to another possible interpretation of the levelling tendency that accelerated throughout the same period.[19] While the drive for *aequitas* does seem to have had a philosophical basis during the Antonine and Severan periods, it can also be argued that Severus facilitated or exploited this process in order to stabilise his dynasty's grip on power.[20] The same theory can also be applied to the sole reign of Caracalla since, according to Dio and Herodian, the emperor's relationship with the senate was far from cordial.[21] This conclusion has serious implications for the way in which we perceive the purpose of the *Constitutio Antoniniana*, specifically that it was a politicised initiative designed to garner a large support base for the emperor at a time when he was mistrustful of many among the senatorial elite.[22]

Re-writing the Severan Past

This situation facing Caracalla at the opening of 212 was arguably even more complicated than the perilous combination of political and military obstacles

---

18   Hdn. 3.5.2 (tr. Whittaker). For Dio's claims, see 76.4.2.
19   Dio 76.8.4; Hdn. 3.8.2–7. For more on the question of senators supporting Albinus and the atmosphere of tension in Rome following the Severan victory, see Daguet-Gagey (2006) 76.
20   Mennen (2011) 136–38.
21   Dio (78.4.1–6.1) describes Caracalla engaging in a purge of illustrious men, while Herodian (4.5.7) claimed that he instilled fear among the senators in an angry speech, following the murder of Geta. While we should exercise caution in accepting Dio's testimony as representative of the entire senatorial order, it remains clear that Caracalla was not a popular ruler among the senate. For more on Dio's perspective, see Davenport (2012).
22   In the aftermath of Caracalla's speech to the senate, Herodian (4.5.7) claimed that the emperor made a point of fixing his gaze upon known associates of Geta among the assembled body. That the emperor might still have questioned many senators' loyalty in the opening months of 212 is plausible. For a suggestion that some among the senate had already agitated against Caracalla, in the attempted coup d'état that resulted in the execution of Plautianus, see Bingham and Imrie (2015) 76–91.

that Septimius Severus had to overcome to secure his grip on imperial power. As noted above, Caracalla's sole principate was founded on the unprecedented act of one incumbent emperor murdering another. It has been argued that this outbreak of violence at the end of 211 was a fatally destructive act, effectively ending any hope for the continued survival of the dynasty: 'by killing his brother and his own wife, who had left him no heirs, Caracalla had personally ruined the Severan dynasty.'[23] Mennen has posited that the emperor found himself in a situation in which he was compelled to do 'everything in his power to forget the dynasty', and create a new imperial image that was, in effect, anti-dynastic.[24] This is an overly simplistic assessment of Caracalla's principate, however, that misinterprets the extant evidence.

Given the act of fratricide that heralded Caracalla's sole principate and the subsequent murders of individuals connected to the dynasty, such as Plautilla, it would clearly have been impossible for the emperor to adopt or continue the pre-existing familial propaganda emphasised through official media by his father.[25] These themes would have drawn too much attention to the memory of Geta, a factor which might have undermined his own legitimacy as emperor, especially if the ancient writers are correct that Caracalla only won the support of groups like the Alban legion through large donatives.[26] This does not equate, however, to a denial of the Severan dynasty at large, since Geta was never the individual from whom Caracalla derived his dynastic legitimacy. As the eldest son of Septimius Severus and Julia Domna, Caracalla had been a

---

23   Mennen (2006) 260. Caracalla's estranged wife, Plautilla, is included among a list of notable individuals murdered on Caracalla's order in the period directly following Geta's assassination; see Dio 78.1.1.

24   Mennen (2006) 260.

25   In the aftermath of the Wars of Succession, Severus' propaganda focused on the strength and unity of the wider Severan family. Themes such as *Felicitas Saeculi* were stressed on coins with accompanying imagery of Julia Domna and both Caracalla and Geta. See BMCRE V 225 for one such example. Furthermore, Severan unity was promoted through larger structures such as the *Septizodium*, and by the central roles played by each of the family members in state occasions such as the *Ludi Saeculares*. For more detail on this, see Gorrie (2004) 61–72; (2001) 653–70.

26   Dio (78.3.1–2) wrote that Caracalla silenced the soldiery by promising great things. Herodian (4.4.8) alleged that the soldiers knew the facts of Geta's murder, but hailed Caracalla as sole emperor nonetheless, after being promised vast sums. The most intriguing account of this moment, however, comes from the *Historia Augusta*. In this source, the author claimed that the legion at Alba initially refused Caracalla entrance to their camp, declaring that they had sworn allegiance to both the sons of Severus. Like the other accounts, the emperor secured their loyalty, though only after promising them large sums of money. For more detail, see HA *Car.* 2.7–8; HA *Geta.* 6.1–2.

Severan emperor since 198, and remained so in 212, regardless of his struggle with his younger brother. While it is true that Geta's demise and the lack of an obvious heir made the question of the eventual succession acute, as the only surviving male descendent of Severus, Caracalla *was* the Severan dynasty.[27] I would argue that it was never Caracalla's intention to renounce his connection to the dynasty.[28] Instead, I would concur with Kemezis that the emperor was compelled to present a re-envisioned account of recent history: 'Instead of two brothers peacefully continuing a dynasty stretching back to Nerva and forward to the infinite future, there was a story of crisis and triumph, in which the true emperor is preserved by the gods from the forces of evil represented by his brother.'[29] It is into this propagandistic revolution that the Antonine Constitution fits, signalling a redefinition of the relationship between the emperor and his subjects.

Before considering the role of the legislation in this process, however, is it worth noting briefly the other ways in which Caracalla reinvented the Severan dynasty in the aftermath of Geta's demise. The first of these is the act of damnatio memoriae ordered by the emperor on his dead brother.[30] Dio claimed that Caracalla's wrath was so extreme that he even ordered the defacement of any foundation stones which had supported Geta's statues, further commanding that any coinage bearing his image was to be melted down.[31] The author also alleged that the emperor engaged in 'unholy rites' by ordering offerings to be made to the *manes* of his brother, thereby condemning him to the underworld for eternity and preventing him from being deified.[32] Even accounting for the hyperbolic nature of Dio's text in criticising Caracalla, the surviving material evidence suggests that the damnatio was carried out with an unparalleled intensity. Getan statuary was destroyed, defaced or removed from public

---

27 Levick (2007) 92.
28 If it was Caracalla's intention to distance himself from the Severi, as Mennen has claimed, then it is odd that the emperor opted to retain elements of obvious continuity, such as his Antonine nomenclature, for example. Furthermore, it is worth noting that Caracalla maintained a close association with his mother from the period of Geta's murder to his own demise. For more detail on the relationship between Caracalla and Julia Domna, see Levick (2007) 90–93; Saavedra-Guerrero (2007) 120–31.
29 Kemezis (2014) 32.
30 In the aftermath of the murder, Caracalla had Geta declared a public enemy, see Hdn. 4.8; HA *Car.* 1.1; Eutrop. 8.19.
31 Dio 78.12.6.
32 Dio 78.12.6.

view and placed in warehouses, presumably to be re-carved and recycled.[33] The number of surviving inscriptions that make reference to Geta is also understandably miniscule. Of the 174 extant inscriptions on which his name appears, only 37 have survived intact.[34] This remarkable rate of attrition is testament to the thorough nature of the process, leading Murphy to comment that 'in few cases has an order to efface a man's name from the monuments been so effectively carried out'.[35] Not even coinage appears to have escaped Caracalla's wrath. The survival of Getan coins demonstrates that the melting of coinage ordered by Caracalla was only partially successful, but a high number of numismatic remains found across the empire do display evidence of defacement and vandalism.[36] Whether this act was the result of a desire to cleanse the empire publically of the evil that Geta had come to represent or, rather, a simple reflection of Caracalla's utter hatred of his dead brother, the evidence suggests that the process was considered by the emperor to be an important element in consolidating his rule in the opening months of 212.

In addition to the destruction of Geta's legacy, Caracalla's own self-image underwent considerable change. One of the most visible elements of this phenomenon is the change in the emperor's official portraiture. While images of Caracalla produced during his adolescence are marked by an Antonine influence, the result of Septimius Severus' attempts to forge a connection between the dynasty and his own, Caracallan portraiture from 212 onwards is characterised by a cropped, militaristic hairstyle and furrowed brow line.[37] Rather than simply accepting the spurious claim offered by the ancient writers that

---

33 Varner (2004) 170–73, 256. Only one full length statue thought to represent Geta survives intact, now in the *Villa del Poggio Imperiale*. Even this has sustained a considerable degree of damage to the facial area.

34 Varner (2004) 182.

35 Murphy (1945) 105. For more recent works on the *damnatio* and its unusual intensity, see Krüpe (2011) and De Jong (2007) 95–111.

36 There are a number of examples from cities such as Ephesus, Pergamum and Stratonikeia where either Getan portraiture or titles (sometimes a combination of both) have been scraped or erased from the flan, the spaces subsequently countermarked in some cases. For more detail on this numismatic phenomenon, see Varner (2004) 171–72.

37 Mennen (2006) 257–58. Dio (76.7.4) remarked that Severus styled himself as the son of Marcus Aurelius and the brother of Commodus. This is an element of Dio's text that can be also observed in the epigraphic record, with Severus tracing his self-styled family line back to the emperor Nerva. For an example of this, see *CIL* VI 954, and Hekster (2012) 243–46. It is also worth noting, however, that both Caracalla and Geta's numismatic portraiture had been in a state of flux, with both men adopting leaner, more soldierly profiles by 209. For more on the numismatic phenomenon, see Pangerl (2013).

the emperor's visage changed and became more severe as his character grew more savage—since it seems a ridiculous assumption that an emperor would knowingly promote a public image of cruelty in his statuary—it has been proposed that Caracalla might have been attempting to tap into another artistic tradition.[38] Leander Touati has suggested that it is possible to compare the later Caracallan portraiture with military figures found on the Great Trajanic Frieze which display similarly tense and stark expressions in many cases. Far from savagery, Leander Touati has argued that these portraits (and the Caracallan style, by extension) are probably an attempt to convey the concept of *virtus* through the portrait medium.[39] Considering Caracalla's popularity with the army, it is understandable that he would seek to emphasise such a quality about his imperial character.[40] In a similar vein, Zanker has suggested that the furrowed brow, intimidating on first sight, might be explained by the emperor emphasising a personal quality of stoicism.[41]

How, then, does the Antonine Constitution fit into this programme of reinvention? As I stated at the opening of this chapter, if the text of the *constitutio* is examined closely, it is possible to identify three ways in which the edict functioned as a powerful vehicle of imperial propaganda, in which Caracalla's version of his struggle with Geta is defined. Firstly, he emphasised his personal religious devotion and piety, publicising the idea of divine providence supporting his reign and promoting an image of the emperor and populace striving together for religious *consensus*.[42] Secondly, he sought to depict himself as the most generous *princeps* to date in an attempt to distance himself further from the image of a fratricide. Thirdly, Caracalla attempted to secure his sole position of imperial power by creating a global patron-client relationship between him and his populace, an initiative which also served to prompt a reconsideration of Roman identity.[43] Indeed, if the text of the *constitutio* is considered, all of these key elements are visible. In essence, the edict allowed Caracalla to promote each of his three propagandistic strands simultaneously and on a massive scale.

---

38 For the ancient accounts of Caracalla's allegedly savage nature, see Dio 78.6.1a, 78.10.2; Hdn. 4.3.3-4; HA *Car.* 2.1-3, 9.3, 11.5.
39 Leander Touati (1991) 117-31.
40 This can also be observed in the emperor's attempts to draw parallels between himself and Alexander the Great, seen in the previous chatper.
41 Zanker (1996) 93-97, 267.
42 Ando (2000) 131-76, 336-405.
43 Kemezis (2014) 32.

A Religious Offering

The emperors of the Severan dynasty are renowned for their individual piety, on the whole. Caracalla himself was often linked with the god Serapis, for example, while the fondness of Elagabalus for eastern deities and cult is infamous.[44] The opening lines of the Antonine Constitution and the tone found throughout the edict reveal that Caracalla was eager to publicise his legislation as a religious act. In the section of the text prefiguring the actual grant of *civitas*, the emperor outlined both the context of the *constitutio* and the motivation underlying it. He claimed that the edict represented an act of thanksgiving to the gods, a way in which the emperor thought he could display his gratitude to them for what he refers to as divine protection against a secretive conspiracy—implying that Geta had been preparing to murder him.[45] He continued by declaring that an appropriate way to thank the gods was to bring more of his people into their temples as fully enfranchised Romans. Indeed, the text of the edict reads:

> Αὐτοκράτωρ Καῖσαρ Μᾶρκος Αὐρήλιος Σεουῆρος Ἀντωνῖνος Εὐσεβὴς λέγει πάντως εἰς τὸ θεῖον χρὴ μᾶλλον ἀναφέρειν καὶ τὰς αἰτίας καὶ λογισμοὺς δικαίως δ'ἂν κἀγὼ τοῖς θεοῖς τοῖς ἀθανατοις εὐχαριστήσαιμι ὅτι τῆς τοιαύτης ἐπιβουλῆς γενομένης σῶον ἐμὲ συνετήρησαν τοιγαροῦν νομίζω οὕτω μεγαλοπρεπῶς καὶ εὐσεβῶς δύνασθαι τῇ μεγαλειότητι αὐτῶν τὸ ἱκανὸν ποιεῖν, εἰ τοὺς ἐν τῇ ἀρχῇ ὁσάκις ἐὰν ὑπεισέλθωσιν εἰς τοὺς ἐμοὺς ἀνθρώπους ὡς Ῥωμαίους εἰς τὰ ἱερὰ τῶν θεῶν συνεισενέγκοιμι.

> The Emperor Caesar Marcus Aurelius Severus Antoninus Pius decrees: It is altogether necessary to attribute the causes and reasons [of recent events] to the divine. I, personally, would rightly thank the immortal gods, since although such a conspiracy [as that of Geta] has occurred, they have watched over me and protected me. I think that I am able, both magnificently and piously, to do something fitting to the gods' majesty, if I manage to bring [all] those in the empire, who constitute my people, to the temples of the gods as Romans.[46]

---

44 For an example of Caracalla being referred to as *philosarapis*, see *IGRR* I 1063. On the religious practice of Elagabalus, see Arrizabalaga y Prado (2010) 165–82.
45 Herodian (4.5.3–4) claimed that, in the course of his speech to the senate following Geta's murder, the emperor revealed a Getan plot to poison Caracalla which had been foiled.
46 *P. Giss.* 40 I, ll. 1–7.

It seems incontrovertible, then, that the primary public motivation for the Antonine Constitution was a religiously inspired one.[47] We should note, moreover, that the 212 edict was not the only way in which Caracalla can be observed engaging in religious devotion. In fact, the emperor seems to have been eager to associate himself with a number of gods throughout his sole reign. This aspect of Caracalla's rule from 212–17 will be considered with specific attention to his imperial coinage, since there is a wealth of iconographic evidence to be found in the numismatic corpus. It is also likely that the emperor was concerned with the matter of *consensus* in state religion as described by Ando.[48] The evidence suggests that there is more to Caracalla's concept and presentation of religious belief than simply devotion, and that these elements of the emperor's reign, including the tone of the *constitutio*, are better explained as part of the wider process of his refashioning the Severan dynasty and focusing it around himself from the outset of 212.

A cursory examination of the numismatic evidence for Caracalla's reign reveals the importance of the Roman religious pantheon to the period of his sole rule. In her analysis of Caracalla's imperial coinage for 212–17, Manders has shown that themes promoting 'divine association', that is to say any themes connecting the emperor with the gods and the divine, or presenting him as *sacerdos*, form the largest iconographic group, some 66.9% of all imperial coin types struck.[49] On one level, these coins might be seen as an extension of the religious thanksgiving that Caracalla proclaimed in the text of the *constitutio*. This hypothesis is supported when it is noted that *providentia* is a prominent theme in the imperial output of this period, usually carrying the legend PROVIDENTIAE DEORVM and depicting a personification of Providentia.[50] Indeed, these coin types further support the theory that Caracalla publically promoted the notion that he had been saved from his brother's machinations and thus that his sole rule was divinely sanctioned.

---

47   For a recent exploration of the religious import of the Antonine Constitution, see Corbo (2013) 125–85. Dal Covolo (2013) 15–20, has gone further, and views the *constitutio* as an important component in the religious development of the Empire and the rise of the Christian church.

48   Ando (2000) 73–276. The issue of *consensus* will be considered later in this chapter.

49   Manders (2012) 232. Similarly, Rowan (2012) 112, has used hoard evidence to conclude that depictions of gods represented 59% of the total found.

50   *RIC* 227; 309a-b; 511a-d; 514; 519; 535; 527a-b; 575a–576. Also see Manders (2012) 241, who lists these examples in connection with Caracalla's coin types promoting 'divine association'. For more on the attributes of Providentia, a virtue associated with the wellbeing of the populace but also, importantly, forming a guarantor of smooth imperial succession, see Noreña (2011) 92–99.

More generally, it has been noted that Caracalla's numismatic iconography is dominated by a 'striking collection' of gods, including Apollo, Diana, Isis, Pluto, Serapis, Venus and Vesta, in the 212–17 period.[51] The number of healing deities included in his imperial and provincial coinage, such as Apollo, Aesculapius and Serapis, has led to questions regarding how far we should accept Dio's statement that the emperor was ill of mind and body.[52] Considering the prominence of religious iconography during this period, it is unsurprising that there have been attempts in the past to identify a reference to the Antonine Constitution within this body of evidence. Euzennat has attempted to link the edict with Caracalla's probable visit to the oracle of Apollo at Claros, for example.[53] As Rowan has rightly argued, however, there is no evidence to support such a connection in the text of the edict; if the oracle of Apollo at Claros was a major influence on Caracalla and the *constitutio*, then we would expect there to be at least a passing mention of it in the body of the text.[54] Furthermore, this hypothesis would rest on the *constitutio* being passed during Caracalla's Germanic campaigns, a factor which does not fit with the 212 dating of the edict.[55]

Another theory connects the *constitutio* with Pluto coin types struck during Caracalla's sole reign. This hypothesis has more traction since it is noteworthy that Pluto reverses were extraordinary for this period and only appear on coins during Caracalla's sole reign.[56] Manders has suggested that the sudden appearance of this deity on Roman coins from 212 might therefore make reference to the *constitutio*, using the agricultural element of the deity to promote a positive consequence of the edict, in the form of an increased corn dole from Egypt resulting from the increased tax yield from the province.[57] She has argued that this connection seems more likely when it is also noted that Serapis also appeared in his own right as a deity on Roman coinage from 212.[58] While this

---

51 For more detail, with examples of each of these types, see Manders (2012) 233–35.
52 Dio 78.15.3. While it is impossible to disprove that Caracalla suffered from a number of ailments, I would argue that Rowan (2012) 113–31, is correct to suggest that there may be a more mundane reason behind the appearance of these deities, in that the emperor might simply have chosen to honour the local cults of the cities that he visited. Indeed, Pergamum was renowned for its *Asclepieion*, and Claros and Grannus are thought to have had healing sanctuaries to Apollo, to give two examples.
53 Euzennat (1976) 68.
54 Rowan (2012) 127.
55 Van Minnen (2016) 218–20; Barnes (2012) 51–52.
56 Manders (2012) 239.
57 Manders (2012) 239.
58 Manders (2012) 239; also see L'Orange (1947) 82.

combination of evidence is circumstantially elegant and persuasive, the fact remains that this would represent an incredibly subtle iconographic allusion to the edict, dependent on the intended audience understanding a new coin type (which contained no specific reference to the *constitutio*) and a rather precise connection to the Egyptian corn supply. Even if we accept that coin types were generally intelligible among ancient consumers, this hypothesis seems unconvincing.[59]

Rather than attempting to identify vague references among the specifics of Caracalla's considerable religious output, Ando has argued that the *constitutio* fits better into a wider social and religious system in which the *consensus* of the populace was crucial.[60] He argues that the Romans understood that divine favour was primarily achieved by the 'universal piety' of the populace, noting that when referring to religious matters, certain sources appear to adopt quasi-medical terminology 'to express the "infection" of the Roman body politic by some foreign "poison".'[61] It is in this context, then, that Ando believes the Antonine Constitution should be interpreted, as an attempt to achieve a powerful *consensus universorum* and secure the lasting favour of the gods:

> Wishing to lead the people of the empire in a unanimous display of consensual piety, and believing that the *populus* of the empire was most properly constituted by its citizen body, Caracalla granted citizenship to all its residents. In other words, the *consensus* of the empire's population would speak more loudly if all were citizens.[62]

This explanation seems to be the strongest in relation to the religious aims of Caracalla in promulgating the *Constitutio Antoniniana*, but more needs to be said here. The emperor's attempt to achieve a nearly universal *consensus* across the empire can be seen to form a component part of the Caracallan worldview promoted following the murder of Geta, a more dangerous one in which the emperor was challenged to triumph over adversity with divine assistance; the participation of his new citizens in securing heavenly favour was therefore essential.[63] By invoking the gods, and referring to his survival and continued prosperity as a matter of divine providence, Caracalla had utilised

---

59   For more on coin targeting and the question of audience comprehension, see Howgego (1995) 70–76.
60   Ando (2000) 277–405.
61   Ando (2000) 392. For ancient examples, see Cic. *Har. Resp.* 9.19, and Tert. *Apol.* 25.2.
62   Ando (2000) 395. Also see Ando (2012) 52–57.
63   Kemezis (2014) 32.

the Antonine Constitution and associated media to provide himself with a solid ideological foundation on which to legitimise his position as the one and only ruler of the Empire.

It is important to note, however, that this was not the only way in which Caracalla characterised the transition from the shared principate to his sole regime. Returning to the emperor's numismatic output from 212 to 217, another feature that becomes apparent is the revolution in the different virtues that were emphasised in this period compared to that which preceded it. It is hardly surprising to discover that there is a decline in coin types promoting traditionally dynastic themes, 'golden age' types or that of *aeternitas*, for example.[64] Of the types that fill this iconographic void, the appearance of *securitas* and *libertas* are of particular note. Manders has depicted the emergence of the former as the successor to the *aeternitas* type, since the coins in question proclaim *securitas perpetua*.[65] Even more illuminating is the sudden, and short-lived, appearance of *libertas* in the coinage of 213. It is not difficult to envisage this iconography being struck in reference to the murder of Geta, though I would argue that the time delay between the murder and the circulation of this type makes it more likely that these coins were struck in support of the *Constitutio Antoniniana*, in which Caracalla made reference to a conspiracy against him.[66] In either case, the appearance of *libertas* in this period following Geta's demise might serve to depict the youngest son of Severus as a tyrannical conspirator against a legitimate emperor. With this in mind, it would seem that Rowan is correct to identify a new 'ideology of power' being emphasised in the opening period of Caracalla's sole rule, a phenomenon which itself fits well with the idea that the emperor offered a re-envisaged version of recent history to consolidate his position.[67]

---

64 Manders (2012) 247. The primary *aeternitas* type struck during the period 198–210 was that of *Concordia aeterna*, which would clearly be of limited value to Caracalla in the context of Geta's murder. For more on this, see Manders (2012) 248.
65 Manders (2012) 248. For examples of these coins, see RIC 309a; 536a–b, and 573 a–b. There are further examples which can only be dated 210–13 but, given this context, it seems more likely that they also derive from the beginning of 212 onwards. See RIC 229a–b; 512a–d; 515 and 520.
66 Manders (2012) 245.
67 Rowan (2012) 111.

The Indulgentissimus Princeps

Another important component of this iconographic revolution is the emperor's continued emphasis of his personal generosity (*indulgentia*). The promotion of *indulgentia* as an imperial quality was not unique to Caracalla. In fact, it appeared at many different points during the Principate, especially from the reign of Trajan onwards, forming one marker of a 'good emperor' and containing a paternalistic quality which reflected the *princeps* protecting and looking after his people.[68] The virtue appears during the reign of Septimius Severus, struck on precious and base metal coinage, primarily with reference to the generosity shown by the emperor towards Carthage and Italy.[69] With the change from shared rule to Caracalla's sole reign, we can observe a significant increase in the number of coins struck bearing a representation of *indulgentia*. If coin types depicting personified virtues are examined in more detail, it becomes clear that Caracalla struck more than double the number of *indulgentia* types than his closest predecessor, devoting close to thirty percent of all such coins to the deity.[70] Schmidt-Dick also noted this thematic concentration under Caracalla, identifying 214 varieties of *denarii* bearing the legend INDVLG FECVNDAE, with another 300 carrying the more general INDVLGENTIAE AVG.[71] An examination of the later Severan emperors' coinage reveals that, while they contain a number of references to similar virtues,

---

68   Buraselis (2007) 79–80, see also Noreña (2011) 276.
69   Severus struck large numbers of coins bearing the reverse legend INDVLGENTIA AVGG IN CARTH, dating to 203–4 CE, following his visit to Carthage. From hoard analysis, Rowan has estimated that this type alone represented about three percent of Severus' total output, while the deity, in general, represented just under 15% of the total Severan 'virtue types'. For more detail, see Rowan (2012) 78; Noreña (2011) 279–80. While the precise indulgence being referred to in these coins remains a mystery, it has been suggested that it could either have been in response to a remission of tax, or a distribution of olive oil. For the fiscal hypothesis, see Babelon (1903) 157–74. Whilst the fiscal hypothesis is logical in the context of Severus visiting Carthage in person, the theory of an oil dole is equally likely, especially when it is noted that there was a similar *indulgentia* type issued in connection with Italy. For more on this, see Pera (1979) 103–26. See also Rowan (2012) 79.
70   Noreña (2011) 279–80, has shown that the only emperors to come close to the Caracallan *indulgentia* output were Septimius Severus, with fifteen percent of all virtue types, and Hadrian, with less than five percent.
71   Schmidt-Dick (2002) 61–62. These types are in addition to the Carthage type described above which appears on Caracallan coinage, on *RIC* 130–31, for example. These latter coins, however, can arguably be attributed to the influence of Severus in ensuring that both the Augusti promoted the generosity displayed towards Carthage.

such as *liberalitas*, the number of *indulgentia* reverses is so meagre as to be arguably insignificant.[72] Rather than forming a natural evolution in numismatic iconography prompted by a general increase in the importance of *indulgentia* to the Roman state, this suggests that the virtue of generosity was a singularly important one to Caracalla's image of his new principate.

A similar trend can also be found in the epigraphic corpus. In addition to an increase in the official use of the virtue through the numismatic medium, the period 212–217 also represents a high-point for unofficial and dedicatory inscriptions associating *indulgentia* with Caracalla personally, referring to the emperor as *indulgentissimus*.[73] In this matter, I concur with Noreña that the upsurge in inscriptions of this nature being produced is probably reflective of a public that was knowledgeable of, and sensitive to, the Caracallan regime's official iconographic emphases.[74] These inscriptions can be found in areas across the empire, both in Rome and in the provinces.[75] In further support of the notion that there was an important ideological link between the emperor and the virtue, it should be noted that references to Caracalla's *indulgentia* were made even in inscriptions not directly dedicated to him. Julia Domna was hailed as the 'mother of the most generous emperor' in an inscription from Germania Superior, for example.[76]

---

72 *Indulgentia* does not feature at all during the reign of Elagabalus, while only five types are attributed to Alexander Severus: *RIC* 1, 2, 381, 382 and 557. Four of these five specimens are dated to 221, meaning that they were struck before Alexander Severus even ascended to the imperial throne. The final example, *RIC* 557, is undated. On the reverse, *Spes* (the virtue was often associated *Spes* and *Clementia* in the numismatic medium) is depicted walking left, holding a flower and raising her skirt. I would suggest that this example was either struck around the same time as the other *indulgentia* types or at the very outset of his reign, with the mint of Rome merely continuing themes struck for him as Caesar before they had received any new directive from the new emperor. For more on the association between *Spes* and *Indulgentia*, see Buraselis (2007) 81.

73 Noreña (2011) 277–79.

74 Noreña (2011) 282. A retrospective knowledge of the importance of *indulgentia* can be observed again under Caracalla's successors. The virtue appears in epigraphic evidence inscribed during the reigns of Elagabalus and Alexander Severus. For inscriptions under Elagabalus, see *CIL* III 6900, VI 1082, VIII 10304 and 10308; for those under Alexander Severus, see *CIL* III 8359 and VIII 8781. Similar to the numismatic material, however, these inscriptions would appear to fit better with later attempts to forge a link between these emperors and Caracalla, similar to the way in which they do so with Alexander the Great iconography. For more detail, see Buraselis (2007) 82–83.

75 For examples in Rome, see *CIL* VI 1065–67; for Cosa, see *CIL* XI 2633; for Narbonese Gaul, see *CIL* XII 1851; for North Africa, see *CIL* VIII 7000, 7094–98, 21828, and *IRT* 429.

76 *CIL* XIII 6531: *matri indulgentissimi principis Marci Aureli Antonini Pii Augusti*.

It is worth stressing here that, similar to the numismatic evidence, this explosion in *indulgentia* iconography took place in such a concentrated way between 212 and 217 that it is unlikely to have been the result of a natural increase in the deity's status, or simple coincidence.[77] It is far more likely that this virtue was of considerable importance to Caracalla in relation to the image that he wanted to construct of his sole principate.[78] With this in mind, it is furthermore important to note that on numerous inscriptions where the emperor is hailed as *indulgentissimus*, the epithet often appears on reworked sections of stone which had borne the name and titulature of Geta, prior to damnatio memoriae being carried out.[79] The localised nature of this evidence (these inscriptions all derive from Numidia and North Africa) means that it might be a coincidence of the surviving evidence. It is interesting to observe, nonetheless, that in a variety of cases, the emperor's *indulgentia* actively overwrites the memory of his murdered brother and thus contributes to the process of damnatio employed by Caracalla in the wider process of refashioning his principate.[80]

How can this important theme, then, be linked to the *constitutio Antoniniana*? The role of the edict as an example of imperial *indulgentia* is not so much in the precise wording of its text, as was the case regarding its religious significance, but rather in its scale and effects. As the imperial period progressed, there seems to have been an increasing link between imperial *indulgentia* and the bestowal of Roman citizenship. In his letter to Trajan requesting *civitas* for Harpocras, for example, Pliny the Younger claimed that he could not properly reward his medical therapist without the emperor's generosity.[81] The underlying association here between *indulgentia* and citizenship is arguably more significant than the act itself in the Trajanic case. The fact that there was such a connection between enfranchisement and *indulgentia* has led Noreña to argue that promoting *indulgentia* would have been the logical choice for Caracalla when publicising the edict of 212:

---

77   Buraselis (2007) 85–86.
78   Perhaps the most intriguing appearance of *indulgentia* can be found in Numidia, where the deity is honoured directly after the Capitoline triad in an inscription. See *CIL* VIII 2194. For more on this, see also Noreña (2011) 278, who declares the positioning of *indulgentia* to represent a decidedly 'odd addition to the Capitoline triad.'
79   For examples, see *CIL* VIII 6307; 6944; 6969; 6998 and 7000.
80   Buraselis (2007) 87.
81   Plin. *Ep.* 10.5.1: *cuius sollicitudini et studio tuae tantum indulgentiae beneficio referre gratiam parem possum.*

The frequent association of this term ... with imperial grants of citizenship in particular suggests that *indulgentia* would have been the most appropriate imperial virtue through which to communicate and publicise the grant of universal citizenship.[82]

In effect, even if the *constitutio* was not wholly motivated by a sense of euergetistic generosity on the part of Caracalla, the emperor emphasised the image of his personal generosity and publically associated it with his act of mass enfranchisement.[83] The extensive promotion of the emperor's *indulgentia* served as an indirect or symbolic reference to the edict, a 'systematic effort by the regime to communicate the emperor's spectacular generosity in granting citizenship to all free inhabitants of the empire—an effort, that is, to attach a specific meaning to the edict that announced this extraordinary decision, and then to disseminate that meaning as broadly as possible.'[84] We must exercise caution, however, not to view the Antonine Constitution solely in terms only of publicising a religious or euergetistic agenda on the part of the emperor. I would argue that the connection forged between Caracalla and his citizens through the *Constitutio Antoniniana* was, in fact, something altogether more binding.

A Social Contract

The literary evidence for the aftermath of Geta's murder suggests that support for Caracalla's new regime was polarised between the army, who had been won over by the promise of massive donatives, and the more hesitant senate.[85] It is against this backdrop that we must view the emperor's attempt to engage with the wider populace through the Antonine Constitution. It has been argued recently that the edict functioned, at least partly, as a redefinition of Roman identity, inasmuch as the vast majority of the populace would owe their franchise to the emperor and would therefore play a tacit role in accepting the version of events offered by Caracalla, namely that the legislation was a response to the treachery of Geta.[86] While I concur that the *constitutio* did, in one sense, compel the populace to become active participants in the emperor's revised history, it is also plausible that Caracalla was determined to secure a more

---

82   Noreña (2011) 282 *passim*.
83   Noreña (2011) 280.
84   Noreña (2011) 280.
85   Dio 78.3.1–6.1; Hdn. 4.4.3–6.5.
86   Kemezis (2014) 32.

tangible form of loyalty from the citizenry by extending the franchise. With this in mind, I argue that it is appropriate to view the Antonine Constitution as an act of patronage on an imperial scale, a piece of legislation designed to establish a personal link and relationship between the emperor and every one of his new citizens.

The system of patronage found during the Principate remained relatively unchanged from that of the Republic, with three fundamental elements: that there must be a reciprocal exchange of goods or services, there must be some degree of personal contact to distinguish the arrangement from a standard business contract, and the parties in the relationship must be of different social backgrounds.[87] One obvious change, however, was the role of the emperor as a patron. The *princeps* was seen as 'the supreme benefactor, whose gifts were intended as a display of regal splendour and generosity, and also as a 'super patron' whose subjects lived under his protection and looked to him for benefactions.'[88] Under the Principate, therefore, the role of the emperor in bestowing civic patronage became increasingly important.[89]

In this context, the gift of citizenship was a special grant inasmuch as it bestowed honour upon both parties in the arrangement, the patron as much as the newly enfranchised protégé. A mass act of enfranchisement and social promotion such as the *Constitutio Antoniniana* might, then, be said to form a logical endpoint in this area of imperial benefaction. On initial examination, this association might appear irreconcilable with Saller's specification that the relation between the patron and client ought to be a personal one, that is to say based upon 'particularistic rather than universalistic criteria', but it is important to remember that while the *constitutio* might form the end of an evolutionary process in patronage, as with the gradual expansion of the franchise, it was nevertheless a revolutionary action.[90] It cannot be expected, therefore, that the Antonine Constitution would conform to all of the strictest of modern parameters of imperial benefaction. In fact, it is wholly appropriate to discuss the edict in terms relevant to Roman patronage and thus to view the *constitutio* as an example of an imperial *beneficium*, a term which Seneca defined

---

87   Saller (1982) 1.
88   Lomas and Cornell (2003) 7. Also see: Saller (1982) 3; Veyne (1990) 102–3, 377–8.
89   Coleman (2003) 61–88. It has been suggested that the reason that provincial cities struck numismatic iconography that would resonate with the *princeps* was in the hope of receiving imperial benefaction: Noreña (2011) 270–71. For more information on civic patronage under the Severans, see Gorrie (2004) 61–72.
90   For the notion of the particularistic nature of patronage based upon a pre-existing personal connection, see Saller (1982) 1, 32–33.

as a grant which someone gives when there is no legal compulsion for them to do so.[91] The bestowal of a *beneficium* might be considered as an example of Caracalla's *indulgentia*, but it must be noted that, in the context of patronage, it can also be viewed as part of a reciprocal exchange relationship, or an arrangement in which there was at least an expectation of some reciprocity.[92]

If the edict is studied closely, there are two potential ways in which Caracalla expected some form of return benefit to be derived from the citizen body. The first of these appears to be a very practical one concerning fiscal revenue. Although severely damaged, the final lines of the Giessen text can be restored to make reference to tax obligations on the part of the newly enfranchised:

Ἄπο δὲ τῶν προσόδων τῶν νῦν ὑπερχουσῶν συντελούντων, ἅπερ ἐκελεύσθη παρὰ Ῥωμαίων ἀπὸ τοῦ κα ἔτους, ὡς δίκαιον ἐκ τῶν διαταγμάτων καὶ ἐπιστολῶν, ἃ ἐξεδόθη ὑφ' ἡμῶν τε καὶ τῶν ἡμετέρων προγόνων Προετέθη ...

Referring to the taxes that exist at present, all are due to pay those that have been imposed upon the Romans from the beginning of their twenty-first year [of age], as it is the law, according to the edicts and rescripts issued by us and our ancestors. Displayed publically ...[93]

Examination of the *Constitutio Antoniniana* can thus reveal at least one way in which Caracalla expected his great *beneficium* to be repaid. In return for being inducted into the citizen body, the emperor ordered that the newly enfranchised would be immediately liable to pay the taxes traditionally levied against the citizenry.[94] The question of finances aside, however, there was an even more fundamental expectation that accompanied the extension of *civitas*, one of personal loyalty and support. From the time of the late Republic and throughout the Principate, *beneficia* appear to have carried an expectation of goodwill towards the patron, an obligation which carried no legal compulsion but was nevertheless treated seriously.[95] Velleius Paterculus recorded that during the civil war between Antony and Octavian, Asinius Pollio refused to

---

91   Sen. *De. Ben.* 3.19.1: *beneficium enim id est quod quis dedit, cum illi liceret et non dare*.
92   Saller (1982) 19–20.
93   *P. Giss.* 40 I, ll. 14–17. For more on the difficult nature of the Giessen text, see Chapter 1 and the appendix accompanying this book. The fiscal importance of the *constitutio* has also been considered in Chapter 2.
94   This is a factor which lends some credence to the argument of an economic rationale underlying the edict, a claim made by Cassius Dio (78.9.5).
95   Saller (1982) 19.

join the latter's cause on the basis that he had previously been the recipient of *beneficia* from Antony.[96] Later, in the opening lines of the *Histories*, Tacitus emphasised his ability to write objectively regarding Galba, Otho and Vitellius because he had received neither *beneficia* nor *iniuria* from them.[97] Admittedly these examples are focused on favours and contracts between members of the elite classes but if the basic premise is accepted that the emperor was looked to by his subjects as a supreme patron and that 'Emperor and subject alike believed that imperial *beneficium*, like any other, created a debt which could be repaid in gratitude and in more concrete forms', then the importance of the Antonine Constitution to Caracalla's consolidation of power in the aftermath of Geta's murder adopts an even greater significance.[98] By extending the franchise in the first half of 212, the emperor initiated a personal tie of loyalty between himself and millions of subjects at the very moment when his rule must have seemed at its most precarious.

In summary then, Caracalla's position as sole ruler was potentially compromised at the outset of 212, owing to his act of fratricide and the subsequent damnatio memoriae of a reputedly popular figure from within the imperial household. The *Constitutio Antoniniana* therefore represented a perfect way in which to secure the favour of a vast number of individuals across the entire empire. The grant of citizenship should not be seen as a simple, superficial attempt by the emperor to divert attention away from his dead brother, but rather as something more substantial. Caracalla attempted to secure the favour and loyalty of his hitherto peregrine subjects through a reciprocal contract in which, in return for taxation and goodwill, the emperor guaranteed them access to the framework of the Roman legal system. With his pre-existing popularity with the military and this new unspoken debt of gratitude among the majority of his people, Caracalla's position would have been strengthened and his uneasy relations with the *ordo senatorius* would thus have presented less of an obstacle to his sole reign than might otherwise have been the case. In this sense, the *constitutio* can be observed to function on simultaneously ideological and practical levels, carrying religious significance but designed to address a political requirement. Moreover, if interpreted in this way, then the Antonine Constitution should be viewed not as an ill-conceived exercise in vanity by a 'bad' emperor, but rather as an astute political manoeuvre designed to explain the murderous events of the recent past and to secure Caracalla's sole regime.

---

96   Vell. Pater. 2.86.3.
97   Tac. *Hist.* 1.1. Also see: Saller (1982) 70.
98   Saller (1982) 69.

Epilogue

Caracalla took an unprecedented legal step in 212, by extending the rights of citizenship to all corners of his realm. In one move, the emperor altered the Roman Empire irrevocably, changing not only the mechanisms through which the majority of imperial subjects related to the state, but also the fundamental nature of Roman identity. It is no understatement that the ramifications of this single piece of legislation were immense. Yet, for all of its significance, the *Constitutio Antoniniana* remains one of the most controversial documents to survive from antiquity. There is surprisingly little direct evidence for the legislation, and what does survive is characterised either by its fragmentary nature or the hostility of the source from which it derives.

There is no way that any one study could possibly address every aspect of the edict: its language, scope, legal and social implications and its rationale. This has prompted scholars to engage with the legislation in very particular ways, questioning the precise text of the Giessen papyrus, assessing potential motivating factors on an individual basis, or studying the longer term consequences of the edict in periods for which there is better evidence. All of these studies have been valuable, and have illuminated important aspects of the troublesome document, but they also present problems of their own, in turn. The difficulty with these individual approaches has been that they risk either giving an inflated sense of importance to the element in question or, more seriously, removing the document from its original environment altogether. At the extreme, the *constitutio* is in danger of becoming abstract, and the connection to its own legal and cultural milieu being lost. The fundamental purpose of this monograph, then, in examining the rationale of the emperor in promulgating the Antonine Constitution, has been to return the focus to the third century.

We have observed that Caracalla's decision to extend the franchise was the result of a combination of factors motivating the emperor to legislate in 212, and that the edict consequently reflects his contemporary concerns and ambitions. On one level, it can be seen as a response to circumstances that Caracalla inherited as an emperor, rather than problems of his own making. Cassius Dio's explanation of the edict, namely that it was introduced in order to reap a massive tax yield to fund the emperor's financial profligacy, has been largely dismissed by modern scholars, owing to the unmistakeable hatred held by the author towards Caracalla. This investigation has argued, however, that it is possible to identify a fiscal initiative to raise capital if the Giessen text is studied in conjunction with other extant media. Of crucial importance to this consideration is the way in which the lacunose Giessen papyrus is reconstructed. If the traditionally problematic reference to the *dediticii* being disbarred from the grant of *civitas* is rejected and replaced with an allusion to additional privileges (*additicia*) being forbidden alongside the rights of citizenship, it can be shown that Caracalla was eager to expand his available tax base.

The numismatic evidence for the period further supports this hypothesis. It confirms, for example, that the emperor engaged in a policy of currency debasement. It would be a mistake, however, to interpret this as the result of a systemic economic crisis, especially since the evidence reveals that the early Severan period represented a high watermark in terms of building activity, funded by the capital raised through war booty and expropriations acquired by Septimius Severus. Rather than economic instability, I have argued that it is more likely that Caracalla required large quantities of physical coinage to fund his military reforms, as well as those undertaken by his father. Since both emperors introduced army pay rises within their programmes of reform, it is appropriate to interpret the fiscal element of the *Constitutio Antoniniana* as a response to a short-term problem of liquidity rather than economic collapse. This is even more convincing when it is noted that a key recipient of the capital raised from this augmented tax yield was the military treasury.

In addition to improving the financial lot of the soldiery, the Antonine Constitution can be seen as a response to a perennial problem of insufficient numbers enrolling for legionary service. By turning nearly every free individual across his empire into citizens, Caracalla had overcome the primary obstacle facing emperors in filling the levies, namely that the soldiers of the legions had to be fully enfranchised upon their enlistment. If this consequence of the *constitutio* is combined with the economic implications of the edict, it strongly suggests that the emperor was eager to reform his military apparatus radically, and that extending the franchise was considered the way to realise that ambition. This aspect of Caracalla's edict should come as little surprise, owing to his close identification with the soldiery and his imitation of Alexander the Great, not to mention his imperial ambitions against Parthia. But it is nevertheless a facet of the *constitutio* that, until recently, has been comparatively understudied.

It is impossible to assess the rationale underlying the *Constitutio Antoniniana* without considering the dynastic crisis that had been prompted by the death of Geta. Caracalla's adolescence and early adult life had been defined, to a large extent, by the fierce rivalry that he shared with his younger brother. While Dio is often a questionable source regarding the life of his bête-noir, his assessment that 'anybody could see that something terrible was bound to result' from the enmity seems all too plausible.[1] The shared principate between the brothers in 211 was a disaster, but Caracalla's eventual success in eliminating Geta nevertheless left him in a delicate position.

Never before had an incumbent emperor been murdered by his colleague in office. If this were not enough to threaten Caracalla's position, the act of fratricide also served to undermine the extensive programme of imperial propaganda engineered by his father, Septimius Severus, in which the brothers were repeatedly presented as a guarantee of imperial harmony and continuity following the bloody civil wars that had ensued from the assassinations of Commodus and Pertinax. The year 212 thus began with Caracalla facing the unenviable prospect of having to rule alone for the first time in his life, while being simultaneously compelled to consolidate and legitimise his precarious position publically. His solution to the problems facing him was to revolutionise the character of the Severan dynasty completely, offering an official version of the events that preceded his murder of Geta. The familial imagery that had been a keystone in Severus' later political communication was discarded in favour of iconography that presented the surviving emperor as a protector of the state whose reign was divinely sanctioned. Where Geta had once served as a symbolic guarantor of concord, he now became emblematic of an evil that Caracalla was compelled to destroy and triumph over. By condemning his brother's memory and reinventing his public image, the emperor had effectively re-written the history of the Severan dynasty and centred the regime around his persona alone.

It is into this context that the Antonine Constitution should be considered, since the edict can be seen to address Caracalla's imperial anxieties in a number of ways. The opening lines of the *constitutio* make it unmistakeably clear that the emperor intended the document to be viewed as an act of piety, a religious thanksgiving for the gods' protection against a plot on his life, concocted by his brother. This forms one facet of a wider religious programme that was complemented by a staggering array of divinely inspired numismatic iconography throughout his sole reign. The act of enfranchisement itself can also be seen to carry a religious dimension, since the grant of *civitas* appears to have been partially prompted by a Caracallan desire to achieve an effective *consensus universorum*, through which the favour of the gods would be ensured in perpetuity.

Further examination of the Giessen text reveals that the emperor also attempted to engage with his wider populace in different ways. The rhetoric

---

1 Dio 78.1.5.

employed by the emperor throughout the Antonine Constitution lends credence to the theory that Caracalla fostered a connection between himself and Alexander the Great. The resulting reaction among population groups in the eastern empire, manifesting in festivals and coinage connecting the emperor to the king, suggests that he was successful in laying claim to Alexander's legacy and the imagery of military virtue that accompanied it. The Alexander mythos formed only one facet of Caracalla's attempt to connect with his populace, though. On one level, he depicted his great edict as an extreme example of imperial *indulgentia*. More than this, however, the Antonine Constitution heralded an even more binding connection between the emperor and his new *cives*. I have argued that it is appropriate to view the edict as an act of patronage carried out on an unprecedented scale. While the expression of patronage had changed slightly from the Republic into the Principate, it is clear that the same expectation of loyalty and goodwill accompanied the gift of *beneficia*. By giving nearly every free person in the empire the rights of *civitas*, Caracalla had affected them on an individual level and had forged a personal connection with them at the very moment when the legitimacy of his sole reign might have been questioned. In this context, the *Constitutio Antoniniana* represents a powerful and elegant solution to the threat posed to Caracalla by dynastic instability and cool relations with the senatorial order in 212.

The Antonine Constitution is one of the most studied documents pertaining to the Roman imperial period, let alone the Severan dynasty. Much effort has been made to examine the value of the edict in the legal sphere, and to explore the legacy and long term effects of the document as the Principate progressed into the era of late antiquity. For too long, however, insufficient work has been done on the *constitutio* in its own historical milieu. And yet, it is only by studying the edict in a properly embedded context that we can ever come to a satisfactory understanding of Caracalla's decision to introduce this revolutionary legislation. I have endeavoured to present a variety of often interdependent factors and pressures that either inspired the emperor or compelled him to act in 212. That the *constitutio* was grounded in the volatile political environment of the Severan dynasty and was designed to address the emperor's crisis of legitimacy is beyond question, but it also allowed him to pursue a longer term military-economic agenda. The *Constitutio Antoniniana* was therefore a product of its time in every sense imaginable. What remains clear at the conclusion of this work, however, is that much of the controversy surrounding the Antonine Constitution stems from the collective impression of Caracalla's personality. A more nuanced discussion of Caracalla's life and regime is needed, removed from the stereotypical image of the 'bad emperor', if we are to continue to make progress in this regard.

Appendix

Text, Translation and Commentary of the Giessen Papyrus

Reconstruction of P. Giss. 40, I

1) [Αὐτοκράτωρ Καῖσαρ Μά]ρκο[ς Α]ὐρή[λιος Σεουῆρος Ἀ]ντωνῖνο[ς] Ε[ὐσεβὴ]ς λέγει
[πάντως εἰς τὸ θεῖον χρὴ] μᾶλλον ἀν[αφέρειν καὶ τὰ]ς αἰτίας κ[α]ὶ [λογι]σμοὺς
[δικαίως δ'ἂν κἀγὼ τοῖς θ]εοῖς τ[οῖ]ς ἀθ[αν]άτοις εὐχαριστήσα[ι]μι ὅτι τῆς τοιαύτη[ς]
[ἐπιβουλῆς γενομένης σφο]ν ἐμὲ συν[ετ]ήρησαν τοιγαροῦν νομίζω [ο]ὕτω με –
5) [γαλοπρεπῶς καὶ εὐσεβ]ῶς δύ[να]σθαι τῇ μεγαλειότητι αὐτῶν τὸ ἱκανὸν ποι –
[εῖν, εἰ τοὺς ἐν τῇ ἀρχῇ ὀσ]άκις ἐὰν ὑ[πε]ισέλθ[ωσ]ιν εἰς τοὺς ἐμοὺς ἀν[θρ]ώπους
[ὡς Ῥωμαίους εἰς τὰ ἱερὰ τῶν] θεῶν συνει[σ]ενέγ[κοιμ]ι Δίδω[μ]ι τοί[ν]υν ἅπα–
[σι τοῖς κατὰ τὴν Ῥωμαϊκ]ὴν οἰκουμένην π[ολειτ]είαν Ῥωμ[αί]ων [μ]ένοντος
[τοῦ δικαίου τῶν πολιτευμ]άτων χωρ[ὶς] τῶν [ἀδδ]ειτικίων Ὀ[φ]είλει [γ]ὰρ τὸ
10) [πλῆθος οὐ μόνον τἆλλα συνυπομέ]νειν πάντα ἀ[λλ]ὰ ἤδη κ[α]ὶ τῇ νίκῃ ἐνπεριει –
[λῆφθαι Τοῦτο δὲ τὸ διάτ]αγμα ἐ[ξαπ]λώσει [τὴν] μεγαλειότητα [το]ῦ Ῥωμα[ί]
[ων δήμου συμβαίνει γὰρ τὴν αὐτή]ν περὶ τοὺς [ἄλλο]υς γεγενῆσθα[ι] ἤπερ δ[ι]α–
[πρέπουσιν ἀνέκαθεν Ῥωμαῖοι τιμῇ κα]ταλειφ[θέντων μηδέν]ων τῶ[ν] ἑκάστης
[χώρας ἐν οἰκουμένῃ ἀπολιτεύτων ἢ ἀτιμ]ήτω[ν Ἀπὸ δὲ τῶν] π[ρ]οσ[όδων τῶν νῦν]
15) [ὑπερχουσῶν συντελούντων, ἅπερ ἐκελεύσ]θη [παρὰ Ῥωμαίων ἀπὸ τοῦ κα ἔτους,][1]
[ὡς δίκαιον ἐκ τῶν διαταγμάτων καὶ ἐπιστολ]ῶ[ν, ἃ ἐξεδόθη ὑφ' ἡμῶν τε]
[καὶ τῶν ἡμετέρων προγόνων Προετέθη ....]

1 W₃K: [Σεβαστὸς Ἀ]ντονῖνο[ς] O: Σ[εβαστὸ]ς λέγει MBSS₂WHW₂

2 WH: ἀν[αβαλόμενον τὰ]ς αἰτίας MS: ἀν[τὰ]ς αἰτίας W₃K: λ[ογι]σμοὺ[ς] S₂WHW₂
W₃OK: λ[ιβ]έλλου[ς] MS

3 WHO: [ζητεῖν, ὅπως ἂν τοῖς θ]εοῖς MS: [τίνι ἂν τρόπῳ ἀξίως τοῖς θ]εοῖς S₂W₂

4 SWHW₂: [συμφορᾶς γενομένης] B: [ἐπιβουλῆς ἄφνω γενομένης] W₃O

5 W₂: [γάλως καὶ φιλανθρώπ]ως S: [γαλομερῶς καὶ θεοπρεπ]ῶς WH: [γαλομερῶς ἂν καὶ εὐσεβ]ῶς W₃O

6 S: [εἰ τοσάκις μυρίους ὀσ]άκις S₂WHW₂: [εἰ τοὺς ξένους ὀσ]άκις M: [εἰ τοὺς βαρβάρους ὀσ]άκις B: [εἰ νῦν ἅπαντας, καὶ ὀσ]άκις W₃O

7 WH: [ἰσοτίμους εἰς τὰ ἱερὰ τῶ]ν θεῶν SW₂: [καὶ ἄλλοι, εἰς τὰ ἱερὰ τῶ]ν θεῶν O: [εἰς τὰς θρησκείας τῶ]ν θεῶν M: [εἰς θρησκείας τῶν ἡμετέρω]ν θεῶν W₃: τοί[ν]υν ἅπα- MBSS₂WHW₂: τοῖ[ς σ]υνάπα- W₃OK

---

[1] The reconstruction of lines 15–17 relies heavily on the edition of Heichelheim (1941) 10–22. Although his suggestions to fill the lacunae are undoubtedly eloquent, they are ultimately speculative, and are primarily included here in the interests of completeness.

8   H: [σιν ὅσοι ἐὰν ὦσι κατὰ τὴ]ν οἰκουμένην S₂W₂: [σιν ξένοις τοῖς κατὰ τὴ]ν οἰκουμένην M: [σιν ἐπηλύταις τοῖς κατὰ τ]ὴν οἰκουμένην B: [σιν τοῖς οὖσι κατὰ τ]ὴν οἰκουμένην S: [σιν τοῖς κατοικοῦσιν τὴ]ν οἰκουμένην W: [σιν ἐν τῇ ἀρχῇ μου κατὰ τ]ὴν οἰκουμένην W₃O: [σιν κατὰ τ]ὴν οἰκουμένην K: π[ολειτ]είαν HW₃K: π[ολιτ]είαν MBSS₂WW₂

9   W₃OK: [παντὸς γένους πολιτευμ]άτων M: [τῷ φίσκῳ τοῦ λόγου ἀπαραβ]άτως B: [πολιτικοῦ σφισιν ἀπαραβ]άτως S: [ξένου οὐδενὸς τῶν πολιτευμ]άτων S₂: [οὐδενὸς ἐκτὸς τῶν πολιτευμ]άτων W: [δὲ ξενου οὐδενὸς τῶν ταγμ]άτων H: [οὐδενὸς τῶν πρὶν ἐλασσωμ]άτων W₂: [ἀδδ]ειτικίων W₃: [δε]δειτικίων MBSS₂WH: [δη]δειτικίων W₂: [ ]δειτικίων K

10 WH: [οὐ μόνον συμπο]νεῖν S: [οὐ μόνον συνκινδυνε]ύειν S₂: deest O

11 MSS₂: [τοῦτο δὲ τὸ ἐμὸν διάτ]αγμα W: [τοῦτο δὲ τὸ ἐμαυτοῦ διάτ]αγμα H: ἐ[ξαπ]λώσει WH: ἐ[κδ]ελώσει S: ἐ[ξο]λώσει S₂: deest O

12 WH: [κελεύω δὲ τὴν αὐτὴν χάρι]ν B: [ων δήμου διὰ τὸ τὴν αὐτὴν τάξι]ν S: [ων δήμου μετὰ τὸ τὴν ἴσην τιμὴ]ν S₂: deest O

13 WH: [τὴν εὐγένειαν Ῥωμαῖοι] S₂: deest MBSW₂W₃OK

14 H: deest MBSS₂WW₂W₃OK

15 H: deest MBSS₂WW₂W₃OK

    H: deest MBSS₂WW₂W₃OK

17 H: deest MBSS₂WW₂W₃OK

M   Meyer, P. M. 1920: *Juristische Papyri: Erklärung von Urkunden zur Einführung in die Juristische Papyruskunde*, Berlin.

B   Bickermann, E. 1926: *Das Edikt des Kaisers Caracalla in P. Giss. 40*, Diss., Berlin.

S   Schönbauer, E. 1931: 'Reichsrecht gegen Volksrecht? Studien über die Bedeutung der Constitutio Antoniniana für die römische Rechtsentwicklung', ZRG 51, 277–335.

S₂ Stroux, J. 1933: 'Die Constitutio Antoniniana', *Philologus* 88, 272–295.

W   Wilhelm, A. 1934: 'Die Constitutio Antoniniana', *American Journal of Archaeology* 38, 178–80.

H   Heichelheim, F. M. 1941: The Text of the "Constitutio Antoniniana" and the Three Other Decrees of the Emperor Caracalla Contained in Papyrus Gissensis 40, *Journal of Egyptian Archaeology* 26, 10–22.

W₂ Weissert, D. 1963: 'Bemerkungen zum Wortlaut des P. Giss. 40 I (Constitutio Antoniniana) Z. 1–9', *Hermes* 91, 239–50.

W₃ Wolff, H. 1976: *Die Constitutio Antoniniana und Papyrus Gissensis 40 I*, Diss., Köln.

O   Oliver, J. H. 1989: *Greek Constitutions of Early Roman Emperors from Inscriptions and Papyri*, Philadelphia.

K   Kuhlmann, P. A. 1994: *Die Giessener Literarischen Papyri und die Caracalla-Erlasse*, Giessen.

Translation

The Emperor Caesar Marcus Aurelius Severus Antoninus Pius decrees: It is altogether necessary to attribute the causes and reasons [of recent events] to the divine. I, personally, would rightly thank the immortal gods, since although such a conspiracy [as that of Geta] has occurred, they have watched over me and protected me. I think that I am able, both magnificently and piously, to do something fitting to the gods' majesty, if I manage to bring [all] those in the empire, who constitute my people, to the temples of the gods as Romans. I therefore give everyone in the Roman world the Roman citizenship: preserving customary law, without additional privileges. It is necessary for the masses not only to share in our burden, but also to be included in victory. This decree will spread the magnificence of the Roman people. For it now happens that the same greatness has occurred for everyone, by the honour in which the Romans have been preeminent since time immemorial, with no-one from any country in the world being left stateless or without honour. Referring to the taxes that exist at present, all are due to pay those that have been imposed upon the Romans from the beginning of their twenty-first year [of age], as it is the law, according to the edicts and rescripts issued by us and our ancestors. Displayed publically ...

General Observations and Dating

Even a cursory glance at the document reveals that *P. Giss.* 40 has suffered extensive wear and damage, most notably on the left-hand side where the text of the *constitutio* is written. From comparison of the left and (largely complete) right sides of the papyrus, it can be estimated that around one third of the upper left side of the document is missing. The damage in this area is compounded by a large vertical tear in the middle of the surviving papyrus which has obliterated yet more script. The lower left-hand section of *P. Giss. 40* is in an even more damaged state. The large tear that has destroyed some of the upper left side extends further into the papyrus and has left only around thirty characters of text remaining. Smaller localised tears and holes in areas suggest that the papyrus has suffered worm-damage, while areas where the top-layer of the document is damaged (more visible on the right side of the papyrus) are the result of damage sustained in the document's afterlife when the museum attempted to glaze it.[2]

The other visible form of damage on *P. Giss. 40* is in the form of dark patches spread over the surface of the papyrus, especially in the upper-right quadrant. This is indicative of water damage sustained in February 1945, when the papyrus was being held in the safe of the Dresdner Bank.[3] This has caused the felt back-layer, added to the artefact by the museum, to become fused to the papyrus. Considering the severely

---

2   Kuhlmann (1994) 1.
3   Kuhlmann (1994) 2.

damaged nature of the Giessen papyrus, it is hardly surprising that much of the academic focus directed towards the document has concerned the necessary reconstruction of the Greek text.

Despite the severe damage to the artefact, however, the availability of high-resolution photographs of the papyrus from the *Giessener Papyri- und Ostraka-Datenbank* has facilitated a far more detailed analysis of the text than was ever possible in the past. The text of *P. Giss. 40* is presented in a legible, cursive script of Koine Greek. Meyer claimed that the text was of a 'careful, clerical' nature, while Kuhlmann has concluded that the papyrus is business-like in appearance and that the script is 'regular and aesthetic'.[4] The characters are clear and of a regular size, 0.3–0.4cm wide in the majority of cases, often using capitalised versions of characters and lunate sigmas (c). In the course of the text, there are larger spaces between the different sections of the documents to allow ease of legibility.[5] This feature permits a more confident estimate regarding the number of missing letters in the various lacunae. The script appears to be of a formal style found throughout the second and third centuries CE. It does not exhibit the elongated chancery stylisation of some official papyri of this period, particularly from the Alexandrian Chancery (*P. Berol. inv. 11532*, for example); the rather more rounded characters group this papyri with those of a bureaucratic context, the attractive calligraphic script reminiscent of literary papyri.[6]

In spite of its aesthetic quality, there are minor irregularities.[7] There are numerous ligatures throughout the papyrus. The appearance of iota varies from a small compact line to a larger, sweeping version that impacts on the line of script below. Epsilons are written sometimes as tall, narrow characters with three short but equidistant bars, while in other places they are written with an extended central bar, joining to other letters. Omicron is presented in a very small form, often higher in the line than other letters, and the letter π is notable for being considerably wider than the majority of the other characters.[8]

Some of the oddities, in particular that of the omicron being reduced in size, exhibit certain traits of the more simplistic style that was to evolve throughout the later third century and from the time of Diocletian into the 'upright ogival majuscule' style of writing that was common throughout late antiquity and the Byzantine era.[9] This apparent combination of stylistic features allows us to assign a time period for this

---

4   Meyer (1910) 25; Kuhlmann (1994) 8–9.
5   *P. Giss.* 40, l.7 for example. Also see Kuhlmann (1994) 216.
6   Cavallo and Maehler (2008) 123.
7   Kuhlmann (1994) 215.
8   Kuhlmann (1994) 215–16, draws attention to these irregularities in more detail.
9   Cavallo & Maehler (2008) 131–2.

artefact with more confidence. The style of writing, when combined with the subject matter of the text, means that a dating of the early third century CE is convincing.

Commentary

Line 1: From the surviving script alone, it is relatively clear that this line is a formulaic list of imperial titles introducing the emperor making the decree. This edition has opted to restore the penultimate word in the line as Εὐσεβής rather than Σεβαστός. The damage to the papyrus around the initial letter of the word makes it difficult to decipher the character beyond all doubt. The shape does bear a close similarity to the larger scale lunate sigmas found throughout the text. Magnification of the high-resolution image of the papyrus, however, appears to reveal a trace of ink concurrent with the middle bar of a capitalised epsilon.[10]

Line 2: The beginning of this line has prompted a variety of different wordings, although the sentiment remains roughly the same. The attribution of certain events to divine powers by Caracalla is repeated from Stroux onwards. This edition supports the version offered by Wilhelm and later Heichelheim, a good compromise between the earlier edition of Stroux and the later one of Weissert. Owing to the visibility of –σμους at the end of the line, it is palaeographically impossible to accept the earlier versions of Meyer, Bickermann and Schönbauer. The suggestion of λογισμούς by Stroux is far more acceptable. This conjecture was supported by Schubart in addition to Wilhelm and Heichelheim, becoming the traditionally accepted reconstruction.[11] In this reconstruction, αἰτίας κ[α]ὶ [λογι]σμοὺς translates as the reasons and causes of recent events to which Caracalla was referring, thus making any attempt to restore λιβέλλους unwarranted.

Line 3: Similar to the second line, there is an underlying sentiment that is brought out in all of the reconstructions. The feeling of gratitude expressed by Caracalla is shown by the nearly complete survival of εὐχαριστήσαιμι ('I would thank'). Owing to the generally literary feel of the text, the slightly more eloquent version offered by Wilhelm and

---

10 A search of the PHI Greek Inscription Database reveals that Εὐσεβής (= Pius) was a title used in relation to Caracalla, usually positioned before Σεβαστός whenever the two titles were used together: see *Apollonia Salbake* 4 (= Robert, *La Carie* II. no.149), *Magnesia* 297 (= *CIL* III 13689) and *Stratonikeia* 91 (= *IStratonikeia* 811) for three such uses of the title. Also see Bureth (1964) 102–4. Kuhlmann (1994) 222–3, has suggested that this usage of the title may explain why Caracallan documents are often confused with those of Antoninus Pius. This confusion can be found even in late antiquity, when the edict was erroneously attributed to Antoninus Pius in Justinian's *Novellae* (78.5) and to Marcus Aurelius by Aurelius Victor (*Caes.* 16.12).

11 Schubart, (1940) 31–38.

Heichelheim is, again, perhaps the closest to the spirit of the original. The genitive τῆς τοιαύτη[ς] is part of a genitive absolute construction, which refers to an unspecified incident that had taken place in the recent past. This event is most probably a conspiracy (ἐπιβουλῆς γενομένης), mentioned in the following line.

Line 4: Of all the editions cited above, Meyer is the only one not to stress the feeling of a struggle or misfortune that Caracalla has been saved from. This edition's text is based upon the versions offered by Schönbauer and Wilhelm, beginning with ἐπιβουλῆς. The alternative version offered by Heichelheim in which the upsilon is omitted is not incorrect, since both essentially infer an attempt made against Caracalla's life, but ἐπιβουλή conveys a more secretive and conspiratorial feeling that is better in keeping with Caracalla's reputed statements in the aftermath of Geta's murder. This version is closer to a passage in Dio where the author described Caracalla addressing the troops in an attempt to persuade them that he was, in fact, the victim of an attempted coup d'état.[12] While we must be careful not to allow Dio's text to influence our reconstruction excessively, it is tempting to imagine that he would have seen the original edict and allowed it to colour the language used in his later account of events.

Line 5: In his commentary, Oliver concluded that it was not possible to discern confidently the two adverbs employed on the papyrus to describe the emperor's great act of gratitude to the gods for saving him.[13] While this edition concurs with Weissert's use of the adverb εὐσεβῶς in the second position, I have opted to agree with Meyer and Stroux that the adverb μεγαλοπρεπῶς is more appropriate for the word at the beginning of the line. Both μεγαλομερής and μεγαλοπρεπής have been used to mean 'magnificence' but the latter appears to carry an added sense of an act befitting a great man, an inference that may be attached to Caracalla's position as emperor.[14]

Line 6: This edition has opted not to accept the version preferred by Stroux, Wilhelm, Heichelheim and Weissert, since their reconstructions leave a vague impression of the people that the emperor intended to bring to the temples of the gods as Roman citizens (see line seven, below).[15] The version by Schönbauer, however, maintains the idea

---

12 Dio (77.3.1) employs the middle voice perfect participle of ἐπιβουλεύω: ὁ δ' Ἀντωνῖνος καίπερ ἑσπέρας οὔσης τὰ στρατόπεδα κατέλαβε, διὰ πάσης τῆς ὁδοῦ κεκραγὼς ὡς *ἐπιβεβουλευμένος* καὶ κινδυνεύων (emphasis added).
13 Oliver (1989) 503.
14 For the adverbial use of μεγαλοπρεπής, see: Hdt. 6.128; Xen. *Anab.* 1.4.17.
15 It is true that one might expect the decree to avoid specifics, owing to the intended impression of grandeur that surrounded it, but this reconstruction is still, perhaps, a little overly complicated.

of the vast scale of Caracalla's plans while at the same time providing a more precise notion of their intended extent. Oliver has noted that the phrase ἐν τῇ ἀρχῇ appearing in the line was again similarly used by Dio when describing the scale of the *constitutio*.[16]

Line 7: All of the reconstructions of this line bear connotations of masses being brought together in religious devotion, further describing Caracalla's debt of gratitude outlined in lines five and six. This edition favours the more pointed reconstruction of Wilhelm and Heichelheim, with its emphasis on the importance of bringing all those under the emperor's authority to the temples as Romans rather than merely assorted subject peoples.[17]

There is a minor disagreement regarding the nature of the final two words of the line, where Caracalla declares that the gift (that he has yet to disclose) will be given to all under his power. The traditionally accepted version only acknowledges one letter space in the lacuna near the end of the line, leaving a reconstruction τοί[ν]υν ἅπα | σιν. This has been challenged by both Wolff and Kuhlmann who have claimed that there is space for two letters in the lacuna, offering the alternative reconstruction τοί[ς σ]υνάπα | σιν. The space does appear to be large enough to fit two lunate sigmas, but it is also possible that the scribe simply left a slightly larger separation between the two words for ease of legibility.

This edition has therefore opted for the more traditional restoration of τοίνυν. The appearance of an inferential particle is the better semantic choice since it refers back to the events that prompted Caracalla's edict rather than leaving the great gift of citizenship entirely separate from its context. The causative link that τοίνυν creates between the two sentences at this juncture makes it the more naturally acceptable choice.

Line 8: It is in this line that the grant of Roman citizenship is outlined. The reconstruction of the lacuna in the middle of the extant script as π[ολιτ]είαν is nearly universally accepted in the different reconstructions of this line.[18] This is of crucial importance, as acceptance of this phrase equates to an agreement that this text is a record of the universal citizenship decree. This edition concurs with the restoration of Heichelheim who is consistent in his emphasis of the *Romanitas* of the grant.

It should be noted that in maintaining the potential *Romanitas* of the edict through the wording τοῖς κατὰ τὴν Ῥωμαϊκὴν οἰκουμένην, this text echoes the Latin description

---

16   Dio 78.9.5; Oliver (1989) 503.
17   This reconstruction fits well with Ando's claim that Caracalla sought *consensus* in religious worship. For more on the matter of *consensus*, see Ando (2000) 73–276.
18   Oliver (1989) 504. Wolff has read the first letter of this word as a *mu*, consequently producing a different restoration. This would fit with his general thesis that *P. Giss.* 40 does not contain the text of the *Constitutio Antoniniana*.

of the decree outlined by Ulpian, who may be safely assumed to have been familiar with the original.[19] The jurist was explicit that the edict affected those *in orbe Romano qui sunt*.[20] The reconstruction of the participle μένοντος at the end of the line is also universally accepted but will be discussed below in connection with line nine.

Line 9: The text of line nine outlines the nature and scale of Caracalla's mass enfranchisement. The majority of the controversy regarding this section of *P. Giss.* 40 regards the prepositional phrase (χωρίς + genitive) contained at the end of the line, a small lacuna obscuring the pivotal word, currently reading only as [...]ειτικιων. In his original reconstruction of the text, Meyer concluded that this word ought to be restored as δεδιτικίων.[21] This is a Hellenised version of the Latin *dediticii*, a term used by Gaius to describe population groups subjugated by Rome via an official act of surrender (*deditio*).[22] While the Greek spelling has been questioned, with δηδειτικίων becoming the preferred option, this reconstruction represented the *communis opinio* for many years.[23]

Despite the traditional academic support for a reconstruction including mention of the *dediticii*, however, it was far from a perfect answer. If the reconstruction of δηδειτικίων was palaeographically correct, it might appear to mean that Caracalla's extension of the franchise was not universal. This immediately presents a dilemma, since the only extant contemporary source that actively described the scale of the *constitutio*, that of Ulpian, mentions no such exception or caveat to the edict.[24] It would seem careless of a jurist of Ulpian's character to omit such an important legal detail.[25]

The potential contradiction in the ancient evidence led some to question the nature of the exclusion inferred by the prepositional phrase χωρίς + genitive. One explanation offered in the past is that the text contained on *P. Giss.* 40 did not, in fact,

---

19 Honoré (2002) 24. Honoré claimed that Ulpian would have advocated the extension of citizenship affected by Caracalla.
20 Dig. 1.5.17. Also see Ando (2016) 8.
21 Meyer (1910) 30–33.
22 Gaius, *Inst.* 1.14. This group is sometimes referred to as the *peregrini dediticii* to distinguish them from a group of similar legal status found later, freedmen convicted of serious crimes during their time in slavery under the terms of the *lex Aelia Sentia* (see: Gaius, *Inst.*, 1.13). For more on these groups, see Rocco (2010) 134, n.16; Wirth (1997) 32–34.
23 Weissert (1963) 239–50. This reconstruction has even been accepted in more recent years. For selected examples, see Moatti (2016) 90–92; Van Minnen (2016) 218–20; Rocco (2010) 134.
24 *Dig.* 1.5.17, see above n.3. Similarly, there is no mention of any exceptions to Caracalla's edict in the course of Dio's hostile summary of the grant (Dio 78.9.5–6).
25 Unless, of course, the compilers of the *Digest* later removed any mention of the *dediticii* instead.

make reference to the grant of *civitas* itself, but rather to some associated grant or supplement.[26] The problem with this, however, is that, without any clear analogies that can be drawn from other texts, such a hypothesis relies upon imagination and speculation.[27]

The inescapably conjectural nature of these analyses has led others to doubt the very existence of any mention of *dediticii* in connection with the *constitutio* text. Benario, for example, has voiced his scepticism, pointing to the silence of Dio on the subject: 'if a significant portion of the population had been barred from the enjoyment of the emperor's gift, Dio would, in all likelihood, not have failed to mention it, since he was a bitter enemy of the ruler.'[28] Whilst the 'unabashed hatred' of Dio for Caracalla is well-known, one must be careful not to exaggerate or assume the intentions of any ancient source.[29]

It is safer simply to observe that if, in the course of the *Institutes*, Gaius was correct that the *dediticii* were completely bereft of political identity and could never, under any condition, hope to attain the rights of Roman citizenship, then there must have been as little requirement to stipulate their exclusion from the terms of the Antonine Constitution as there would have been for the slave population. The idea that Caracalla's edict made specific mention of one population group, whose ineligibility would already likely have been automatically assumed, seems a rather tautological explanation of the status quo.[30] Moreover, the fact remains that the fundamental existence of δηδειτικίων in the ninth line of *P. Giss.* 40 is far from assured; the hapax legomenon forms a problematic and unsatisfying suggestion for the complement of χωρίς.[31] With this in mind, it is appropriate to seek an alternative explanation regarding this area of the text preserved on the Giessen papyrus.

The publication of materials relating to the Antonine document known as the *Tabula Banasitana* has changed the nature of this debate and allows for an analysis of the *Constitutio Antoniniana* removed from the difficulties presented by the *dediticii*. The *tabula* is a bronze tablet containing three letters dating to the latter half of the second century CE, discovered near the ancient settlement of Banasa in Morocco in 1957.[32] The first document is a letter, dating to *c.* 168, which was addressed from the

---

26 This hypothesis has been championed most famously by Sherwin-White (1973a) 380, but has also been taken up by Jones (1936) 223–235, and Préaux (1953) 218.
27 Lukaszewicz (1990) 97–99. Also see Kuhlmann (2012) 49.
28 Benario (1954) 188.
29 For more on Dio's fierce hatred of Caracalla, see: Millar (1964) 150. For further discussion of Dio's assessment of the *constitutio*, see Chapter 2.
30 Lukaszewicz (1990) 96–98.
31 Lukaszewicz (1990) 95.
32 *IAM* 2.1, 94 = *AE* 1961, 142. For an annotated edition of the Tabula of Banasa, see: Oliver (1972) 336–40.

emperors Marcus Aurelius and Lucius Verus to the governor of Mauretania Tingitana and concerned the enfranchisement of a local notable known as Julian the Zegrensian (who had petitioned for a grant of citizenship despite not being the leader of his community) and his family. The second letter, dated early in 177 and from Marcus Aurelius and Commodus, was addressed to the provincial governor and concerned the citizenship of the family of the new chieftain of the Zegrensians, another Julian (who is sometimes assumed to be the son of the subject of the previous letter preserved in the inscription).[33] The final document in the tablet is an extract from a *commentarius*, which recorded the grant of *civitas* to the younger Julian, and would have made the conferral valid.

Of particular importance to any analysis of the Antonine Constitution is the way in which certain qualifications were placed upon the grant of *civitas* to the Mauretanian and his descendants in the course of the earlier *tabula*. The grant of citizenship in this case was applied both *salvo iure gentis* and *sine diminutione tributorum et vectigalium populi et fisci*.[34] The first of these clauses states that the grant of *civitas Romanorum* would not exclude the recipient from the legal framework and obligations of their parent communities, thereby preserving customary law (*ius gentium*). The second of the clauses found in the *tabula* forms a clear statement that the newly enfranchised individual would not enjoy the fiscal immunity experienced by citizens under the early years of the Principate, and would be fully obligated to make tax payments.[35]

A similarity between the Latin of the *Tabula Banasitana* and the Greek of the *Constitutio Antoniniana* texts can be identified when reconstructing the controversial eighth and ninth lines of Caracalla's edict. The modern consensus on this portion of the text is that the clause immediately following the grant of *civitas* in the papyrus ought to read: μένοντος τοῦ δικαίου τῶν πολιτευμάτων.[36] The underlying sentiment here, that even the mass enfranchisement of 212 honoured the existence of local custom, seems to form an easily identifiable Greek equivalent of *salvo iure gentis*.[37]

The existence of these Latin formulae tempering the grant of citizenship allows for another interpretation to be made of the problematic ninth line of *P. Giss.* 40. If the μένοντος clause bridging lines eight and nine of *P. Giss.* 40 is agreed to form a Hellenised

---

33   Oliver (1972) 338; Sherwin-White (1973b) 88.
34   *IAM* 2.1, 94. l.37.
35   Sherwin-White (1973b) 86–98.
36   Kuhlmann (2012) 47; see above for translation.
37   Sasse (1958) 48–58, has shown that the genitive participle μένοντος, found in the eighth line of *P. Giss.* 40, is relatively common in Greek legal texts, and that in at least forty-seven cases, the construction is identical to that of the Giessen papyrus, with the participle employed in a genitive absolute construction. In this case, it can clearly be seen to mirror the Latin ablative absolute construction in the *salvo* clause of the *Tabula Banasitana*.

construction preserving the local *ius gentium*, then it is logical that the exclusionary clause which follows it should similarly mirror the Latin construction found in the *Tabula Banasitana*, which emphasised the newly enfranchised citizens' liability to pay taxes. In every edition of the *constitutio* text that includes mention of the *dediticii*, the Greek χωρίς is always translated meaning 'except'. An alternative translation for this term, however, would be 'without'.[38] This alternative translation would certainly seem to mirror the Antonine document, with χωρίς representing a Hellenised version of *sine*.

An objection to this translation of χωρίς, in connection to the *dediticii*, has been voiced by Lukaszewicz, since he believes that such a wording would infer a complete denial of the continued existence of the *dediticii* as a political class.[39] This problem can easily be overcome, though, by removing the *dediticii* from the equation altogether. In the years since the discovery of the *constitutio* text, there have been attempts made to reconstruct the text of the Giessen papyrus without making any reference to the *dediticii*.[40] Unfortunately, however, the majority of these attempts were made long before the discovery of the Antonine *tabula* and, as a result, are almost entirely conjectural, often plagued by their own grammatical and palaeographical problems.[41]

If χωρίς is understood to mean 'without' rather than 'except', an attempt can to be made to assess whether the end of the ninth line of *P. Giss.* 40 is equivalent to the Latin *sine diminutione tributorum et vectigalium populi et fisci* found in the *Tabula Banasitana*.[42] Instead of δηδειτικίων, it has been suggested that the lacuna might be better reconstructed as αδδειτικίων.[43] Whilst admittedly a hapax legomenon in its own right, it is no more controversial than δηδειτικίων.

The adjectival noun, translating as 'additional', may be understood to make reference to the system of fiscal *immunitas* enjoyed historically by citizens under the earlier Principate. Kuhlmann disagrees that the χωρίς τῶν ἀδδειτικίων clause represents a direct transliteration of *sine diminutione tributorum et vectigalium populi et fisci*, however, doubting that it makes specific reference to fiscal immunity alone.[44] He questions how far the sentiment from the Latin construction can be inferred from one word alone, arguing that if Oliver was correct in his assumption regarding the focus of *additicia*, then it must represent a hitherto unrecognised Greek *terminus technicus*.[45]

---

38 Lukaszewicz (1990) 98.
39 Lukaszewicz (1990) 98–99.
40 Böhm (1963) 278–355; Heichelheim (1941) 10–22; Laqueur (1927) 15–28.
41 For a detailed objection to some of the earlier attempts to remove the *dediticii* from the text of the edict, see Lukaszewicz (1990) 99.
42 Wolff (1977) 99–102.
43 Kuhlmann (2012) 48–50; Oliver (1989) 504.
44 Kuhlmann (1994) 237. For examples of the term in the Latin corpus which Kuhlmann identifies, see *Dig.* 50.16.98.1 and Tert. *Resurr.* 52.
45 Van Minnen (2016) 219; Kuhlmann (1994) 236–37.

This conclusion would ultimately infer that the χωρίς clause found in the *constitutio* text was, in fact, a very general one designed to facilitate and overcome any short term problems that the Roman authorities might encounter in the aftermath of such a mass act of enfranchisement. While I agree with Kuhlmann that the precise text of the edict must be read in this general sense, among all of the innumerable benefits that the Giessen papyrus might theoretically make reference to in the controversial clause, fiscal privileges were probably among the foremost concerns of both Caracalla and his newly enfranchised populace.[46] The sense of Caracalla's edict thus moves away from the idea of a grant in which a specific population group was forbidden access to the benefits of Roman *civitas*. Instead, the *constitutio* text can be interpreted as a more formulaic piece of legislation, one in which the newly enfranchised were simultaneously assured that their new legal status would not preclude their engagement with local customary law in the provinces, while being reminded that their enfranchisement would result in an obligation to pay taxes levied against the citizen population.

The revised wording obviously does not meld flawlessly with the Latin construction seen in the text of the *Tabula Banasitana*, but this is hardly surprising owing to the nature of the transliteration process from Latin into Greek.[47] Until the discovery of other materials relating to the *constitutio*, students of this document must accept that linguistic questions and arguments will persist.[48] The removal of the troublesome *dediticii* from the wording of this document, however, would appear to fit more comfortably with the rest of the extant evidence, none of which makes any reference to a population group disbarred from Caracalla's otherwise universal edict.[49]

Line 10: Although far less controversial than the previous line, the appearance of νίκη in this line has prompted disagreement on what is being alluded to. Johnson disputed any notion that the 'victory' being referred to was in connection to the assassination of Geta in late 211. He advocated a theory linking it to the German campaign of 213, instead.[50] Such a conclusion would, of course, have the resulting effect of questioning the date of the *constitutio*, inferring a promulgation date of 213 at the earliest, rather than the preceding year, as is most widely accepted. There is a further fundamental

---

46 This hypothesis is considered in greater detail in Chapter 2.
47 Oliver (1989) 500.
48 Lukaszewicz (1990) 98–101.
49 In addition to the contemporaneous legal evidence, the idea that the *Constitutio Antoniniana* was an entirely universal one is maintained in later literature. Sidonius Apollinaris, for example, claimed that: 'none but the barbarian and slave is foreign' (*Ep.* 1.6.2).
50 Johnson (1961) 226, n.2. Also see Oliver (1989) 501. This hypothesis has been proven incorrect in recent years, see Van Minnen (2016).

APPENDIX   151

problem with Johnson's hypothesis, however, in that he has attempted to assign a particular event to an area of the edict which is clearly rhetorical. The appearance of 'victory' in this line is incontrovertible, but this edition favours a more general interpretation, in keeping with the literary tone of the text, rather than referring to any episode specifically.

Lines 11–13: These lines have prompted little variation between the various scholars who reconstructed the papyrus. The general idea of a spread in the greatness or magnificence of the Romans is preserved through the survival of μεγαλειότητα (μεγαλειότης = majesty) in line eleven and γεγενῆσθαι in line twelve. Line thirteen signals the beginning of the worst areas of damage to the papyrus, with significantly fewer characters surviving in this and subsequent lines when compared to those above. The reconstruction assigning the spread of greatness to a timeless Roman honour is accepted both by Wilhelm and Heichelheim.[51]

Lines 14–17: These lines are so damaged that only Heichelheim has attempted any significant reconstruction. In line fourteen, he continues the notion of the spread of Rome's magnificence by suggesting that the decree stated that no one would be left stateless (ἀπολίτευτος) or dishonoured (ἀτίμητος). The latter would appear to be a fair reconstruction, fitting with the three extant letters in that section of the line, but lines 15–17 are based on so few surviving characters that, although interesting and eloquent solutions to the lacunae have been proposed, we are faced with the inescapable conclusion that we cannot be certain regarding the content of this line or any subsequent in the first column of *P. Giss. 40*.

---

51   Stroux follows a similar line, but employs notion of nobility (εὐγένεια) rather than honour.

ILLUSTRATION 1   *Giessen, University Library, P. Giss. 40 / P. Giss. inv. 15.*

APPENDIX

Bibliography

Adler, A. (2012), 'Cassius Dio's Agrippa-Maecenas Debate: an operational code analysis', *AJP* 133: 477–520.
Alföldy, G. (1968), *Die Hilfstruppen der römischen Provinz Germania inferior*, Dusseldorf.
Alston, R. (1994), 'Roman Military Pay from Caesar to Diocletian', *JRS* 84: 113–23.
Amelotti, M. (1995), 'Reichsrecht, Volksrecht, Provinzialrecht: Vecchi problem e nuovi documenti', *SDHI* 211: 213–14.
Ando, C. (2000), *Imperial Ideology and Provincial Loyalty in the Roman Empire*, London.
Ando, C. (2011), *Law, Language and Empire in the Roman Tradition*, Philadelphia.
Ando, C. (2012), *Imperial Rome, AD 193–284: the critical century*, Edinburgh.
Ando, C. (2016), 'Sovereignty, Territoriality and Universalism in the Aftermath of Caracalla', in C. Ando (ed.), *Citizenship and Empire in Europe, 200–1900: The Antonine Constitution after 1900 Years* [Stuttgart, 2016]: 7–28.
Andreau, J. (2002), 'Twenty Years after Moses I. Finley's *The Ancient Economy*', in W. Scheidel and S. von Redden (eds), *The Ancient Economy* [Edinburgh, 2002]: 35–52.
Arangio-Ruiz, V. (1949), 'Chirographi di Soldati', *Studi in onore di Siro Solazzi*, Naples.
Arrizabalaga y Prado, L. (2010), *The Emperor Elagabalus, fact or fiction?*, Cambridge.
Athanassiadi, P. (1992), *Julian: an intellectual biography*, London.
Babelon, E. (1903), 'Les monnaies de Septime Sévère, de Caracalla et de Geta relatives à l'Afrique', *RIN* 16: 157–74.
Badian, E. (1958), 'Alexander the Great and the Unity of Mankind', *Historia* 7: 425–44.
Bagnall, R. S. (2000), '*P. Oxy.* 4527 and the Antonine plague in Egypt: death or flight?', *JRA* 13: 288–92.
Baharal, D. (1996), *Victory of Propaganda, the dynastic aspect of the imperial propaganda of the Severi: the literary and archaeological evidence AD 193–235*, London.
Baharal, D. (2003), 'Caracalla, Alexander the Great, and education in Rome', in P. Defosse (ed.), *Hommages à Carl Deroux III. Histoire et épigraphie, Droit (Collection Latomus)* [Brussels, 2003]: 27–36.
Balty, J. C. (1988), 'Apamea in Syria in the Second and Third Centuries AD', *JRS* 78: 91–104.
Bancalari Molina, A. (2001), 'Sobre los effectos del Edicto de Caracalla: consideraciones histórico-jurídicas', *Studi classici e orientali* 47: 167–82.
Bang, M. (1906), 'Ein versetztes Fragment des Cassius Dio', *Hermes* 41: 623–29.
Barnes, T. D. (1967), 'The family and career of Septimius Severus', *Historia* 16: 87–107.
Barnes, T. D. (2012), 'The date of the *Constitutio Antoniniana* once more', in B. Pferdehirt and M. Scholz (eds), *Bürgerrecht und Krise: Die Constitutio Antoniniana 212 n. Chr. und ihre innenpolitischen Folgen* [Mainz, 2012]: 51–52.

Beard, M; North, J. and Price, S. (1998), *Religions of Rome, vol. I: a history*, Cambridge.

Bell, H. I. (1947), 'The Constitutio Antoniniana and the Egyptian Poll-Tax', *JRS* 37: 17–23.

Benario, H. W. (1954), 'The Dediticii of the Constitutio Antoniniana', *TPAPA* 85: 188–96.

Bickermann, E. (1926), *Das Edikt des Kaisers Caracalla in P. Giss. 40*, Diss., Berlin.

Bingham, S. (2013), *The Praetorian Guard: A History of Rome's Elite Special Forces*, London.

Bingham, S. and Imrie, A. (2015), 'The Prefect and the Plot: a reassessment of the murder of Plautianus', *JAH* 3: 76–91.

Bird, H. W. (1971), 'Suetonian influences in the Later Lives of the Historia Augusta', *Hermes* 99: 129–34.

Birley, A. R. (1988), *Septimius Severus: the African emperor*, London.

Boak, A. E. R. (1955), *Manpower Shortage and the Fall of the Roman Empire in the West*, Ann Arbor.

Bodel, J. P. (2001), *Epigraphic Evidence: ancient history from inscriptions*, London.

Böhm, R. (1963), 'Studien zur civitas Romana, II: Eine falsche Lesart bei Aelius Aristides In Romam 65', *Aegyptus* 43: 54–67.

Boissevain, P. (1901), *Cassii Dionis Cocceiani: Historiarum Romanarum quae supersunt*[3], Berlin.

Bonner, S. (1977), *Education in Ancient Rome: from Cato the Elder to the Younger Pliny*, London.

Bosworth, A. B. (1980), 'Alexander and the Iranians', *JHS* 100: 1–21.

Boteva, D. (1999), 'Following in Alexander's footsteps: the case of Caracalla', *Ancient Macedonia: Sixth International Symposium, vol. 1*: 181–88.

Bowman, A. K., Garnsey, P. and Cameron, A. (eds.) (2005), *The Cambridge Ancient History, Vol. 12: The Crisis of Empire AD 193–337*[2], Cambridge.

Bowman, A. K. and Wilson, A. (eds) (2009a), *Quantifying the Roman Economy*, Oxford.

Bowman, A. K. and Wilson, A. (2009b), 'Quantifying the Roman Economy: Integration, Growth, Decline?', in A. K. Bowman and A. Wilson (eds), *Quantifying the Roman Economy* [Oxford, 2009]: 3–86.

Bowman, A. K. and Wilson, A. (eds) (2011), *Settlement, Urbanisation and Population*, Oxford.

Bradeen, D. W. (1959), 'Roman citizenship *per magistratum*', *CJ* 54: 221–28.

Brunt, P. A. (1965), 'The aims of Alexander', *G&R* 12: 203–15.

Bryen, A. (2016), 'Reading the Citizenship Papyrus (P. Giss. 40), in C. Ando (ed.), *Citizenship and Empire in Europe, 200–1900: The Antonine Constitution after 1900 Years* [Stuttgart, 2016]: 29–44.

Bruun, C. (2007), 'The Antonine Plague and the 'third century crisis'', in O. Hekster, G. de Kleijn and D. Slootjes (eds), *Crises and the Roman Empire: proceedings of the seventh international workshop, Impact of Empire (Nijmegen, June 20–24, 2006)* [Leiden, 2007]: 201–17.

Buraselis, K. (2007), *ΘΕΙΑ ΔΩΡΕΑ: Das Göttlich-kaiserliche Geschenk, Studien zur Politik der Severer und zur Constitutio Antoniniana*, Vienna.

Buraselis, K. (2013), 'Constitutio Antoniniana', in R. S. Bagnall, K. Broderson, C. B. Champion, A. Erskine and S. Huebner (eds), *The Encyclopaedia of Ancient History* [Oxford, 2013]: 1747–48.

Bureth, P. (1964), *Les Titulatures impériales dans les papyrus, les ostraca et les inscriptions d'Égypte (30 a.C–284 p.C.)*, Brussels.

Burnett, A. (1987), *Coinage in the Roman World*, London.

Buttrey, T. V. (1961), 'Dio, Zonares and the Value of the Roman *Aureus*', *JRS* 51: 40–45.

Cagnat, R. (1882), *Étude historique sur les impôts indirects chez les Romains*, Paris.

Campbell, B. (2002), *Warfare and Society in Imperial Rome, 31 BC–AD 284*, London.

Carlà, F. (2007), '*Tu tamen praefecti mihi studium et annonam in necessariis locis praebe*: prefettura al pretorio e *annona militaris* nel III secolo d.c.', *ZPE* 56: 82–110.

Carlsen, J. (1999), 'Gli alimenta imperial e privati in Italia: ideologia e economica', in D. Vera (ed.), *Demografia, sistemi agrari, regimi alimentari nel mondo antico* [Bari, 1999]: 273–88.

Cavallo, G. and Maehler, H. (2008), *Hellenistic Bookhands*, New York.

Coleman, K. M. (2003), 'Euergetism in its place: where was the amphitheatre in Augustan Rome?', in K. Lomas and T. Cornell (eds), *Bread and Circuses: euergetism and municipal patronage in Roman Italy* [London, 2003]: 61–88.

Connolly, S. (2010), 'Constantine answers the veterans', in S. McGill, C. Sogno and E. Watts (eds), *From the Tetrarchs to the Theodosians: Later Roman History and Culture, 284–450 CE* [Cambridge, 2010]: 93–116.

Corbier, M. (2005), 'The Economy of the Empire', in A. K. Bowman, P. Garnsey and A. Cameron (eds), *The Cambridge Ancient History, Vol. 12: The Crisis of Empire, AD 193–337*² [Cambridge, 2005]: 327–49.

Corbier, M. (1977), 'L'*aerarium militare*', in *Armées et fiscalité dans le monde antique. Paris 14–16 octobre 1976*, Paris: 197–234.

Corbo, C. (2013), *Constitutio Antoniniana: ius philosophia religio*, Naples.

Cotton, H. (2007), 'The impact of the Roman army in the province of Judaea/Syria Palaestina', in L. de Blois and E. Lo Cascio (eds), *The Impact of the Roman Army, 200 BC–AD 476* [Leiden, 2007]: 393–407.

Cowan, R. (2002), *Aspects of the Severan Field Army: the praetorian guard, legio II Parthica, and legionary vexillations AD 193–238*, Diss., Glasgow.

Croisille, J.-M. (ed.) (1990), *Neronia IV: Alejandro Magno, modelo de los emperadores romanos*, Brussels.

Crook, J. A. (1955), *Consilium Principis, Imperial Councils and Counsellors from Augustus to Diocletian*, Cambridge.

Daguet-Gagey, A. (2006), 'C. Fulvius Plautianus, *Hostis Publicus* Rome, 205–208 après J.-C.', in M.H. Quet (ed.), *La "Crise" de L'Empire Romain de Marc Aurèle à Constantin* [Paris, 2006]: 65–94.

BIBLIOGRAPHY

Dahmen, K. (2008), 'Alexander in gold and silver: reassessing third century AD medallions from Aboukir and Tarsos', *AJN* 20: 493–546.

Dahmen, K. (2007), *The Legend of Alexander the Great on Greek and Roman Coins*, London.

Dal Covolo, E. (2013), 'La Constitutio Antoniniana e lo sviluppo delle relazione tra l'Impero e la Chiesa nell'età dei Severi', *Saec. Christ.* 20: 15–20.

Davenport, C. (2012), 'Cassius Dio and Caracalla', *CQ* 62: 796–815.

Davies, J. K. (1998), 'Ancient economies: models and muddles', in H. Parkins & C. Smith (eds), *Trade, Traders and the Ancient City* [London, 1998]: 221–52.

Davies, J. K. (2001), 'Hellenistic economies in the post-Finley era', in Z. Archibald, J. K. Davies, V. Gabrielsen and G. Oliver (eds), *Hellenistic Economies* [London, 2001]: 11–62.

De Blois, L. (ed.) (2001), *Administration, Prosopography and Appointment Policies in the Roman Empire*, Leiden.

De Blois, L. (2002), 'Monetary policies, the soldiers' pay and the onset of the crisis of the third century AD', in P. Erdkamp (ed.), *The Roman Army and the Economy* [Amsterdam, 2002]: 90–110.

De Blois, L. and Lo Cascio, E. (eds) (2007), *The Impact of the Roman Army: 200 BC–AD 476*, Leiden.

De Blois, L. (2014), 'The Constitutio Antoniniana (AD 212): Taxes or Religion?', *Mnemosyne* 67.6: 1014–21.

De Callataÿ, F. (2005), 'The Graeco-Roman Economy in the Super-long run: Lead, Copper and Shipwrecks', *JRA* 18: 361–72.

De Giovanni, L. (2006), 'La giurisprudenza severiana tra storia e diritto: le « Institutiones » di Elio Marciano', *Athenaeum* 94: 487–505.

De Jong, J. (2007), 'Propaganda or Pragmatism? Damnatio memoriae in the third century papyri and imperial representation', in S. Benoist and A. Daguet-Gagey (eds), *Mémoire et histoire: Procedures de condamnation dans l'antiquité romain* [Metz, 2007]: 95–111.

De Martino, F. (1975), *Storia della constituzione romana, IV.2²*, Naples.

De Vos, M. (2013), 'The rural landscape of Thugga: Farms, presses, mills and transport', in A. Bowman and A. Wilson (eds), *The Roman Agricultural Economy: organization, investment and production* [Oxford, 2013]: 143–218.

DeLaine, J. (1997), *The baths of Caracalla: a study in the design, construction, and economics of large-scale building projects in imperial Rome*, Portsmouth RI.

Depeyrot, G. and Hollard, D. (1987), 'Pénurie d'argent-métal et crise monétaire de IIIᵉ siècle après J.-C.', *Histoire et Mesure* 2: 57–85.

Develin, R. (1971), 'The army pay rises under Severus and Caracalla, and the question of the *annona militaris*', *Latomus* 30: 687–95.

Du Plessis, P. (2010), *Borkowski's Textbook on Roman Law⁴*, Oxford.

Duncan-Jones, R. (1964), 'The Purpose and Organisation of the Alimenta', *PBSR* 19: 123–46.
Duncan-Jones, R. (1990), *Structure and Scale in the Roman Economy*, Cambridge.
Duncan-Jones, R. (1994), *Money and Government in the Roman Empire*, Cambridge.
Duncan-Jones, R. (1996), 'The Impact of the Antonine Plague', *JRA* 9: 108–36.
Dušanić, S. (1982), 'The issue of military *diplomata* under Claudius and Nero', *ZPE* 47: 149–71.
Dušanić, S. (1986), 'Pre-Severan *diplomata* and the problem of 'special grants'', in W. Eck and H. Wolff (eds), *Heer und Integrationspolitik: Die Römischen Militärdiplome als historiche Quelle*, [Köln, 1986]: 190–240.
Eck, W. (1999), 'The Bar Kokhba Revolt: the Roman point of view', *JRS* 89: 76–89.
Erdkamp, P. (1998), *Hunger and the Sword. Warfare and Food Supply in Roman Republican Wars, 264–30 BC*, Amsterdam.
Erdkamp, P. (2002), 'Introduction', in P. Erdkamp (ed.), *The Roman Army and the Economy* [Amsterdam 2002]: 5–16.
Euzennat, M. (1976), 'Une dédicace volubilitaine a l'Apollon de Claros', *Antiquités Africaines* 10: 63–68.
Finley, M. I. (1973), *The Ancient Economy*, Los Angeles.
Formisano, M. and C. Petrocelli (2003), *P. Flavio Vegezio Renato. L'arte della guerra romana*, Milan.
Forni, G. (1953), *Il reclutamento delle legioni da Augusto a Diocleziano*, Milan.
Frederick, D. (2002), 'Architecture and Surveillance in Flavian Rome', in A. J. Boyle and W. J. Dominik (eds), *Flavian Rome: Culture, Image, Text* [Leiden, 2002]: 199–227.
Fuhrmann, C. (2012), *Policing the Roman Empire: soldiers, administration and public order*, Oxford.
Galsterer, H. (1988), '*Municipium Flavium Irnitanum*: a Latin town in Spain', *JRS* 78: 78–90.
García, P. A. (2009), *Caracalla: la configuración de un tirano*, Madrid.
Gardner, J. F. (2001), 'Making citizens: the operation of the *lex Irnitana*', in L. De Blois (ed.), *Administration, Prosopography and Appointment Policies in the Roman Empire* [Amsterdam, 2001]: 315–29.
Garnsey, P. (1968), 'Trajan's Alimenta: some problems', *Historia* 17: 367–81.
Garnsey, P. (1970), *Social Status and Legal Privilege in the Roman Empire*, Oxford.
Garnsey, P. and Saller, R. (1987), *The Roman Empire: Economy, Society and Culture*, Los Angeles.
Garnsey, P. (2004), 'Roman Citizenship and Roman Law in the Late Empire', in S. Swain and M. Edwards (eds), *Approaching Late Antiquity: the transformation from Early to Late Empire* [Oxford, 2004]: 133–55.
Gascarino, G. (2008), *L'esercito romano. Armamento e organizazione, vol. II: da Augusto ai Severi*, Rimini.

Gascou, J. (1999), 'Hadrien et le droit Latin', ZPE 127: 294–300.
Gaudemet, J. (1967), *Institutions de l'antiquité*, Paris.
Gilliam, J. F. (1952), 'The Minimum Subject to the *Vicesima Hereditatum*', AJP 73: 397–405.
Gilliam, J. F. (1957), 'Enrollment in the Roman Imperial Army', *Eos* 48: 207–16.
Gilliam, J. F. (1961), 'The Plague under Marcus Aurelius', AJP 82: 225–51.
Gilliam, J. F. (1965), 'Dura Rosters and the *Constitutio Antoniniana*', *Historia* 14: 74–92.
Gitler, H. and Ponting, M. (2007), 'Rome and the East: a study of the chemical composition of Roman silver coinage during the reign of Septimius Severus AD 193–211', *Topoi*, Suppl. 8: 375–97.
Gonzalez, J. and Crawford, M. H. (1986), 'The *Lex Irnitana*: a new copy of the Flavian Municipal Law', JRS 76: 147–243.
González-Fernández, A. and Fernández Ardanaz, S. (2010), 'Algunas cuestiones en torno a la promulgación de la Constitutio Antoniniana', *Gérion* 28: 157–91.
Gorrie, C. (2001), 'The Septizodium of Septimius Severus revisited: the monument in its historical and urban context', *Latomus* 60: 653–70.
Gorrie, C. (2002), 'The Severan Building Programme and the Secular Games', *Athenaeum* 90: 461–81.
Gorrie, C. (2004), 'Julia Domna's building patronage, imperial family roles and the Severan revival of moral legislation', *Historia* 53: 61–72.
Green, P. (1990), *Alexander to Actium: the historical evolution of the Hellenistic age*, Berkeley.
Greene, K. (1986), *The Archaeology of the Ancient Economy*, London.
Griffin, M. T. (1976), *Seneca: a philosopher in politics*, Oxford.
Grünewald, T. (1999), *Räuber, Rebellen, Rivalen, Rächer: Studien zu Latrones im römischen Reich*, Stuttgart.
Guey, J. (1948), 'Les animaux célestes du nouvel édit Caracalla', CRAI 92: 128–30.
Guey, J. (1947), 'Les éléphants de Caracalla', REA 49: 248–73.
Haas, C. (1997), *Alexandria in Late Antiquity: topography and social conflict*, London.
Haensch, R. (2001), '*Milites legionis* im Umfeld ihrer Provinz. Zur Rekrutierungspraxis, sozialen Position und zur 'Romanisierung' der Soldaten der niedergermanischen Legionen im 2. und 3. Jahrhundert', in L. de Blois (ed.), *Administration, Prosopography and Appointment Policies in the Roman Empire* [Leiden, 2001]: 84–109.
Hagedorn, D. (1996), 'Noch einmal zum Volljährigskeitsalter in Ägypten nach der Constitutio Antoniniana', ZPE 113: 224–26.
Hammond, M. (1957), 'The composition of the senate, AD 68–235', JRS 47: 74–81.
Hannestad, N. (1984), *Roman Art and Imperial Policy*, Aarhus.
Harker, A. (2008), *Loyalty and Dissidence in Roman Egypt: the case of the Acta Alexandrinorum*, Cambridge.
Harl, K. (1996), *Coinage in the Roman Economy 300 BC–AD 700*, London.

Hassall, M. (1987), 'Romani e non Romani', in J. Wacher (ed.), *Il mondo di Roma imperiale, vol. III: la società e religione, Parte nona: la società* [Bari, 1989]: 165-84.

Hauken, T. (1998), *Petition and Response: an epigraphic study of petitions to Roman emperors, 181-249*, Bergen.

Haynes, I. P. (2001), 'The Impact of Auxiliary recruitment on Provincial Communities from Augustus to Caracalla', in L. de Blois (ed.), *Administration, Prosopography and Appointment Policies in the Roman Empire* [Leiden, 2001]: 62-83.

Heichelheim, F. M. (1941), 'The text of the "Constitutio Antoniniana" and the three other decrees of the emperor Caracalla contained in Papyrus Gissensis 40', *Journal of Egyptian Archaeology* 26: 10-22.

Hekster, O. (2002), *Commodus: an emperor at the crossroads*, Amsterdam.

Hekster, O. (2003), 'Coins and Messages. Audience targeting on coins of different denominations', in L. de Blois et al. (eds), *Representation and Perception of Roman Imperial Power* [Amsterdam, 2003]: 20-35.

Hekster, O., de Kleijn, G. and Slootjes, D. (eds) (2007), *Crises and the Roman Empire: proceedings of the seventh international workshop, Impact of Empire (Nijmegen, June 20-24, 2006)*, Leiden.

Hekster, O. (2008), *Rome and its empire, AD 193-284*, Edinburgh.

Hekster, O. (2012), 'The empire after his death', in M. Van Ackeren (ed.), *A Companion to Marcus Aurelius* [London, 2012]: 234-48.

Hekster, O. (2015), *Emperors and Ancestors: Roman Rulers and the Constraints of Tradition*, Oxford.

Hermann, P. (1972), 'Überlegungen zur Datierung der Constitutio Antoniniana', *Chiron* 2: 519-30.

Heuss, A. (1954), 'Alexander der Große und die politische Ideologie im Altertum', *A&A* 4: 65-104.

Hijmans S. E. (1994), 'Castor, Caracalla, and the so-called Statue of Sol in the North Carolina Museum of Art', *BABesch* 69: 165-74.

Hitchner, B. (2009), 'Coinage and Metal Supply', in A. Bowman and A. Wilson (eds), *Quantifying the Roman Economy* [Oxford, 2009]: 281-86.

Honoré, T. (1994), *Emperors and Lawyers*[2], Oxford.

Honoré, T. (2002), *Ulpian: pioneer of human rights*[2], Oxford.

Honoré, T. (2004), 'Roman Law AD 200-400: from *Cosmopolis* to *Rechtstaat*?', in S. Swain and M. Edwards (eds), *Approaching Late Antiquity: the transformation from Early to Late Empire*, Oxford: 109-32.

Hope, V. (2000), 'Status and social identity in the Roman world', in J. Huskinson (ed.), *Experiencing Rome: culture, identity and power in the Roman Empire* [London, 2000]: 125-52.

Hopkins, K. (1980), 'Taxes and Trade in the Roman Empire (200 BC-AD 400)', *JRS* 70: 101-25.

Hopkins, K. (2002), 'Rome, Taxes, Rents and Trade', in W. Scheidel and S. von Redden (eds), *The Ancient Economy* [Edinburgh, 2002]: 190–232.

Horsmann, G. (1991), *Untersuchungen zur militärischen Ausbildung im republikanischen Kaiserzeitlichen Rom*, Boppard am Rhein.

Hose, M. (2007), 'Cassius Dio: a senator and historian in the age of anxiety', in J. Marincola (ed.), *A Companion to Greek and Roman Historiography* [Oxford, 2007]: 461–67.

Howe, L. L. (1966), *The Praetorian Prefects from Augustus to Diocletian*[2], Chicago.

Howgego, C. (1995), *Ancient History from Coins*, London.

Howgego, C. (2007), 'Coinage and Identity in the Roman Provinces', in C. Howgego, V. Heuchert and A. Burnett (eds), *Coinage and Identity in the Roman Provinces* [Oxford, 2007]: 1–18.

Ibbetson, D. (2015), 'Sources of Law from the Republic to the Dominate', in D. Johnston (ed.), *The Cambridge Companion to Roman Law* [Cambridge, 2015]: 25–44.

Icks, M. (2011), *The Crimes of Elagabalus: the life and legacy of Rome's decadent boy emperor*, London.

Illés, I. A. (2013), *The Genesis and the Dating of the lex Flavia municipalis*, Diss., Szeged.

Imrie, A. (2014), 'A Case of Mistaken Identity: Julia Domna as Concordia in *RIC* 380 and 381', *RBN* 160: 307–15.

Jahn, J. (1984), 'Zur Entwicklung römischer Soldzahlungen von Augustus bis auf Diokletian', *Studien zu den Fundmünzen der Antike* 2: 53–74.

Johnson, A. C., Coleman-Norton, P. R. and Bourne, F. C. (2003), *Ancient Roman Statutes: a translation with introduction, commentary, glossary and index*, Clark N.J.

Johnston, A. (1983), 'Caracalla's Path: the numismatic evidence', *Historia* 32: 58–76.

Jones, A. H. M. (1936), 'Another Interpretation of the 'Constitutio Antoniniana'', *JRS* 26, 223–35.

Jones, A. H. M. (1974), *The Roman Economy*, Oxford.

Jongman, W. (2007a), 'The early Roman empire: Consumption', in W. Scheidel (ed.), *The Cambridge Economic History of the Greco-Roman World* [Cambridge, 2007]: 592–618.

Jongman, W. (2007b), 'Gibbon was right: the decline and fall of the Roman economy', in O. Hekster, G. de Kleijn, & D. Slootjes (eds), *Crises and the Roman Empire: proceedings of the seventh international workshop, Impact of Empire (Nijmegen, June 20–24, 2006)* [Leiden, 2007]: 183–200.

Jongman, W. (1988), *The Economy and Society of Pompeii*, Amsterdam.

Jucker, H. (1981), 'Römische Herrscherbildnisse aus Ägypten', *ANRW* II, 12, 2: 667–725.

Junkelmann, M. (1986), *Die Legionen des Augustus*, Mainz.

Kalb, W. (1975), *Roms Juristen, nach ihrer Sprache dargestellt*, Aalen.

Kantor, G. (2016), 'Local Law in Asia Minor after the Constitutio Antoniniana', in C. Ando (ed.), *Citizenship and Empire in Europe, 200–1900: The Antonine Constitution after 1900 Years* [Stuttgart, 2016]: 45–62.

Kehoe, D. P. (2007), 'The early Roman empire: Production', in W. Scheidel (ed.), *The Cambridge Economic History of the Greco-Roman World* [Cambridge, 2007]: 543–69.

Kehoe, D. P. (2006), *Law and Rural Economy in the Roman Empire*, Ann Arbor.

Kelly, B. (2011), *Petitions, Litigation and Social Control in Roman Egypt*, Oxford.

Kemezis, A. (2014), *Greek Narratives of the Roman Empire under the Severans: Cassius Dio, Philostratus and Herodian (Greek Culture in the Roman World)*, Cambridge.

Kemmers, F. (2009), 'From Bronze to Silver: coin circulation in the early third century AD', *RBN* 155: 143–58.

Kemmers, F. (2011), 'Out of the Shadow: Geta and Caracalla reconsidered', in S. Faust and F. Leitmeir (eds), *Repräsentationsformen in severischer Zeit* [Berlin, 2011]: 270–90.

Kerneis-Poly, S. (1996), 'Les *numeri* ethniques de l'armée romaine au IIe et IIIe siècles', *RSA* 26: 69–94.

Kienast, D. (2011), *Römische Kaisertabelle: Grundzüge einer römischen Kaiserchronologie*, Darmstadt.

King, A. (1999), 'Diet in the Roman World: A Regional Inter-site Comparison of the Mammal Bones', *JRA* 12: 168–202.

Kissel, T. K. (1995), *Untersuchungen zur Logistik des römischen Heeres in den Provinzen des griechischen Ostens (27 v. Chr.–235 n. Chr.)*, St. Katharinen.

Klauser, T. 1944 (1948), 'Aurum Coronarium', *Mitteilungen des deutschen archaeologischen Instituts. Römische Abteilung* 59: 129–53.

Kraft, K. (1951), *Zur Rekrutierung der Alen und Kohorten an Rhein und Donau*, Bern.

Kron, G. (2002), 'Archaezoological Evidence for the Productivity of Roman Livestock Farming', *MBAH* 21: 53–73.

Kron, G. (2005), 'Anthropometry, Physical Anthropology, and the Reconstruction of Ancient Health, Nutrition, and Living Standards', *Historia* 54: 68–83.

Kron, G. (2008), 'The Much Maligned Peasant. Comparative perspectives on the productivity of the Small Farmer in Classical Antiquity', in L. de Ligt and S. Northwood (eds), *People, Land and Politics: demographic developments and the transformation of Roman Italy 300 BC–AD 14* [Leiden, 2008]: 79–119.

Krüpe, F. (2011), *Die Damnatio Memoriae: Über die Vernichtung von Erinnerung. Eine Fallstudie zu Publius Septimius Geta (189–211 n. Chr.)*, Gutenberg.

Kuhlmann, P. (1994), *Die Giessener Literarischen Papyri und die Caracalla-Erlasse: Edition, Übersetzung und Kommentar*, Giessen.

Kuhlmann, P. (2012), 'Die Constitutio Antoniniana: Caracallas umfassende Bürgerrechtsverleihung auf dem Papyrus Gissensis 40', in B. Pferdehirt and M. Scholz (eds) (2012), *Bürgerrecht und Krise: Die Constitutio Antoniniana 212 n.Chr. und ihre innenpolitischen Folgen* [Mainz, 2012]: 51–2.

Kühnen, A. (2008), *Die imitatio Alexandri in der römischen Politik*, Münster.

Lange, C. and Madsen, J. M. (eds) (2016), *Cassius Dio: Greek Intellectual and Roman Politician*, Leiden.

Langenegger, W. (2010), 'Zur Entwicklung der Denargewichte der Münzstätte Rom von Septimius Severus bis Aemilianus (193–253 n. Chr.), *Jahrbuch für Numismatik und Geldgeschichte* 60: 167–81.

Laqueur, R. (1927), 'Das erste Edikt Caracallas auf dem Papyrus Gissensis 40', *Nachrichten der Giessener Hochschulgesellschaft* 61: 15–28.

Lavan, M. (2016), 'The Spread of Roman Citizenship, 14–212 CE: Quantification in the face of high uncertainty', *Past and Present* 230: 3–46.

Leander Touati, A. M. (1991), 'Portrait and historical relief. Some remarks on the meaning of Caracalla's sole ruler portrait', in A. M. Leander Touati, E. Rystedt and Ö. Wikander (eds), *Munuscula Romana* [Stockholm, 1991]: 117–31.

Le Bohec, Y. (2000), *The Imperial Roman Army*, London.

Le Roux, P. (1982), *L'armée romaine et l'organisation des provinces ibériques d'Auguste à l'invasion de 409*, Paris.

Letta, C. (1994), 'Il "naufragio" di Caracalla in Cassio Dione, nell' Historia Augusta e nei commentary degli Arvali', *ZPE* 103: 188–90.

Levick, B. (1969), 'Caracalla's Path', *Hommages à Marcel Renard* (*Collection Latomus*) 102: 426–457.

Levick, B. (1985), *The Government of the Roman Empire: a sourcebook*, London.

Levick, B. (2007), *Julia Domna: Syrian Empress*, London.

Lewis, N. (1979), 'Ἀφῆλιξ before and after the Constitutio Antoniniana', *BASP* 16: 117–20.

Lewis, N. (1983), *Life in Egypt under Roman Rule*, Oxford.

Lichtenberger, A. (2011), *Severus Pius Augustus: Studien zur sakralen Repräsentation und Rezeption der Herrschaft des Septimius Severus und seiner Familie (193–211 n. chr.)*, Leiden.

Link, S. (1993), 'Anachoresis: Steuerflucht im Ägypten der frühen Kaiserzeit', *Klio* 75: 306–20.

Littman, R. J. and M. L. Littman (1973), 'Galen and the Antonine Plague', *AJP* 94: 243–55.

Lo Cascio, E. (1984), 'Dall "antoninianus" al "laurato grande": L'evoluzione monetaria del III secolo alla luce della nouva documentazione di età diocleziana', *Opus* 3: 133–201.

Lo Cascio, E. (1994), 'The size of the Roman Population: Beloch and the meaning of the Augustan Census figures', *JRS* 84: 23–40.

Lo Cascio, E. (2005a), 'The age of the Severans', in A. K. Bowman, P. Garnsey and A. Cameron (eds), *The Cambridge Ancient History, Vol. 12: The Crisis of Empire, AD 193–337*^{2} [Cambridge, 2005]: 137–55.

Lo Cascio, E. (2005b), 'The government and administration of the empire in the central decades of the third century', in A. K. Bowman, P. Garnsey and A. Cameron (eds), *The Cambridge Ancient History, Vol. 12: The Crisis of Empire, AD 193–337*^{2} [Cambridge, 2005]: 156–69.

Lo Cascio, E. (2007), 'The early Roman empire: the state and the economy', in W. Scheidel (ed.), *The Cambridge Economic History of the Greco-Roman World* [Cambridge, 2007]: 619–50.

Lomas, K. and Cornell, T. (eds) (2003), *Bread and Circuses: Euergetism and Municipal Patronage in Roman Italy*, London.

L'Orange, H. P. (1947), *Apotheosis in Ancient Portraiture*, Oslo.

Lukaszewicz, A. (1989), 'Alexandrie sous les Sévères et l'historiographie', in L. Criscuolo and G. Geraci (eds), *Egitto e storia antica dall'ellenismo all'eta araba, Bilancio di un confront, Atti del Colloquio Internazionale Bologna, 31 agosto–2 settembre 1987* [Bologna, 1989]: 491–96.

Lukaszewicz, A. (1990a), 'Zum Papyrus Gissensis 40 I 9 (Constitutio Antoniniana)', *JJP* 20: 90–101.

Lukaszewicz, A. (1990b), 'Some Berlin Papyri reconsidered', *ZPE* 82: 129–32.

Lukaszewicz, A. (1993), *Aegyptiaca Antoniniana: Działalność Karakalli w Egipcie (215–216)*, Warsaw.

Lusnia, S. S. (2004), 'Urban planning and sculptural display in Severan Rome: reconstructing the Septizodium and its role in dynastic politics', *AJA* 108: 517–44.

Manders, E. (2012), *Coining Images of Power: Patterns in the Representation of Roman Emperors on Imperial Coinage, AD 193–284*, Leiden.

Mann, J. C. (1983), *Legionary Recruitment and Veteran Settlement during the Principate*, London.

Mann, J. C. and M. M. Roxan (1988), 'Discharge certificates of the Roman army', *Britannia* 19: 341–47.

Marasco, G. (1994), 'L'inscription de Takina et la politique sociale de Caracalla', *Mnemosyne* 47: 495–511.

Mathisen, R. W. (2006), 'Peregrini, barbari and cives Romani: concepts of citizenship and the legal identity of barbarians in the later Roman Empire', *American Historical Review* 111: 1011–40.

McKinnon, M. (2004), *Production and Consumption of Animals in Roman Italy*, Portsmouth R.I.

Meckler, M. (1999), 'Caracalla the intellectual', in E. dal Covolo and G. Rinaldi (eds), *Gli imperatori Severi: Storia Archeologia Religione* [Rome, 1999]: 39–46.

Mennen, I. (2006), 'The image of an emperor in trouble (legitimation and representation of power by Caracalla)', in L. De Blois, P. Funke and J. Hahn (eds), *The Impact of Imperial Rome on Religions, Ritual and Religious Life in the Roman Empire* [Leiden, 2006]: 253–67.

Mennen, I. (2011), *Power and Status in the Roman Empire AD 193–284*, Leiden.

Meyer, P. M. (1910), *Griechische Papyri im Museum des Oberhessischen Geschichtsvereins zu Gießen (Urkunden No. 36–57)*, Leipzig.

Meyer, P. M. (1920), *Juristische Papyri: Erklärung von Urkunden zur Einführung in die Juristische Papyruskunde*, Berlin.

Millar, F. (1962), 'The Date of the Constitutio Antoniniana', *JEA* 48: 124–31.

Millar, F. (1964), *A Study of Cassius Dio*, Oxford.

Millar, F. (1977), *The Emperor in the Roman World*, London.
Millar, F. (1979), 'Review: Die Constitutio Antoniniana und Papyrus Gissensis, by H. Wolff', *JRS* 69: 235.
Milner, N. P. (1993), *Vegetius: Epitome of Military Science*, Liverpool.
Moatti, C. (2016), 'The Notion of *Res Publica* in the Age of Caracalla', in C. Ando (ed.), *Citizenship and Empire in Europe, 200–1900: The Antonine Constitution after 1900 Years* [Stuttgart, 2016]: 63–98.
Modrzejewski, J. M. (1990), *Droit Imperial et Traditions Locales dans l'Egypte Romaine*, Aldershot.
Mordine, M. J. (2013), '*Domus Neroniana*: the Imperial Household in the age of Nero', in E. Buckley and M. T. Dinter (eds), *A Companion to the Neronian Age* [London, 2013]: 102–17.
Morizot, P. (2002), 'Impact de l'armée romaine sur l'economie de l'Afrique', in P. Erdkamp (ed.), *The Roman Army and the Economy* [Amsterdam, 2002]: 345–74.
Morley, N. (2007), 'The early Roman empire: Distribution', in W. Scheidel (ed.), *The Cambridge Economic History of the Greco-Roman World* [Cambridge, 2007]: 570–91.
Mullen, A. (2007), 'Linguistic Evidence for 'Romanization': continuity and change in Romano-British onomastics: a study of the epigraphic record with particular reference to Bath', *Britannia* 38: 35–61.
Murphy, G. J. (1945), *The Reign of the Emperor L. Septimius Severus from the Evidence of the Inscriptions*, Philadelphia.
Navarro, I. L. (2008), 'Caelestia animalia Mauretaniae: une breve reflexion a propositoi del edicto de Banasa', *Ktèma* 33: 413–20.
Nicolet, C. (1980), *The World of the Citizen in Republican Rome*, Los Angeles.
Niebuhr, B. G. (1849), *Lectures on Roman History²*, Vol. 3, London.
Noreña, C. (2011), *Imperial Ideals in the Roman West: representation, circulation, power*, Cambridge.
Oliver, J. H. (1955), 'Free men and dediticii', *AJP* 76: 279–97.
Oliver, J. H. (1972), 'Text of the Tabula Bansitana, AD 177', *AJP* 93, 336–40.
Oliver, J. H. (1974), 'Minutes of a trial conducted by Caracalla in Antioch in AD 216', in *Mélanges helléniques offerts à George Daux*, Paris: 289–94.
Oliver, J. H. (1978), 'On the Edict of Severus Alexander (*P. Fayum* 20)', *AJP* 99: 474–85.
Oliver, J. H. (1989), *Greek Constitutions of Early Roman Emperors from Inscriptions and Papyri*, Philadelphia.
Pangerl, A. (2013), 'Porträttypen des Caracalla und des Geta auf römischen Reichsprägungen—Definition eines neuen Caesartyps des Caracalla und eines neuen Augustustyps des Geta', *Archäologisches Korrespondenzblatt* 43: 99–114.
Parker, A. J. (1992), *Ancient Shipwrecks in the Mediterranean and Roman Provinces* (*BAR Series*), Oxford.

Pavis d'Esurac, H. (1974), 'Réflexions sur la *classis Africana Commodiana*', in J. Thréheux (ed.), *Mélanges d'histoire ancienne offerts à William Seston* [Paris, 1974]: 397–408.

Pera, R. (1979), 'Probabili significati della scritta *INDULGENTIA AVGG IN CARTHAGINEM* ed *INDULGENTIA AVGG IN ITALIAM* su alcune monete di Settimio Severo e Caracalla', *RIN* 80: 103–26.

Perez, A. A. (2009), 'Taxation in the times of the Principate', *Gerión* 27: 207–17.

Picard, C. (1948), 'Note sur les *caelestia animalia* (éléphants) de l'édit de Caracalla', *CRAI* 92: 134–35.

Potter, D. S. (2014), *The Roman Empire at Bay: AD 180–395*², London.

Potter, D. S. (2004), *The Roman Empire at Bay: AD 180–395*, London.

Préaux, C. (1953), *Les raisons de l'originalité de l'Egypte (Museum Helveticum 10)*, Basel.

Rees, R. (2007), 'Diocletian and the Efficacy of Public Law', in J. W. Cairns and P. Du Plessis (eds), *Beyond Dogmatics: Law and Society in the Roman World* [Edinburgh, 2007]: 105–24.

Riess, W. (2001), *Apuleius und die Räuber: Ein Beitrag zur historischen Kriminalitätsforchung*, Stuttgart.

Rilinger, R. (1988), *Humiliores-Honestiores: Zu einer sozialen Dichotomie im Strafrecht der römischen Kaiserzeit*, Munich.

Rivas, E. A. (2009), 'La ciudadanía Romana bajo los Severos', *Revista de Estudios Histórico-Jurídicos* 31: 87–123.

Rives, J. B. (1999), 'The decree of Decius and the religion of Empire', *JRS* 89: 35–54.

Rocco, M. (2010), 'The Reasons Behind the Constitutio Antoniniana and its Effects on the Roman Military', *Acta Classica Universitatis Scientiarum Debreceniensis* 46: 131–55.

Rodger, A. (1996), 'Jurisdictional limits of the *lex Irnitana* and the *lex de Gallia Cisalpina*', *ZPE* 110: 189–206.

Roebuck, D. and De Loynes de Fumichon, B. (2004), *Roman Arbitration*, Oxford.

Rohrbacher, D. (2013), 'The Sources of the *Historia Augusta* Re-examined', *Histos* 7: 146–80.

Rohrbacher, D. (2016), *The Play of Allusion in the Historia Augusta*, Madison.

Roos, A. G. (1915), 'Herodian's method of composition', *JRS* 5: 195–202.

Rostovtzeff, M. (1957), *The Social and Economic History of the Roman Empire*, 2 Vols., Oxford.

Roth, J. P. (1998), *The Logistics of the Roman Army at War (264 BC–AD 235)*, Leiden.

Roth, J. P. (2002), 'The army and economy in Judaea and Palestine', in P. Erdkamp (ed.), *The Roman Army and the Economy* [Amsterdam, 2002]: 375–97.

Rowan, C. (2012), *Under Divine Auspices: divine ideology and the visualisation of imperial power in the Severan period*, Cambridge.

Rubin, Z. (1980), *Civil War Propaganda and Historiography*, Brussels.

Saavedra-Guerrero, M. D. (2007), 'El poder, el miedo y la ficción en la relación del emperador Caracalla y su madre Julia Domna', *Latomus* 66: 120–31.

Safrai, Z. (1994), *The Economy of Roman Palestine*, New York.
Sahin, S. and French, D. (1987), 'Ein Dokument aus Takina', *EA* 10: 133–45.
Saller, R. P. (1982), *Personal Patronage under the Early Empire*, Cambridge.
Sasse, C. (1958), *Die Constitutio Antoniniana*, Wiesbaden.
Sasse, C. (1962), *Literaturübersicht zur Constitutio Antoniniana*, Warsaw.
Scheidel, W. (ed.) (2001), *Debating Roman demography*, Leiden.
Scheidel, W. and S. von Redden (eds.) (2002), *The Ancient Economy*, Edinburgh.
Scheidel, W. (2007a), 'A model of real income growth in Roman Italy', *Historia* 56: 322–46.
Scheidel, W. (ed.) (2007b), *The Cambridge Economic History of the Greco-Roman World*, Cambridge.
Scheidel, W. (2008a), 'Roman population size: the logic of the debate', in L. de Ligt and S. J. Northwood (eds), *People, land and politics: demographic developments and the transformation of Roman Italy, 300 BC–AD 14* [Leiden, 2008]: 17–70.
Scheidel, W. (2008b), 'The comparative economics of slavery in the Greco-Roman world', in E. Dal Logo & C. Katsari (eds), *Slave Systems, ancient and modern*, [Cambridge, 2008]: 105–26.
Scheidel, W. (2010), 'Real wages in early economies: evidence for living standards from 1800 BCE–1300 CE', *Journal of the Economic and Social History of the Orient* 53: 425–62.
Scheidel, W. (2012a), 'Roman wellbeing and the economic consequences of the 'Antonine Plague', in E. Lo Cascio (ed.), *L'impatto delle "peste antonina"* [Bari, 2012]: 265–95.
Scheidel, W. (2012b), 'Approaching the Roman Economy', in W. Scheidel (ed.), *The Cambridge Companion to the Roman Economy* [Cambridge, 2012]: 1–21.
Schmidt-Dick, F. (2002), *Typenatlas der römischen Reichsprägung von Augustus bis Aemilianus. Zweiter Band: Geographische und männliche Darstellungen*, Vienna.
Schönbauer, E. (1931), 'Reichsrecht gegen Volksrecht? Studien über die Bedeutung der Constitutio Antoniniana für die römische Rechtsentwicklung', *ZRG* 51: 277–335.
Schubart, W. (1940), 'Zur Constitutio Antoniniana', *Aegyptus* 20: 31–38.
Scott, R. (2010), 'Text and Context in Byzantine Historiography', in L. James (ed.), *A Companion to Byzantium* [Oxford, 2010]: 251–62.
Seeck, O. (1910), *Geschichte des Untergangs der antiken Welt³, Vol. 1*, Stuttgart.
Sessa, A. (2014), 'Cittadinanza espansiva ed espansione della cittadinanza: politiche di integrazione e motivazione culturale al reato: tra la Roma antica e il mondo attuale', *SDHI* 80: 171–205.
Seston, W. and M. Euzennat (1961), 'La citoyenneté romaine au temps de Marc Aurèle et de Commode, d'après la *Tabula Banasitana*', *CRAI* 105: 317–24.
Shaw, B. (1984), 'Bandits in the Roman Empire', *Past and Present* 105: 3–52.
Sheldon, R. M. (2010), *Rome's Wars in Parthia: blood in the sand*, London.

Sherman, C. L. (1928), 'The Constitutio Antoniniana in the light of the Γνώμων τοῦ Ἰδίου Λόγου', *TPAPA* 59: 33–47.
Sherwin-White, A. N. (1973a), *The Roman Citizenship*², Oxford.
Sherwin-White, A. N. (1973b), 'The Tabula of Banasa and the Constitutio Antoniniana', *JRS* 63: 86–98.
Simelon, P. (2010), 'Caracalla: entre apothéose et damnation', *Latomus* 69: 792–810.
Simon, E. (1995), 'Die constitution Antoniniana und einer syrischer Porträt', in C. Schubert and K. Broderson (eds), *Rom und der griechische Osten: Festschrift für H. Schmitt zum 65. Geburtstag dargebracht von Schülern, Freunden und Münchener Kollegen* [Stuttgart, 1995]: 249–50.
Smith, R. E. (1972), 'The Army Reforms of Septimius Severus', *Historia* 21: 481–500.
Sohm, R. (1911), *Institutionen: Geschichte und System des römischen Privatrechts*¹⁴, Berlin.
Southern, P. (2015), *The Roman Empire from Severus to Constantine*², Oxford.
Speidel, M. A. (2009a), 'Specialisation and promotion in the Roman imperial army', in M. A. Speidel (ed.), *Heer und Herrschaft im Römischen Reich der Hohen Kaiserzeit* [Stuttgart, 2009]: 283–304.
Speidel, M. A. (2009b), 'Les longues marches des armées romaines. Reflets épigraphiques de la circulation des militaires dans la province d'Asie au IIIᵉ siècle apr. J.-C.', *Cahiers Glotz* 20: 199–210.
Speidel, M. A. 1992 (2009), 'Roman Army Pay Scales', in M. A. Speidel (ed.), *Heer und Herrschaft im Römischen Reich der Hohen Kaiserzeit* [Stuttgart, 2009]: 349–80.
Speidel, M. A. 2000 (2009), 'Sold und Wirtschaftlige der römischen soldaten', in M. A. Speidel (ed.), *Heer und Herrschaft im Römischen Reich der Hohen Kaiserzeit* [Stuttgart, 2009]: 407–37.
Speidel, M. A. (2012), 'Being a soldier in the Roman imperial army: expectations and responses', in C. Wolff (ed.), *Le metier de soldat dans le monde romain* [Lyon, 2012]: 175–91.
Speidel, M. P. (1978), *Guards of the Roman armies*, Bonn.
Speidel, M. P. (1994), *Riding for Caesar: The Roman Emperor's Horse Guards*, London.
Spencer, D. (2002), *The Roman Alexander: reading a cultural myth*, Exeter.
Stewart, A. (1993), *Faces of Power: Alexander's image and Hellenistic politics*, Oxford.
Strobel, K. (2007), 'Strategy and army structure between Septimius Severus and Constantine the Great', in P. Erdkamp (ed.), *A Companion to the Roman Army* [Oxford, 2007]: 267–85.
Stroux, J. (1933), 'Die Constitutio Antoniniana', *Philologus* 88: 272–95.
Sutherland, C. H. V. (1974), *Roman Coins*, London.
Tarn, W. W. (1948), *Alexander the Great, Vol. 2: sources and studies*, Cambridge.
Thomas, C. (2004), 'Claudius and the Roman army reforms', *Historia* 53: 424–52.

Thomas, J. D. and R. W. Davies (1977), 'A new military strength report on papyrus', *JRS* 67: 50–61.

Tofini, S. M. and P. Chiarucci (1994), 'Nuovi rinvenimenti ad Albano', *Documenta Albana, Vol. 2*, Rome.

Torrent, A. (2011), *La Constitutio Antoniniana. Reflexiones sobre el Papiro Giessen 40 I*, Madrid.

Trapp. M. (2007), 'Philosophy, scholarship and the world of learning in the Severan Period', in S. Swain, S. Harrison and J. Elsner (eds), *Severan Culture* [Cambridge, 2007]: 470–88.

Tuori, K. (2007), 'Legal Pluralism and the Roman Empires', in J. W. Cairns and P. Du Plessis (eds), *Beyond Dogmatics: Law and Society in the Roman World* [Edinburgh, 2007]: 39–52.

Turchin, P. and W. Scheidel (2009), 'Coin hoards speak of population declines in ancient Rome', *PNAS* 106: 17276–79.

Ureche, P. (2009), 'Tactics, strategies and fighting specifics of the *cohortes equitate* in Roman Dacia', in O. Ţentea & C. Opriş (eds), *Near and Beyond the Roman Frontier: Proceedings of a colloquium held in Târgovişte, 16–17 October 2008* [Bucharest, 2009]: 329–38.

Van Beek, B. and M. Depauw (2013), 'Quantifying Imprecisely Dated Sources: a new inclusive method for charting diachronic change in Graeco-Roman Egypt', *Ancient Society* 43: 101–14.

Van Minnen, P. (2001), 'P. Oxy. LXVI 4527 and the Antonine Plague in the Fayyum', *ZPE* 135: 175–77.

Van Minnen, P. (2016), 'Three Edicts of Caracalla? A New Reading of P. Giss. 40', *Chiron* 46: 205–21.

Varner, E. R. (2004), *Mutilation and Transformation: damnatio memoriae and Roman imperial portraiture*, Leiden.

Veyne, P. (1990), *Bread and Circuses: Historical Sociology and Political Pluralism*, London.

Walker, D. R. (1977), *The Metrology of the Roman Silver Coinage, Vol. 2*, Oxford.

Walker, P. L. et al. (2009), 'The Causes of Porotic Hyperostosis and Cribra Orbitalia: A Reappraisal of the Iron Deficiency-Anemia Hypothesis', *AJPhA*, 139: 109–25.

Wallace, S. L. (1938), *Taxation in Egypt from Augustus to Diocletian*, Princeton.

Watkins, T. H. (1989), 'Vespasian and Italic right', *CJ* 84: 117–36.

Watson, G. R. (1969), *The Roman Soldier*, New York.

Weber, W. (1999), 'The Antonines', in S.A. Cook, F. E. Adcock & M. P. Charlesworth (eds), *The Cambridge Ancient History, vol. XI: the imperial peace AD 70–192*, [Cambridge, 1999]: 347–48.

Weisser, T. (2011), *Caracalla und Geta—Bruderhass statt Bruderliebe*, Norderstedt.

Weissert, D. (1963), 'Bemerkungen zum Wortlaut des P. Giss. 40 I (Constitutio Antoniniana) Z. 1–9', *Hermes* 91: 239–50.

Whittaker, C. R. (1969), tr., *Herodian: History of the Roman Empire from the time of Marcus Aurelius, Books. 1–4*, London.

Whittaker, C. R. (1994), *Frontiers of the Roman Empire: a social and economic study*, Baltimore.

Whittaker, C. R. (2002), 'Supplying the Army: Evidence from Vindolanda', in P. Erdkamp (ed.), *The Roman Army and the Economy* [Amsterdam, 2002]: 204–34.

Wilhelm, A. (1934), 'Die Constitutio Antoniniana', *AJA* 38: 178–80.

Williams, W. (1974), 'Caracalla and the Rhetoricians. A note on the "*cognition de Goharienis*"', *Latomus* 33: 663–67.

Williams, W. (1979), 'Caracalla and the Authorship of Imperial Edicts and Epistles', *Latomus* 38: 67–89.

Wilson, A. (2009), 'Approaches to Quantifying Roman Trade', in A. Bowman and A. Wilson (eds), *Quantifying the Roman Economy* [Oxford, 2009]: 213–49.

Witcher, R. E. (2006), 'Broken pots and meaningless dots? Surveying the rural landscapes of Roman Italy', *PBSR* 74: 39–72.

Witschel, C. (1999), *Krise-Rezession-Stagnation? Der Nesten des Römischen Reiches im 3. Jahrhundert n. Chr.*, Frankfurt am Main.

Wolff, H. (1977), *Die Constitutio Antoniniana und Papyrus Gissensis*, Köln.

Woolf, G. (1990), 'Food, poverty and patronage. The significance of the epigraphy of the Roman alimentary schemes in early imperial Italy', *PBSR* 68: 197–228.

Zanker, P. (1996), *The Mask of Socrates: the image of the intellectual in antiquity*, Oxford.

Zingale, L. M. (1999), 'Diritto romano e papyri: in margine ad alcuni contributi giusromanisti', *Aegyptus* 79: 81–87.

Index of Names

Aesculapius   84, 124
Alexander Severus   31 n. 133, 62, 108, 115, 128 n. 72, 128 n. 74
Alexander the Great   5, 7, 9, 38, 42, 71, 97 n. 77, 99, 101, 103–109, 111–112, 121 n. 40, 128 n. 74, 135, 137
   Influence on Caracalla   9, 38, 42, 100–101, 104–107, 111
   Tomb of   110–111
Ammianus Marcellinus   88
Antoninus Pius   12, 30, 55, 56 n. 28, 76–77, 143 n. 10
Augustus (emperor)   62, 73, 96, 110
Augustus (title)   18, 21, 23, 26–27, 29
Aurelius Victor   30, 143 n. 10

Caligula   76 n. 122, 105
Caracalla   1–12, 21, 23–33, 35–53, 54 n. 22, 56, 59–67, 70–73, 75–76, 78–83, 86, 91–130, 132–137, 140, 143–148, 150
   As Caesar   21
   As Indulgentissimus   78, 128–129
   Legitimacy   21, 49, 113, 118–119, 137
   Piety   106, 114, 121–122, 125, 136
   Portraiture   105, 107, 120–121
   Rivalry with Geta   8 n. 30, 10, 24–30, 45, 113, 120–121, 135
Cassius Dio   2, 5–6, 8, 31–33, 50, 72, 97, 132 n. 94, 134–136, 146 n. 24
   Hostility towards Caracalla   9, 14, 32, 37, 65, 72, 94, 98
Cicero   33, 35
Clodius Albinus   18–22, 61 n.52, 116, 117 n. 19
Commodus   8, 12–14, 16, 21, 59, 63, 68, 79, 86, 106, 120 n. 37, 136, 148

Didius Julianus   15, 16 n. 33, 18, 79, 116
Domitian   54, 60, 76 n. 122, 90–91, 93 n. 57

Elagabalus   63 n. 62, 65 n. 67, 74, 108, 122, 128 n. 72, 128 n. 74

Faustina the Younger   21

Gaius (jurist)   34, 47 n. 214, 67, 146–147
Galba   13, 133

Geta   7–8, 10, 22–29, 41, 44–45, 49, 81 n. 3, 92, 112–114, 117 n. 21, 118–122, 125, 126 n. 64, 129–130, 133, 135–136, 141, 144, 150
   As Augustus   27
   As Caesar   23
   Assassination   8, 13, 16, 29 n. 123, 44, 49, 81 n. 3, 92, 107, 109 n. 48, 113–114, 118 n. 23, 136, 150
   Damnatio memoriae   119, 129, 133

Hadrian   35, 54–55, 56 n. 28, 77–78, 85, 89, 127 n. 70
Hercules   106
Herodian   12–18, 22, 25–29, 31 n. 132, 37, 81, 113, 116–117, 118 n. 26, 122 n. 45
Historia Augusta   13, 15 n. 26, 16, 17 n. 39, 24, 30, 44 n. 193, 55, 81, 104, 118 n. 26

Julia Domna   21, 28 n. 117, 29, 93 n. 58, 118, 119 n. 28, 128
Julian ('the Apostate')   110

Laetus, Julius   17, 22
Laetus, Q. Aemilius   13–15

Macrinus   94, 108
Marcus Aurelius   12, 30, 35, 56, 68, 115, 120 n. 37, 143 n. 10, 148
Modestinus (jurist)   33, 35, 46

Nero   54 n. 14, 76 n. 122, 85, 87 n. 32, 110

Paul (jurist)   34 n. 146, 35, 114
Pertinax   11–18, 59, 79, 136
Pescennius Niger   16–19, 21, 111, 116
Plautianus   24–26, 117 n. 22
Plautilla   118
Pliny the Elder   104
Pliny the Younger   73, 86, 129
Plutarch   9, 100, 102–103, 112
Pluto   124

Septimius Severus   15–18, 30, 53, 55 n. 24, 63, 75, 79, 81, 92, 93 n. 57, 111, 114, 116, 118, 120, 127, 135–136

Septimius Severus (cont.)
    Death   8, 12, 25, 27–29
    March on Rome   16–17
Serapis   122, 124
Sidonius Apollinaris   30, 150 n. 49

Tacitus   84, 133
Tiberius   83
Trajan   23, 54–55, 73 n. 109, 85, 89, 110, 127, 129

Ulpian   2, 33, 35–36, 46, 67, 146

Vegetius   86, 88, 90
Vespasian   53–55, 84, 85 n. 18
Vitellius   84, 85 n. 18, 133

Xiphilinus   32, 71

Index of Places

Adiabene 20
Alexandria (Egypt) 28, 42, 111
Alexandria (on the Issus) 108
Antioch 20, 28–29

Britain 18, 22 n. 69, 27, 91
Byzantium 19

Carthage 87, 127
Ctesiphon 23

Eboracum (York) 27
Egypt 19, 24, 40, 42, 54, 57, 58 n. 38, 66 n. 69, 78, 124

Gaul 21, 24, 55 n. 26, 85, 128 n. 75

Hatra 23

Ilium (Troy) 111
Issus 20, 108

Lepcis Magna 106
Lugdunum (Lyon) 21 n. 67, 22, 87

Mauretania Tingitana 54 n. 22, 76, 78, 148
Mesopotamia 20, 23, 91

Osrhoene 20

Pannonia 16–17, 19
Parthia 9, 20, 23, 61, 91, 110–111, 135
Perinthus 19

Rome 4, 13, 15–18, 20–23, 26–28, 33, 50, 53 n. 12, 59, 67, 84, 87, 93, 103–104, 106 n. 36, 116, 117 n. 19, 128, 146, 151

General Index

Aequitas   113, 114 n. 7, 117
Aerarium Militare   73 n. 109, 83, 96, 98, 135
Antonine Constitution (Constitutio
   Antoniniana)   1–11, 24, 29–33, 35–36,
      38–39, 41–45, 47–51, 59, 61, 65–66,
      67 n. 75, 68–69, 71 n. 100, 72, 74–75,
      78–80, 82–83, 86–87, 91, 93, 95–98,
      100–104, 111–115, 117, 119, 121–126,
      129–137, 140, 145 n. 18, 147–148, 150
   Dating   1 n. 1, 44, 124, 141, 143
   Fiscal significance   8, 31, 50–51, 65–72, 75,
      82–83, 96–97
   Military application   49, 67, 79, 81–83,
      93–98, 135
   Religious significance   49, 121–127,
      129–130, 133, 136, 145
Antonine Dynasty   12, 35, 53, 56, 117
Antonine Plague   13 n. 15, 56–58
Antoninianus (coin type)   63–64, 79
Army   12, 17, 19, 21–22, 54, 60, 79–81, 83,
      85–86, 91–94, 96–97, 99, 113 n. 3, 116, 121,
      130, 135
   Expenditure   9, 31, 55, 56 n. 28, 81, 83, 86,
      89–90, 92–94, 98
   Pay rise   60, 81, 83, 91 n. 52, 92, 93 n. 57,
      135
   Severan reforms   91–92
Aurum Coronarium   56, 61, 62 n. 55, 115
Auxilia   83, 87 n. 32, 88–90
   Conditions of service   88–90, 92

Citizenship   3, 6, 9, 11, 30, 33, 41, 45–46, 50,
      66, 67 n. 81, 68, 70–71, 79–80, 86–87, 95,
      102–103, 115, 122, 125, 129–131, 133–135,
      137, 141, 145, 146 n. 19, 147–148, 150
Coinage   7, 21 n. 67, 26, 28, 36 n. 159, 51, 52 n.
      12, 55, 60–62, 63 n. 61, 80, 91, 92 n. 53,
      95, 106–109, 119–120, 123–124, 126, 127 n.
      71, 135, 137
   Iconography   7, 26, 28, 63, 104–109, 112,
      118 n. 25, 123–124, 126, 128–129, 131 n. 89,
      136
Concordia   26, 28, 126 n. 64
   Augustorum   28
Consensus   121, 123, 125, 136, 145 n. 17

Currency   59–60, 62, 63 n. 62, 64, 65 n. 67,
      79, 95, 135
   Debasement   53 n. 12, 55 n. 24, 59 n. 46,
      60, 62, 64–65, 79–80, 91, 95, 135
   Fineness   55, 61, 62 n. 59
   Weight   59, 62, 63 n. 61, 64

Damnatio Memoriae   119, 120 n. 35, 129, 133
Dediticii   9, 47–48, 66–70, 71 n. 100, 82, 135,
      146–147, 149–150
Digest, Justinianic   2, 33–34, 67, 86,
      146 n. 25
Dilectus   84–85, 87

Economy   51–54, 56, 59–61, 64, 65 n. 67, 71,
      79, 95
Equites Singulares Augusti   60, 90

Flavian Period   53, 67 n. 81, 73 n. 109, 89

Giessen Papyrus (Papyrus Gissensis)   2–4, 6,
      8–9, 11, 31, 39–45, 47–48, 65, 67–69, 71,
      75, 99–100, 134–135, 139–140, 142–144,
      147, 148 n. 37, 149–150
   Discovery   1, 39 n. 172
   Reconstruction   3, 6, 8, 24 n. 84, 44–45,
      47–48, 65–66, 69–70, 135, 139, 142–146,
      148–151
   Survival   3, 39, 47, 93–94, 134, 141–142

Indulgentia   76, 78 n. 124, 106 n. 32, 114,
      127–130, 132, 137

Jurists   8, 33–36, 38, 43, 116

Legions   9, 17–22, 45, 74, 82–83, 85–86, 88, 89
      n. 40, 90, 91 n. 49, 93, 95–97, 118, 135
   Recruitment   82–87, 90, 97

Patronage   108, 131–132, 137
Praetorian Guard   13–15, 17, 22, 46 n. 202, 56,
      84, 90
Propaganda   7–8, 10, 16, 18, 112, 114, 118, 121,
      136
Providentia   123

GENERAL INDEX

Roman Law   33, 35, 37–38, 43, 45, 46 n. 202, 47, 51, 61
   Ius civile   45–46
   Ius gentium   46, 148–149
   Versus customary law   34, 46–47, 66, 68, 70, 102, 103 n. 18, 148, 150
Romanitas   11, 47 n. 207

Sassanid Persia   110
Secular Games (Ludi Saeculares)   24, 26, 118 n. 25
Senate   12, 14 n. 18, 15–17, 21, 23, 28–29, 84, 94, 116, 117 n. 22, 122 n. 45, 130

Severan Dynasty   6, 10–11, 35, 93 n. 58, 106, 112, 114, 118–119, 122–123, 136–137
   Building programme   42, 53–54, 59–60, 78, 135
Stoicism   103, 121

Taxation   5 n. 22, 31, 37, 51, 53, 54 n. 22, 57, 58 n. 40, 62, 65–66, 68, 72–75, 78, 82, 92, 96–97, 124, 127 n. 69, 132–135, 148
Theodosian Code   86

Vicesima Hereditatum   51, 72–74, 96, 98
Virtus   111, 121